Finding Our Way

8 July 22

Finding Our Way

Rethinking Ethnocultural Relations in Canada

▶ *Will Kymlicka* ◀

OXFORD
UNIVERSITY PRESS

OXFORD

UNIVERSITY PRESS

70 Wynford Drive, Don Mills, Ontario M3C 1J9
http://www.oupcan.com

Oxford New York
Athens Auckland Bangkok Bogotá Buenos Aires Calcutta Cape Town
Chennai Dar es Salaam Delhi Florence Hong Kong Istanbul
Karachi Kuala Lumpur Madrid Melbourne Mexico City Mumbai
Nairobi Paris São Paulo Singapore Taipei Tokyo Toronto Warsaw

and associated companies in
Berlin Ibadan

Oxford is a trade mark of Oxford University Press

Canadian Cataloguing in Publication Data

Kymlicka, Will
Finding our way : rethinking ethnocultural relations in Canada

Includes bibliographical references and index.
ISBN 0-19-541314-8

1. Multiculturalism – Canada. I. Title.

FC105 M8K95 1998   305.8'00971   C98-930747-6
FC1035 A1K95 1998

Design: Max Gabriel Izod
Copyright © Oxford University Press Canada 1998

3 4 - 01 00

This book is printed on permanent (acid-free) paper ∞.
Printed in Canada

Contents

Acknowledgements

For several years I have been working on the issue of the rights of ethno-cultural groups within liberal democracies. In the past, however, my work has been more theoretical than practical, focusing on the way liberal-democratic political theorists have dealt with issues of ethnocultural diversity. The motivation for this book came in part from discussions with officials at the Department of Canadian Heritage of the federal government, who wanted to know what (if anything) these debates among political theorists could tell us about public policy in Canada. In fact, the origins of this book lie in a series of five short papers I wrote for the Department in the fall of 1995. I would like to thank the members of the Department for their interest and comments, and for their advice about useful references. Brian Gilhuly, Dhiru Patel, Barb Preston, and Judy Young have been particularly generous in their assistance.

Over the last few years, I have had the good fortune to be able to try out my ideas on a number of audiences, in Canada and abroad. One can learn a great deal about Canada by trying to explain it to non-Canadians, and I'd like to thank the following people for their invitations to do just that: Veit Bader and Govert den Hartogh (Amsterdam), Xavier Arbos and Ferran Requejo (Barcelona), Nenad Dimitrjevic and Tibor Varady (Budapest); Steven Lukes (Florence), Phillipe Van Parijs (Louvain), Francisco Colom (Madrid), Patrizia Nanz (Milan), Yoav Peled (Tel Aviv), James Anaya (University of Iowa), Rainer Bauböck (Vienna), James Harf (Ohio State), Daniel Ortiz (University of Virginia), and Ian Shapiro (Yale). I'd also like to thank John Jaworsky and Magda Opalski of Forum Eastern Europe for including me in their workshops on managing ethnocultural diversity in Riga and Kiev.

Closer to home, I'm grateful for invitations from Peter Benson (to the McGill Legal Theory Workshop); Joseph Carens (to the University of Toronto Politics department); David Elkins, Steven Lee, and Alain Prujiner (to a conference on 'International Dimensions of Federalism', organized by the Canadian Centre for Foreign Policy Development); David Hawkes (to a 'Fundamental Issues' seminar at the Royal Commission on Aboriginal Peoples); Norman Hillmer (to the conference on '50 Years of Canadian Citizenship', organized by the Association for the Study of National History); Wsevolod Isajiw (to the conference on 'Shaping Ethnicity Towards the Millennium' at the Robert Harney Program in Ethnic, Immigration and Pluralism Studies at the University of Toronto); Roger Gibbins and Guy Laforest (to the Institute for Research on Public Policy's workshop on 'Beyond the Impasse: Exploring a Canada-Quebec Partnership'); Irene Kamchen (to the annual meeting of the Canadian Ethnocultural Council); Michael Keating and John McGarry (to a conference on 'Minority Nationalism in a Changing World Order' at the University of Western Ontario); Lukas Sosoe (to a conference on 'Démocratie, pluralisme, et citoyenneté' at the Université de Montréal); Eric Vernon (to the workshop on 'Social Cohesion Through Social Justice' organized by the Canadian Jewish Congress); Jeremy Webber (to the 'Conference on the Report of the Royal Commission on Aboriginal Peoples' at McGill University); and Doug Williams (to a workshop on 'Individual and Collective Rights' at the federal Department of Justice).

I learned a great deal from the questions and comments of the audiences on each of these occasions. Academics usually talk only to other academics, and often only to academics from their own discipline. But these presentations have given me the chance to try out my ideas on a mixture of academics, government officials, and members of non-governmental organizations. I hope the wider perspective this has provided will be evident throughout the book.

For written comments on some or all of the chapters, I'm grateful to Katherine Fierlbeck, Roger Gibbins, Amy Gutmann, Richard Iton, Les Jacobs, B.B. Kymlicka, Guy Laforest, John MacKinnon, Wayne Norman, Arthur Ripstein, Lois Sweet, Zack Taylor, and Brian Walker. For help with the publishing process, I thank Ric Kitowski at Oxford University Press, my editor, Sally Livingston, and my agent, Bev Slopen.

Above all, I would like to thank Sue Donaldson. I couldn't have written this book without her common sense and critical acumen, combined with her constant support, wit, and love.

In our 130-year existence, Canadians have managed to build a prosperous, tolerant, peaceful, free, and democratic society in what is one of the most ethnoculturally diverse countries in the world. We have become so accustomed to our diversity that we often fail to notice how exceptional Canada is in this regard. Consider immigration. We debate the best overall level of immigration, and the criteria that should be used in selecting immigrants (age, language, skills, family reunification, refugee status, etc.). But almost everyone accepts that we should continue to seek immigrants, and that immigration is an important part of our development as a country.

Yet such acceptance of immigration is exceedingly rare in the world; it is found only in a handful of other former British settler societies (the United States, Australia, and New Zealand) and Israel. There is no longer a single European country that seeks immigrants. Some of them grant asylum to refugees, and allow earlier immigrants to sponsor members of their immediate families—as they are required to do under international law. But of the 184 members of the United Nations, the number that go beyond these minimal legal requirements and actively encourage immigration can be counted on the fingers of two hands.

Moreover, among this small group, Canada has for decades had the most ambitious immigration policy. While the United States is often seen as the paradigmatic 'immigrant country', Canada's per capita rate of immigration is much higher, and the proportion of foreign-born people in Canada (16 per cent) is now double that in the United States (8 per cent). It is not surprising, therefore, that most of the important policy innovations regarding immigration in the post-war era—from the 'point system' for selecting immigrants to the adoption of 'multiculturalism' as a regulative principle governing their integration—originated in Canada, before being adopted by other immigrant countries.

Aboriginal peoples are another vital component of diversity in Canada. Indigenous peoples are found in many countries. But with the possible exception of New Zealand (where the Maori form 15 per cent of the population), there is no Western country in which indigenous peoples have achieved a more prominent political status. The provisions relating to Aboriginal peoples in Canada's 1982 Constitution—both those sections affirming the existence of Aboriginal rights and the section requiring the government to negotiate the meaning of these rights with the Aboriginal peoples themselves—are virtually unique in the world. These provisions have in effect guaranteed that Aboriginal people will have 'a seat at the table' for all future constitutional negotiations that affect their interests. This new status was evident during the dramas of the Meech Lake and Charlottetown Accords, and in the work of the recent Royal Commission on Aboriginal Peoples. Although the task of defining Aboriginal rights remains largely unfinished, at least Aboriginal people in Canada are now the subjects, not just the objects, of public policy and political decisions. The experience and expertise gained by Aboriginal people in this process has had international repercussions. Among the indigenous people who began lobbying the United Nations to draft an international declaration of the rights of indigenous peoples in the 1980s, the most active and effective have been those from Canada.

Another fundamental form of diversity in Canada involves French Canadians and the issues of bilingualism and federalism. Canada is not alone in granting official status to a minority language. On the contrary, this is quite common in countries where the minority is a national rather than an immigrant minority. By 'national minority' I mean a historical society, with its own language and institutions, whose territory has been incorporated (often involuntarily, as is the case with Quebec) into a larger country. Other national minorities include Puerto Ricans in the United States, Catalans in Spain, and the Flemish in Belgium. I call such groups 'national' minorities because they tend to view themselves as 'nations' and to form nationalist movements in defence of their language rights and collective autonomy. Wherever such minority nationalisms arise, the language of the incorporated minority is often given some form of official recognition, although Canada's bilingualism policy is more wide-ranging than most.

What is truly unique in Canada, however, is the use of federalism to accommodate the existence of such a regionally concentrated national minority. Before 1867, no country (with the possible exception of Switzerland) had adopted federalism for the purpose of creating a political unit within which a linguistically distinct national minority would form a majority and govern itself. And no other country has developed as rich a body of experience concerning the relationship between federalism and minority nationalism.

Americans often take credit for inventing the idea of federalism. But the 'federalist revolution' that is currently sweeping the world is based on the Canadian/Swiss model of federalism, in which federal units enable national minorities to govern themselves, rather than the American one, in which federal subunits are simply territorial subdivisions with no ethnocultural significance. It is not surprising, then, that as more and more countries consider adopting federalism as a mechanism for accommodating ethnocultural diversity—countries like Spain, Belgium, South Africa, and Russia—it is Canada they look to as a model.

In short, Canada is a world leader in three of the most important areas of ethnocultural relations: immigration, indigenous peoples, and the accommodation of minority nationalisms. Many other countries have one or more of these forms of diversity, but very few have all three, and none has the same wealth of historical experience in dealing with them. Leslie Laczko, my colleague at the University of Ottawa, recently published a study measuring the levels of ethnocultural diversity in Western democracies, in which he concluded that Canada was almost off the scale in its overall score. Canada is a 'statistical outlier', as he put it, because it combines so many different forms of diversity, all of which are central to our social and political life.[1]

That we have managed to cope with all these forms of diversity simultaneously while still managing to live together in peace and civility is, by any objective standard, a remarkable achievement. We take in our stride a level of immigration that in most countries would provoke xenophobic nationalism; we have learned to live with a vigorous minority nationalism that in many countries would lead to anarchy or civil war; and we have institutionalized, even constitutionalized, the rights of indigenous peoples at a time when many countries are still trying to deny the rights, if not the very existence, of indigenous peoples within their borders.

As a result, Canada is now seen as a model by many other countries. Western Europeans want to know how we've managed to accept so many immigrants without provoking a neo-fascist backlash; Scandinavians want to know about our approach to indigenous rights; Eastern Europeans want to know about the accommodation of national minorities. In all of these areas Canada has relevant experience and expertise to offer the world.

I'm not saying that Canada has 'solved' any of these issues. Far from it. For one thing, ethnocultural relationships are inevitably accompanied by various strains and tensions for which there is no ultimate solution. We can only hope to 'manage', not to solve, conflicts arising from ethnocultural diversity. People who seek a 'solution' to ethnocultural conflicts are either hopelessly idealistic or murderously genocidal. Certainly we have serious conflicts and problems; this book is devoted to discussing them. But, for better or worse, so far we have in fact managed these problems. We have lived together, more or less peacefully; we have adapted our institutions and policies to changing circumstances and new aspirations; we have debated with each other in an open and civil manner; and in the process we have learned a great deal about what sorts of accommodations are necessary and desirable in a pluralistic country, and what sorts of policies are unfeasible and unjust. This experience has been hard-won, achieved only after years of painful struggles, humiliating misunderstandings, and cruel indifference. Nevertheless, we have learned some very important lessons over the years—lessons that many other countries want and need to learn if they too are to survive and prosper.

In the last few years I have received several invitations to other countries to discuss 'the Canadian model' of ethnocultural relations. This is a task I perform with a certain satisfaction and pride. Canada is not a major world power, and is often almost invisible on the international stage. We rarely make it onto CNN, or the BBC World News, or the pages of *Le Monde*. But in this one area, Canada is an internationally recognized leader, in terms not only of specific public policies, but also of the judicial decisions and academic studies that analyse and evaluate these policies. I firmly believe that other countries can learn from our experience, and that we can help other peoples avoid unnecessary conflicts and injustices. And audiences in other countries—whether the US, Britain, Australia, the Netherlands, Spain, Italy, Austria, Latvia, or Ukraine—seem genuinely interested in Canada's successes in this area.

Yet I have also felt a growing ambivalence about the task of presenting 'the Canadian model' to foreign audiences. For at the very time that I am encouraging others to consider seriously the lessons from Canada, I know that more and more Canadians themselves are disillusioned with the basic institutions and principles that underlie the Canadian model. Foreign audiences are eager to hear about Canada, and want to learn the secrets of our success. But growing numbers of Canadians deny that ours is a success story—and indeed would scoff at the very idea. So I have been in the position of trying to encourage foreign audiences to take seriously a set of practices and principles that are increasingly dismissed and derided at home. This is a paradoxical position to be in, and an increasingly untenable one. How can I describe as successes the very policies that Canadians themselves increasingly describe as failures?

Moreover, I find the current temper of disillusionment rather perplexing. It is no surprise that many Canadians are questioning some of our institutions and policies—public policy regarding ethnocultural relations has moved quickly on several fronts in recent years, and some stock-taking and soul-searching is natural and appropriate. Nor does it bother me that many people are concluding that some of these policies are mistaken. That too is natural and appropriate in a democracy. And in any event, many of these recent policy changes were clearly experimental, designed with the expectation that they would be reformulated as we learned from their initial implementation.

What does surprise and dishearten me is the near hysteria that accompanies much of this debate. Otherwise sensible and intelligent people have lost their perspective on these matters. They invoke apocalyptic scenarios of segregation and violence—as if Canada had learned nothing from its history, had developed no safety cushions, no margin of error. It is not uncommon to hear commentators point ominously to Bosnia or South Africa, as if we were on some slippery slope to civil war or apartheid.

What this reflects, it seems to me, is a dramatic loss of confidence. Canadians used to have this confidence; in fact it is one of the most important components of the Canadian experience, one of the most important of our hard-won lessons. A nice illustration of this point is provided in a study by three American social scientists comparing immigration and refugee policies in nine industrialized democracies over the last few decades. The study found that every one of these countries except Canada had faced a crisis over such policies. Canada was spared this crisis, the authors argued, largely because of the 'self-confidence of the Canadian public', who believed throughout the 1970s and 1980s that whatever problems arose in the admission or integration of immigrants could be managed. As a result, problems that in other countries led to a far-right backlash, or to hasty and ill-conceived restrictive legislation, were dealt with in Canada in a sober, pragmatic way.[2]

This confidence was well founded, based on years of trial and error and patient learning. But over the last few years we seem to have lost it, and now that it is gone, Canadians are exhibiting a variety of pathological responses. Some people, dismayed by the excesses of political correctness and frightened by the cacophony of new voices, retreat into individual apathy and private complaint. Others adopt extreme and simplistic solutions. If we no longer feel confident that we can solve the problem of conflicting national identities in English and French Canada, let's avoid the problem entirely by separating into two countries. If we no longer feel confident that we can solve the stresses caused by high levels of immigration, let's avoid the problem entirely by dramatically restricting immigration.

These are not solutions to our problems, but desperate attempts to sidestep them. This, to me, is the most distressing aspect of the Canadian situation. Canadians' former sense of confidence and optimism that our problems were manageable has been replaced with the feeling that things are out of control. We talk and behave as if we've learned nothing from our experience, as if everything is now up for grabs, and nothing is secure or settled. These fears are, I believe, deeply misplaced. Part of my aim in writing this book, therefore, is to provide a kind of reality check. I want to provide a map of ethnocultural relations that might put things back into perspective, and maybe even restore the confidence needed to tackle our unresolved issues more effectively. My aim is less to provide specific policy recommendations than to emphasize the lessons we have already learned, and the ample resources we can draw upon in tackling our remaining problems. In short, this book is an attempt to persuade Canadians of the message I have tried to convey in other countries: that Canada provides an important model of how a pluralistic country can live, not in utopian harmony, but in peace, civility, and justice.

• • •

The book is divided into two parts, reflecting the two major sources of ethnocultural diversity in Canada. It is true that Canada is a 'British settler society', in the sense that it emerged from the union of four British colonies, and that British colonists and colonial administrators established many of the dominant institutions that still govern us. But the British have never been alone on this territory, and they have become an ever-decreasing percentage of the population. We can divide Canada's increasing ethnocultural diversity into two broad categories.

The first sources of ethnocultural diversity are, of course, the people who were here before the British, namely the Aboriginal peoples and French Canadians. They formed complete and functioning societies, long-settled on their own territory, with their own institutions operating in their own languages, prior to being incorporated into British North America. Although this incorporation was involuntary, the result of colonization and conquest, efforts have been made to turn it into a more voluntary federation of peoples through the signing of treaties with Aboriginal peoples and the negotiation of Confederation with French Canadians. Today, however, neither group is satisfied with its status within Canada. As I noted earlier, these groups can be called 'national minorities', since they see themselves as 'nations' within Canada and have historically sought various forms of self-government so as to maintain their status as culturally distinct and self-governing societies within the larger state.

My use of the term 'self-government', while familiar in the Aboriginal context, may seem unusual in the context of Quebec, where demands have usually been phrased in terms of 'distinct society', 'special status', 'asymmetrical federalism', or 'sovereignty-association'. But the demands of the two groups share an important feature: they rest, at least in part, on the sense that both are distinct 'nations' or 'peoples' whose existence pre-dates that of the Canadian state. As nations or peoples, they claim the right to self-determination, which may take the form of an independent state, but may also take the form of voluntary federation into a larger state if the group so chooses. When choosing to enter into such a federation, the community relinquishes some of its powers to the larger state but reserves others for itself, including the powers necessary to ensure the development of its culture.

I am using the term 'self-government rights' to designate this package of beliefs and desires: the sense of being a nation, on its historical territory, that has exercised its self-determination by entering a larger state through some form of federation or treaty, and that sees certain rights and powers as flowing both from its status as a founding people and from the terms of federation. Aboriginal peoples and the Québécois are not simply demanding a general decentralization of power, to promote administrative efficiency or local democracy. Rather, they are demanding recognition as distinct peoples and as founding partners in the Canadian state who have maintained the right to govern themselves and their land in certain areas. This package of beliefs and desires is found, I think, among both Aboriginal people and the Québécois today, and underlies many Québécois demands, including those framed in the language of 'distinct society' or 'sovereignty-association'.

Learning to accommodate the diversity resulting from the presence of our 'nations within' is a long-standing concern, going back to the Royal Proclamation of 1763, which guaranteed Aboriginal rights, and the Quebec Act of 1774, which guaranteed autonomy for the Canadiens of Quebec. Yet these groups still do not feel that their nationhood has been properly recognized, or that their national rights have been properly respected. Today, the demands of the Québécois and Aboriginal peoples for autonomy and national recognition are inextricably linked, for better or worse, with our system of federalism. Chapters 9 to 13 of this book are devoted to discussing the complicated relationship between federalism and minority nationalism in Canada, and to explaining why it has proven so difficult for federalism to accommodate the aspirations of our nations within.

I will begin, however, by examining the other major source of ethno-cultural diversity in Canada: mass immigration. This too has been a long-standing feature of Canadian history, beginning with the Irish immigrants in the 1830s, and recurring in waves in this century. As a result, Canada now contains people whose ancestral roots lie in all four corners of the world.

Needless to say, these groups have very different histories from the 'nations within'. They are the result not of the involuntary incorporation of complete societies settled in their historic lands, but of the decisions of individuals and families to leave their original homelands for a new life. This choice was more or less voluntary, at least in the sense that they chose to come while many of their friends and family chose to stay, and it was made by people who knew that they were entering a new society with its own established laws and institutions.

Sometimes I will refer to these groups as 'immigrant groups', since their origins in Canada lie in the act of immigration. But for certain groups, particularly those from Northern Europe, these origins lie quite far in the past, so that the bulk of the group's members today are not immigrants themselves but the children, grandchildren or even great-grandchildren of the original immigrants. It seems slightly odd, therefore, to describe German Canadians or Ukrainian Canadians as 'immigrant groups'. Many people use the term 'ethnic groups' instead, and I too will use that term in several places. But as we will see, the fact that these groups were formed initially through immigration is pivotal in understanding their status in Canada, and in understanding how and why they differ from our 'nations within'. Throughout this book, therefore, I will use 'immigrant group' and 'ethnic group' interchangeably to refer to those groups formed through acts of immigration, to distinguish them from the Aboriginal and French-Canadian 'national' groups.

Historically, immigrant/ethnic groups have sought and achieved social and political integration in Canada—not self-government—although they have also wanted some accommodation of their ethnocultural distinctiveness. Today, Canada's approach to the accommodation of groups formed by immigration is labelled 'multiculturalism'. The first half of this book is devoted to an explanation and evaluation of this approach, which, as I will try to show, has been more successful than many people think.

In particular, Chapter 1 reviews the evidence concerning the impact of 'multiculturalism' on the integration of ethnic groups. Many people believe that the policy of multiculturalism is undermining the historical tendency of ethnic groups to integrate, and instead is encouraging them to live separately and apart. On this view, ethnic groups are increasingly seeking to create and maintain their own societal institutions—educational, economic, legal, and political—in the hope that these will enable them to prosper without integrating into the societal institutions of either French or English Canada. I will show that this view is manifestly false. On the contrary, immigrant groups integrate more quickly and more effectively today than they did before the adoption of the multiculturalism policy, and they do so more successfully in Canada than in any country that does not have such a policy. If we examine the evidence, it turns out that the benefits of multiculturalism have been seriously underestimated, and its drawbacks overestimated.

What explains this widespread misunderstanding? Part of the answer, I think, is that neither defenders nor critics have explained how multiculturalism fits into the broader context of government policies affecting ethnocultural relations, including employment, education, and citizenship policies. Chapter 2 tries to situate multiculturalism within this broader setting, and to show that multiculturalism is best understood not as a rejection of integration, but rather as a vehicle for adjusting the terms of integration. Illustrations of this point are provided in Chapter 3, which looks more closely at a range of specific policies associated with multiculturalism in Canada, in order to see how each of them affects the aspirations and institutional capacities of immigrant groups.

Canadians' concerns about multiculturalism are not limited to issues of integration. There is also the concern that multiculturalism entails an obligation to accept or at least to tolerate the traditional practices of ethnocultural groups, even when these violate our basic notions of human dignity and individual rights. Many people worry that multiculturalism involves granting 'group rights' that stand in inherent conflict with individual rights, and that 'respect for cultural diversity' will be used to justify illiberal practices. This raises the question of the limits of tolerance, which is explored in Chapter 4. I try to show that there are in fact definite limits to our tolerance of illiberal practices, and that these limits are neither arbitrary nor ad hoc, but reflect a consistent working out of our basic constitutional principles. In these first four chapters, which attempt primarily to describe and evaluate multiculturalism policies as they now exist, I hope to show that multiculturalism is a coherent, defensible, and indeed successful approach to the integration of ethnic groups in Canada.

The next three chapters explore potential directions for multiculturalism in the future. Multiculturalism has always been an evolving policy, responding to new needs and circumstances, and it will continue to evolve as new challenges arise. Chapters 5 to 7 try to identify some of the most important of these challenges. One pivotal issue is race relations, discussed in Chapter 5. Some people argue that multiculturalism may have succeeded among white immigrant groups, but that this is less true for non-white groups. Others argue that it is working for Asians and East Indians, but not for African Canadians. The assumption that the immigrant multiculturalism model is not working for visible minorities is, I believe, premature. Indeed, it is largely the result of the implicit, often unconscious, adoption of American assumptions about race relations.

Blacks in the United States are not an 'immigrant' group: they were transported there involuntarily as slaves, and until recently were discouraged if not legally prevented from integrating into the mainstream society, even as new immigrants from overseas were welcomed and encouraged to integrate. This gulf between Blacks and immigrant groups is one of the fundamental facts affecting race relations in America. But visible minorities in Canada, including most African Canadians, are recent immigrants, and there is at least some evidence that the immigrant multiculturalism model is working to integrate these groups. More needs to be done, however, and Chapter 5 discusses some of the new policy directions we should be considering.

Chapter 6 asks whether multiculturalism can be extended to include various non-ethnic identity groups, in particular gays and lesbians, and people with disabilities. The 'ethnic revival' is often considered one part of a broader movement towards a 'politics of identity', in which a wide range of previously disadvantaged groups seek public recognition for their distinctive identities and needs. All these groups are seeking not only the common rights of Canadian citizenship, but also certain forms of group-specific rights. In this respect they raise many of the same issues as ethnic groups. In fact, in the United States the term 'multiculturalism' is often used to refer to all forms of identity politics. While I think this all-encompassing use of the term 'multiculturalism' is confusing, the model of accommodation developed in the immigrant context does have some relevance for thinking about other forms of identity politics as well.

Chapter 7 addresses issues of group representation in the political process, particularly proposals to guarantee seats in Parliament for members of certain groups. Such an arrangement has been proposed not only in the context of ethnic and national groups, but also for women and other identity groups. My aim is not to defend any particular proposal for group representation, for there are serious theoretical and practical difficulties with such proposals, but rather to emphasize the importance of ensuring a voice for minorities in political decision-making. Multiculturalism has helped make Canadian society more open and inclusive, but these gains may be ephemeral if the political process is not also made more representative.

The final chapter in Part 1 contains a plea for a truce in the rhetorical wars over multiculturalism. The public debate, to date, has largely consisted of trading epithets of 'racism', 'intolerance', 'divisiveness', and 'apartheid'. Chapter 8 attempts to outline what a more informed and fruitful debate would look like.

Throughout Part 1, my conclusions are comparatively optimistic. I hope to show that multiculturalism is working well, and that fears of ethnocultural separatism are misplaced. I also hope to show that this general integrationist pattern is not limited to 'white' ethnic groups; that racism in Canada need not be an insurmountable barrier to the integration of Canadians of Asian, Arab, or African descent; and that the multiculturalism model of integration offers useful lessons for thinking about some of the new challenges facing Canadian society and democracy.

My arguments in Part 2, however, are more ambivalent. Indeed, the outlook for accommodation of our 'national' differences is not particularly promising. In recent years, both the Québécois and Aboriginal peoples have strongly asserted their distinctive national identities. For them, Canada is a single country that contains more than one 'nation': their citizenship is Canadian, but their national identity is Québécois, Cree, etc. As a result Canada is, sociologically speaking, a 'multination' state, and like all multination states it must find a way to accommodate minority nationalisms.

After a brief introduction in Chapter 9, Chapter 10 turns to a discussion of the nature of minority nationalisms in Canada, and why their claims to self-government rights and national recognition have been so difficult to satisfy. Canada's system of federalism is intended, in part, to help satisfy these demands, but in fact federalism itself is now part of the problem. The sort of 'multination' federalism desired by most Québécois and Aboriginal people rests on a model of federalism fundamentally opposed to the model of symmetrical federalism that is endorsed by the (non-Aboriginal, non-Québécois) majority in Canada.

I will use the term 'English-speaking Canada' to refer to this non-Aboriginal, non-Québécois majority. This term is not entirely accurate, but I prefer it to the other term that is sometimes used: the 'Rest of Canada'. After all, the 'rest of Canada' is not simply a disconnected set of individuals or groups who have nothing in common other than the fact that they are neither Québécois nor Aboriginal. They share many common institutions, operating predominantly in the English language, and English is known and used almost universally by its members. 'English-speaking Canadians' also share, to a large degree, a particular kind of political identity and political culture, including a strong commitment to a model of symmetrical federalism that conflicts with the model of federalism adopted by most Québécois and Aboriginal people in Canada.

The 'national unity' strategy followed by the federal government for the last ten years—which combines a vague recognition of Quebec's distinctiveness with a simultaneous emphasis on provincial equality and shared values—can be seen as an attempt to paper over the differences between these two models of federalism. In Chapter 11 I discuss why this strategy was (and remains) doomed to failure.

If there is no way to paper over these differences, the only way to keep Canada together may be to persuade English-speaking Canadians to accept a multination model of federalism. But what could persuade English-speaking Canadians to adopt such a model? Polling suggests that support for 'special status' or 'distinct society' has, if anything, decreased over the last ten years. And many previous attempts to persuade English-speaking Canadians to adopt this model have had no success. Chapter 12 analyses why these previous attempts failed, and offers a somewhat different set of arguments why English-speaking Canadians might come to accept such a multination conception of Canada and of Canadian federalism. I am not very optimistic about this prospect, but it may be our only chance to keep Canada together.

Finally, in Chapter 13 I discuss whether such a multination federalism, even if it were accepted by English-speaking Canadians, could endure. I offer some guarded reasons for thinking it might, although there are no guarantees that it would not be simply a stepping-stone to the inevitable dissolution of Canada.

The two parts of this book offer very different pictures. The needs and aspirations of Canada's immigrant groups differ significantly from those of its national groups, as do their challenges to the political order. This situation is not unique to Canada. Recent studies by comparative political scientists and normative political theorists have emphasized the vital importance of the distinction between two kinds of ethnocultural groups throughout the world.[3] And, like most other Western democracies, Canada has had much greater success in accommodating immigrant ethnicity than in accommodating minority nationalism.

The conclusion offers some general reflections on the Canadian experiment in managing ethnocultural relations. Although the two parts of the book describe two very different sides of ethnocultural relations in Canada, there is one thing they share: in each case, we seem unable or unwilling to learn from our own experience. Our history can tell us a great deal about what works and what does not, in the context both of immigrant ethnic groups and of national minorities. We have the experience to manage ethnocultural relations in a fair and mutually beneficial way. Yet we seem to have lost the will, or the confidence, to learn from this experience, and to act on the lessons of our past successes and failures. This is perhaps the most surprising and disheartening aspect of our current debate.

Part One

▶ *The Merits of Multiculturalism* ◀

Chapter 1

► *Setting the Record Straight* ◄

In 1971 Canada embarked on a unique experiment by declaring a policy of official 'multiculturalism'. According to Pierre Trudeau, the prime minister who introduced it in the House of Commons, the policy had four aims: to support the cultural development of ethnocultural groups; to help members of ethnocultural groups overcome barriers to full participation in Canadian society; to promote creative encounters and interchange among all ethnocultural groups; and to assist new Canadians in acquiring at least one of Canada's official languages.[1] This policy was officially enshrined in law in the 1988 Multiculturalism Act, excerpts of which are reproduced in the Appendix to this book.

Although the multiculturalism policy was first adopted by the federal government, it was explicitly designed as a model for other levels of government, and it has been widely copied. 'Multiculturalism programs' can now be found not just in the multiculturalism office in Ottawa, but also at the provincial and municipal levels of government and in a wide range of public and private institutions, including schools and businesses.

Such programs are now under attack, perhaps more so today than at any time since 1971. In particular, they are said to be undermining the historical tendency of immigrant groups to integrate, encouraging ethnic separatism, putting up 'cultural walls' around ethnic groups, and thereby eroding our ability to act collectively as citizens. It is understandable that Canadians have had anxieties about multiculturalism, and it would be a mistake to ascribe all of them to xenophobia or prejudice. The process of integrating immigrants from very different backgrounds, including every conceivable race, religion, and language group, who share little in common, is never easy, and historically Canada has been fortunate in having avoided serious ethnic conflict. Canadians have naturally worried that any dramatic change in our approach to integration—such as the adoption of the multiculturalism policy—would change this dynamic, igniting ethnic separatism and conflict.

Thus it is worth having a vigorous discussion about multiculturalism. So far, though, the debate so far has generated much more heat than light.

virtues within boundaries

One reason is that it has been carried on without enough attention to the empirical evidence; as we will see, the critics of multiculturalism are simply uninformed about the consequences of the policy.

But defenders of multiculturalism, including the federal government itself, must also share part of the blame. Virtually every study of the policy in Canada has concluded that it has been 'barely explained at all to the Canadian public', and that 'no serious effort was made by any senior politician to define multiculturalism in a Canadian context'.[2] Insofar as the policy has been defended, the usual approach has been simply to invoke 'cultural diversity' and 'tolerance', as if these were self-evidently or unqualifiedly good things. In fact, both diversity and tolerance have limits. Diversity is valuable, but only if it operates within the context of certain common norms and institutions; otherwise it can become destabilizing. Similarly, tolerance is a virtue, but only within certain boundaries; otherwise it can threaten principles of equality and individual rights. It is on these questions of the limits or boundaries of multiculturalism that defenders have been strangely inarticulate.

As a result, the debate over multiculturalism in the last few years has taken on an air of unreality. On the one hand, uninformed critics level unfounded charges of ethnocultural separatism, without regard for the evidence; on the other hand, defenders invoke 'diversity' and 'tolerance' as a mantra, without explaining the common institutions and principles that define the context within which diversity and tolerance can flourish.

To bring some order to this confusion, in this chapter I will focus on the evidence regarding the impact of multiculturalism since its adoption in 1971, to show that critics of the policy are indeed misinformed. The following two chapters will try to explain the larger context that defines and limits multiculturalism's commitment to tolerance and diversity.

1. THE DEBATE

The debate over multiculturalism has heated up recently, largely because of two best-selling critiques: Neil Bissoondath's *Selling Illusions: The Cult of Multiculturalism in Canada* (1994) and Richard Gwyn's *Nationalism Without Walls: The Unbearable Lightness of Being Canadian* (1995).[3] Bissoondath and Gwyn make very similar claims about the results of the policy. In particular, both argue that multiculturalism has promoted a form of ethnic separatism among immigrants. According to Bissoondath, multiculturalism has led to 'undeniable ghettoization'.[4] Instead of promoting integration, it encourages immigrants to form 'self-contained' ghettos 'alienated from the mainstream', and this ghettoization is 'not an extreme of multiculturalism but its ideal: a way of life transported whole, a little outpost of exoticism preserved and protected'. He approvingly quotes Arthur Schlesinger's claim that multiculturalism reflects a 'cult of ethnicity' that 'exaggerates differences, intensifies resentments and antagonisms, drives even deeper the awful wedges between races and nationalities', producing patterns of 'self-pity and self-ghettoization' that lead to 'cultural and linguistic apartheid'.[5] According to Bissoondath, multiculturalism policy does not encourage immigrants to think of themselves as Canadians; even the children of immigrants 'continue to see Canada with the eyes of foreigners. Multiculturalism, with its emphasis on the importance of holding on to the former or ancestral homeland, with its insistence that *There* is more important than *Here*, encourages such attitudes.'

Gwyn makes the same claim, in very similar language. He argues that 'official multiculturalism encourages apartheid, or to be a bit less harsh, ghettoism.'[6] The longer multiculturalism policy has been in place, 'the higher the cultural walls have gone up inside Canada'. Multiculturalism encourages ethnic leaders to keep their members 'apart from the mainstream', practising 'what can best be described as mono-culturalism'. In this way the Canadian state 'encourages these gatekeepers to maintain what amounts, at worst, to an apartheid form of citizenship'.

Bissoondath and Gwyn are hardly alone in these claims; they are repeated endlessly in the media. To take just one example, Robert Fulford recently argued in *The Globe and Mail* that the policy encourages people to maintain a 'freeze-dried' identity, reducing intercultural exchange and relationships, and that time will judge it to be one of Canada's greatest 'policy failures'.[7]

It is important—indeed urgent—to determine whether such claims are true. Surprisingly, however, neither Bissoondath nor Gwyn provides any empirical evidence for his views. In order to assess their claims, therefore, I have collected some statistics that may bear on the question of whether multiculturalism has promoted ethnic separatism, and discouraged or impeded integration. I will start with evidence from within Canada, comparing ethnic groups before and after the adoption of the multiculturalism policy in 1971 (section 2). I will then consider evidence from other countries, particularly countries that have rejected the principle of official multiculturalism, to see how Canada compares with them (section 3).

2. THE DOMESTIC EVIDENCE

How has the adoption of multiculturalism in 1971 affected the integration of ethnic groups in Canada? To answer this question requires some account of what 'integration' involves. It is one of the puzzling features of the Gwyn and Bissoondath critiques that neither defines exactly what he means by integration. However, we can piece together some of the elements they see as crucial: adopting a Canadian identity rather than clinging exclusively to one's ancestral identity; participating in broader Canadian institutions rather than participating solely in ethnic-specific institutions; learning an official language rather than relying solely on one's mother tongue; having inter-ethnic friendships, or even mixed marriages, rather than socializing entirely within one's ethnic group. Such criteria do not form a comprehensive theory of 'integration', but they seem to be at the heart of Gwyn's and Bissoondath's concerns about multiculturalism, so they are a good starting-point.

Let us begin with the most basic form of integration: the decision of an immigrant to become a Canadian citizen. If the Gwyn/Bissoondath thesis were true, one would expect naturalization rates to have declined since the adoption of multiculturalism. In fact, naturalization rates have increased since 1971.[8] This is particularly relevant because the economic incentives to naturalize have lessened over the last 25 years. Canadian citizenship is not needed in order to enter the labour market in Canada, or to gain access to social benefits. There are virtually no differences between citizens and permanent residents in their civil rights or social benefits; the right to vote is the only major legal benefit gained by naturalization.[9] The primary reason for immigrants to take out citizenship, therefore, is that they identify with Canada; they want to formalize their membership in Canadian society and to participate in the political life of the country.

Moreover, if we examine which groups are most likely to naturalize, we find that it is the 'multicultural groups'—immigrants from non-traditional source countries, for whom the multiculturalism policy is most relevant—that have the highest rates of naturalization. By contrast, immigrants from the United States and United Kingdom, who are not seen in popular discourse as 'ethnic' or 'multicultural' groups, have the lowest rates of naturalization.[10] In other words, those groups that are most directly affected by the multiculturalism policy have shown the greatest desire to become Canadian, while those that fall outside the multiculturalism rubric have shown the least desire to become Canadian.

Let's move now to political participation. If the Gwyn/Bissoondath thesis were true, one would expect the political participation of ethnocultural minorities to have declined since the adoption of multiculturalism in 1971. After all, political participation is a symbolic affirmation of citizenship, and reflects an interest in the political life of the larger society. Yet there is no evidence of decline in such participation.[11] To take one relevant indicator, between Confederation and the 1960s, in the period prior to the adoption of multiculturalism, ethnic groups became increasingly under-represented in Parliament, but since 1971 the trend has been reversed, so that today they have nearly as many MPs as one would expect, given their percentage of the population.[12]

It is also important to note the way ethnocultural groups participate in Canadian politics. They do not form separate ethnic-based parties, either as individual groups or as coalitions, but participate overwhelmingly within pan-Canadian parties. Indeed, the two parties in Canada that are closest to being ethnic parties were created by and for those of French or English ancestry: the Parti/Bloc Québécois, whose support comes almost entirely from Quebecers of French ancestry, and the Confederation of Regions

Party, whose support came almost entirely from New Brunswickers of English Loyalist ancestry.[13] Immigrants themselves have shown no inclination to support ethnic-based political parties, and instead vote for the traditional national parties.

This is just one indicator of a more general point: namely, that immigrants are overwhelmingly supportive of, and committed to protecting, the country's basic political structure. We know that, were it not for the 'ethnic vote', the 1995 referendum on secession in Quebec would have succeeded. In that referendum, ethnic voters overwhelmingly expressed their commitment to Canada. More generally, all the indicators suggest that immigrants quickly absorb and accept Canada's basic liberal-democratic values and constitutional principles, even if their home countries are illiberal or non-democratic.[14] As Freda Hawkins puts it, 'the truth is that there have been no riots, no breakaway political parties, no charismatic immigrant leaders, no real militancy in international causes, no internal political terrorism. . . . immigrants recognize a good, stable political system when they see one.'[15] If we look at indicators of legal and political integration, then, we see that since the adoption of multiculturalism in 1971 immigrants have been more likely to become Canadians, and more likely to participate politically. And when they participate, they do so through pan-ethnic political parties that uphold Canada's basic liberal-democratic principles.

This sort of political integration is the main aim of a democratic state. Yet from the point of view of individual Canadians, the most important forms of immigrant integration are probably not political, but societal. Immigrants who participate in politics may be good democratic citizens, but if they can't speak English or French, or are socially isolated in self-contained ethnic groups, then Canadians will perceive a failure of integration. So let us shift now to two indicators of societal integration: official language acquisition and intermarriage rates.

If the Gwyn/Bissoondath thesis were true, one would expect to find that the desire of ethnocultural minorities to acquire official language competence has declined since the adoption of multiculturalism. If immigrant groups are being 'ghettoized', are 'alienated from the mainstream', and are attempting to preserve their original way of life intact from their homeland, then presumably they have less reason than they did before 1971 to learn an official language.

In fact, demand for classes in English and French as second languages (ESL; FSL) has never been higher, and actually exceeds supply in many cities. According to the 1991 Census, 98.6 per cent of Canadians report that they can speak one of the official languages.[16] This figure is staggering when one considers how many immigrants are elderly and/or illiterate in their mother tongue, and who therefore find it extremely difficult to learn a new language. It is especially impressive given that the number of immigrants who arrive with knowledge of an official language has declined since 1971.[17] If we set aside the elderly—who make up the majority of the Canadians who cannot speak an official language—the idea that there is a general decrease in immigrants' desire to learn an official language is absurd. The overwhelming majority do learn an official language, and insofar as such skills are lacking, the explanation is the lack of accessible and appropriate ESL/FSL classes, not lack of desire.[18]

Another indicator worth looking at is intermarriage rates. If the Gwyn/Bissoondath thesis were true, one would expect intermarriage to have declined since the adoption of a policy said to have driven 'even deeper the awful wedges between races and nationalities' and to have encouraged groups to retreat into 'monocultural' ghettos and hide behind 'cultural walls'. In fact, intermarriage rates have consistently increased since 1971. There has been an overall decline in endogamy, both for immigrants and for their native-born children. Moreover, and equally important, we see a dramatic increase in social acceptance of mixed marriages.[19] Whereas in 1968 a majority of Canadians (52 per cent) disapproved of Black-white marriages, the situation is now completely reversed, so that by 1995 an overwhelming majority (81 per cent) approved of such marriages.[20]

Unlike the previous three indicators of integration, intermarriage is not a deliberate goal of government policy; it is not the business of governments either to encourage or to discourage intermarriage. But changes in intermarriage rates are useful as indicators of a broader trend that is a legitimate government concern: namely, the extent to which Canadians feel comfortable living and interacting with members of other ethnic groups. If Canadians feel comfortable living and working with members of other groups, inevitably some people will become friends with, and even lovers of, members of other ethnic groups. The fact that intermarriage rates have gone up is important, therefore, not necessarily in itself, but rather as evidence that Canadians are more accepting of diversity. And we have direct evidence for this more general trend. Canadians today are much more willing to accept members of other ethnic groups as co-workers, neighbours, or friends than they were before 1971.[21]

Other indicators point to the same trends. For example, despite Gwyn's and Bissoondath's rhetoric about the proliferation of ethnic 'ghettos' and 'enclaves', studies of residential concentration have shown that permanent ethnic enclaves do not exist in Canada. Indeed, 'it is scarcely sensible to talk of "ghettos" in Canadian cities.'[22] What little concentration does exist is more likely to be found among older immigrant groups, like the Jews and Italians, whose arrival preceded the multiculturalism policy. Groups that have arrived primarily after 1971, such as Asians and Afro-Caribbeans, exhibit the least residential concentration.[23]

In short, whether we look at naturalization, political participation, official language competence, or intermarriage rates, we see the same story. There is no evidence to support the claim that multiculturalism has decreased the rate of integration of immigrants, or increased the separatism or mutual hostility of ethnic groups. As Orest Kruhlak puts it, 'irrespective of which variables one examines, including [citizenship acquisition, ESL, mother-tongue retention, ethnic association participation, intermarriage] or political participation, the scope of economic involvement, or participation in mainstream social or service organizations, none suggest a sense of promoting ethnic separateness.'[24]

3. THE COMPARATIVE EVIDENCE

We can make the same point another way. If the Bissoondath/Gwyn thesis were correct about the ghettoizing impact of our official multiculturalism policy, we would expect Canada to perform worse on these indicators of integration than other countries that have not adopted such a policy. Both Gwyn and Bissoondath contrast the Canadian approach with the American, which exclusively emphasizes common identities and common values, and refuses to provide public recognition or affirmation of ethnocultural differences. If Canada fared worse than the US in terms of integrating immigrants, this would provide some indirect support for the Bissoondath/Gwyn theory.

In fact, however, Canada fares better than the United States on virtually any dimension of integration. Its naturalization rates are almost double those of the US.[25] Canada's rates of political participation and official language acquisition are higher, and its rates of residential segregation are lower.[26] In addition Canadians show much greater approval for intermarriage. In 1988, when 72 per cent of Canadians approved of interracial marriages, only 40 per cent of Americans approved, and 25 per cent felt they should be illegal![27] And ethnicity is less salient as a determinant of friendship in Canada than in the United States.[28]

On every indicator of integration, then, Canada, with its multiculturalism policy, fares better than the United States, with its repudiation of multiculturalism. We would find the same story if we compared Canada with other immigrant countries that have rejected multiculturalism in favour of an exclusive emphasis on common identities—such as France.[29] Canada does better than these other countries not only in actual rates of integration, but also in the day-to-day experience of ethnic relations. In a 1997 survey, people in twenty countries were asked whether they agreed that 'different ethnic groups get along well here'. The percentage of those agreeing was far higher in Canada (75 per cent) than in the United States (58 per cent) or France (51 per cent).[30]

This should not surprise us, since Canada does better than virtually any other country in the world in the integration of immigrants. The only comparable country is Australia, which has its own official multiculturalism policy—one largely inspired by Canada's, although of course it has been adapted to Australia's circumstances.[31] The two countries that lead the world in the integration of immigrants are countries with official multiculturalism policies. They are much more successful than any country that has rejected multiculturalism.

In short, there is no evidence to support the claim that multiculturalism is promoting ethnic separateness or impeding immigrant integration. Whether we examine the trends within Canada since 1971 or compare Canada with other countries, the conclusion is the same: the multiculturalism program is working. It is achieving what it set out to do: helping to ensure that those people who wish to express their ethnic identity are respected and accommodated, while simultaneously increasing the ability of immigrants to integrate into the larger society. Along with our fellow multiculturalists in Australia, Canadians do a better job of respecting ethnic diversity while promoting societal integration than citizens of any other country.

4. Explaining the Debate

This finding raises a genuine puzzle. Why do so many intelligent and otherwise well-informed commentators agree that multiculturalism policy is impeding integration? Part of the explanation is that many critics have simply not examined the actual policy to see what it involves. For example, both Gwyn and Bissoondath claim that, in effect, multiculturalism tells new Canadians that they should practise 'monoculturalism', preserving their inherited way of life intact while avoiding interacting with or learning from the members of other groups, or the larger society.[32] If this were a plausible interpretation of the policy's aims, it would be only natural to assume that ethnocultural separatism is increasing in Canadian society.

In reality, as we shall see in the next chapter, and as the government's documents make clear, the main goals of multiculturalism policy (and most of its funding) have been to promote civic participation in the larger society and to increase mutual understanding and co-operation between the members of different ethnic groups. Unfortunately, neither Gwyn nor Bissoondath quotes or cites a single document published by the multiculturalism unit of the federal government—not one of its annual reports, demographic analyses, public education brochures, or program funding guidelines. Their critiques are thus doubly unreal. They describe a (non-existent) policy of promoting 'monoculturalism' among ethnocultural groups, and then blame it for a (non-existent) trend towards 'apartheid' in Canadian society. They have invented a non-existent policy to explain a non-existent trend.

But if the Bissoondath and Gwyn accounts are so ill-informed, why have they been so influential? Both books were generally well reviewed, and often praised for their insight into ethnocultural relations in Canada. Why were so many Canadians persuaded by their claims about growing ethnocultural separatism, even though these claims had no empirical support, and indeed are contradicted by the evidence? Why were so many

Canadians persuaded by their mistaken characterization of the policy?

Part of the answer, I think, is that defenders of the policy have been strangely inarticulate. The federal government has not clearly explained the aims of the policy, nor has it provided criteria for evaluating its success. Even though the policy has been demonstrably successful, the government itself has made little attempt to demonstrate its success; so far as I can tell, it has never attempted to gather together the various findings on integration discussed in this chapter, or to monitor them systematically so as to measure changes in integration over time.

Collecting and publicizing this sort of information would provide Canadians with the tools to question and deflate the exaggerated claims and misinformed critiques we find in Gwyn and Bissoondath. Yet even if this information were more widely available, it would likely not entirely alleviate public anxiety about multiculturalism. Lack of information cannot, by itself, explain public attitudes. In the absence of information, why do so many Canadians assume that multiculturalism has had negative consequences? Why are they fearful of multiculturalism, rather than confident about it?

Part of the problem may be that Canadians have no clear sense of the limits of multiculturalism. They are not sure that certain 'non-negotiable' principles or institutions will be protected and upheld, even if they conflict with the desires or traditions of some immigrant groups. Canadians are not averse to multiculturalism within limits, but they want to know that those limits exist. They value diversity, but they also want to know that this diversity will be expressed within the context of common Canadian institutions, and that it doesn't entail acceptance of ethnic separatism. Similarly, Canadians are generally tolerant, but they also believe that some practices, such as clitoridectomy, are intolerable, and they want to know that they won't be asked to 'tolerate' the violation of basic human rights.

So long as Canadians feel insecure about the limits of multiculturalism, publicizing statistics about the beneficial effects of multiculturalism will have only limited success in changing public attitudes. The statistics may look good today, but what about tomorrow? Perhaps the policy has worked until now to promote integration, but only because the full 'logic' of multiculturalism has not yet been implemented. Perhaps the logic of multiculturalism is to undermine the very idea that there are any principles or institutions that all citizens must respect and adhere to. It is this sort of insecurity that explains, at least in part, the popularity of the Bissoondath/Gwyn account. Until defenders of multiculturalism explain its limits, these sorts of critiques will continue to strike a chord among Canadians, touching deeply felt anxieties about ethnocultural relations.

I think it is possible to address these concerns. In order to do so, however, we need to understand how multiculturalism fits into a larger set of government policies regarding ethnocultural relations in Canada. It is precisely this larger context that is typically ignored in debates about multiculturalism. Both critics and defenders of multiculturalism often talk as if the adoption of the policy in 1971 ushered in an entirely new era in ethnic relations in Canada, overturning the government policies developed over the previous 150 years of immigration. This is a very misleading picture. In many respects, the government policies that encouraged the historical integration of immigrants remain firmly in place. After all, multiculturalism is not the only—or even the primary—government policy affecting the place of ethnic groups in Canadian society; it is just one small piece of the pie. Many aspects of public policy affect these groups, including policies relating to naturalization, education, job training and professional accreditation, human rights and anti-discrimination law, civil service employment, health and safety, even national defence. It is these other policies that are the major engines of integration, for they encourage, pressure, even legally force immigrants to take steps towards integrating into Canadian society.

The idea that multiculturalism promotes ethnic separateness stems in large part, I think, from a failure to see how multiculturalism fits into this larger context of public policy. When we do situate multiculturalism within this larger context, we see that it is not a rejection of integration, but a renegotiation of the terms of integration—a renegotiation that, as the next two chapters will show, was in general not merely justified but overdue.

Chapter 2

▶ *Putting Multiculturalism into Perspective* ◀

Multiculturalism is often described as a set of demands made by ethnocultural groups upon the state. In one sense this is quite correct. Yet in another sense multiculturalism is best understood as a response by ethnocultural groups to the demands that the state imposes on them in its efforts to promote integration. From this perspective, the first step towards understanding multiculturalism is to understand the pressures—both positive (incentives) and negative (barriers)—that the state exerts in order to persuade immigrants to integrate into Canadian society.

Unfortunately, it is precisely these pressures that critics of multiculturalism typically ignore. There seem to be two reasons for this oversight. First, the critics tend to view multiculturalism in isolation, as if it were the most important or even the only policy affecting the status of immigrant groups in Canada. Second, they have a mistaken idea of the state's role in culture: they assume that a liberal state is, or should be, 'neutral' with respect to people's ethnocultural identities. On this view, the official affirmation and recognition of ethnocultural identities provided by multiculturalism is a dramatic and dangerous departure from the normal operations of the democratic state. In reality, however, the state is deeply and inextricably involved in shaping the ethnocultural identities of its citizens through its efforts to promote a very definite form of cultural integration. Multiculturalism neither rejects nor undermines these efforts. It simply seeks to ensure that they are fair.

This chapter begins by exploring the many ways in which the state promotes cultural integration (section 1); it then considers the various options that ethnocultural minorities face in responding to this pressure to integrate (section 2). Multiculturalism represents a very specific response to demands for integration, and can best be understood if we distinguish it from other possible responses, such as marginalization or separatism. In particular, I will try to show what separatism involves, and how multiculturalism differs in theory and practice from separatism (section 3).

1. STATES AND CULTURES

I've said that the state pressures ethnocultural groups into accepting a certain form of cultural integration. But what does 'integration' mean here? There are many forms of integration, and the state does not (and should not) promote all of them. For example, a liberal-democratic state does not seek to promote *religious* integration. Even if the majority of citizens belong to a particular faith, the state does not treat this as the 'official religion', nor does it encourage new citizens to join this church. There is no need for the state to require immigrants to integrate in terms of religion; in fact, that would be a violation of liberal principles, which provide the strongest possible guarantees of freedom of conscience, and which insist on separation of church and state.

Some theorists argue that liberal-democratic states should treat culture generally in the same way as religion: as something that people should be free to pursue in their private lives, but that is not the concern of the state. Just as liberalism precludes the establishment of an official religion, so too it should preclude the establishment of official cultures that have preferred status over other possible cultural allegiances.

On this view, modern governments should avoid supporting any particular societal culture or ethnonational identity. Indeed, some theorists argue that this is precisely what distinguishes liberal 'civic nations' from illiberal 'ethnic nations'. Ethnic nations take the reproduction of a particular ethnonational culture and identity as one of their most important goals. Civic nations, by contrast, are 'neutral' with respect to the ethnocultural identities of their citizens, and define national membership purely in terms of adherence to certain principles of democracy and justice.[1]

For example, Michael Walzer argues that liberalism involves a 'sharp divorce of state and ethnicity'. The liberal state stands above all the various ethnic and national groups in the country, 'refusing to endorse or support their ways of life or to take an active interest in their social reproduction': it is 'neutral with reference to [the] language, history, literature, calendar' of these groups. The clearest example of such a civic nation, according to Walzer, is the United States, whose ethnocultural neutrality is reflected in the fact that it has no constitutionally recognized official language.[2] For immigrants to become American, therefore, is simply a matter of affirming their allegiance to the principles of democracy and individual freedom defined in the American Constitution.

If one accepts this view of ethnocultural neutrality, then demands by immigrants for multiculturalism will seem a dramatic and dangerous departure from established liberal principles. And indeed this conception of neutrality has been explicitly invoked by critics of multiculturalism in Canada. Thus Preston Manning rejects multiculturalism on the grounds that 'the role of the federal government should be neutral to the culture just as it is toward religion.'[3] Similarly, Richard Gwyn argues against multiculturalism by equating it with the state affirmation of religion: 'official multiculturalism is as much beside the point as would be a Multi-Religion Act and a Department of Multi-Religionism. One of our nation-building achievements was to separate church and state; we've now smudged it by conjoining state and race.'[4] This is a misleading conception of the role of the state, particularly in Canada, but even in the United States. In fact, we can see its fallacy most clearly if we look at the United States.

Contrary to Walzer's view, the American government very actively promotes not only a particular set of political principles, but also a particular kind of sociocultural integration. Immigrants who wish to become American citizens are required to swear allegiance to the Constitution, and they must do so *in English*. It is a legal requirement for immigrants (under the age of 50) seeking American citizenship to learn the English language and American history. It is also a legal requirement for children to learn the English language and American history in schools; it is a *de facto* requirement for employment in government that the applicant speak English; court proceedings and other government activities are typically conducted only in English; and the resulting legislation and bureaucratic forms are typically provided only in English. All levels of American government—federal, state, and municipal—have insisted that there is a legitimate governmental interest in promoting a common language, and the Supreme Court has repeatedly affirmed that claim in upholding laws that mandate the teaching and use of English in schools and government functions. As Gerald Johnson put it, 'It is one of history's little ironies that no polyglot empire of the old world has dared to be so ruthless in imposing a single language upon its whole population as was the liberal republic "dedicated to the proposition that all men are created equal".'[5]

In short, the United States has deliberately promoted integration into a societal culture based on the English language. I use the term 'societal culture' to emphasize that it involves a common language and social institutions, rather than common religious beliefs, family customs, or personal lifestyles. Societal cultures within a modern liberal democracy are inevitably pluralistic, containing Muslims, Jews, and atheists as well as Christians; gays as well as heterosexuals; rural farmers as well as urban professionals; socialists as well as conservatives. Such diversity is the inevitable result of the rights and freedoms guaranteed to citizens in a liberal democracy—including freedom of conscience, association, speech, and political dissent, and rights to privacy—particularly when combined with an ethnically diverse population.

Thus a societal culture is a territorially concentrated culture centred on a shared language that is used in a wide range of societal institutions, including schools, media, law, the economy, and government. Participation in such a culture provides access to meaningful ways of life across the full range of human activities—social, educational, religious, recreational, economic—encompassing both public and private spheres. The American government has deliberately promoted integration into such a societal culture: it has encouraged citizens to view their life-chances as tied up with participation in common societal institutions that operate in the English language. Nor is the United States at all unique in this respect. Promoting integration into a societal culture is part of the 'nation-building' project in which all liberal democracies have engaged.

When I speak of the 'integration' of ethnic groups, then, I mean integration in this very specific sociocultural sense: the extent to which immigrants and their descendants integrate into an existing societal culture and come to view their life-chances as tied up with participation in the range of social institutions, based on a common language, which define that societal culture.

The common 'culture' that English-speaking Americans share obviously does not run very deep, since it does not preclude differences in religion, personal values, family relationships, or lifestyle choices. But while this sort of common culture is thin, it is far from trivial. On the contrary, as I will explain below, whenever pressures to integrate into such a common societal culture have been applied to national minorities, rather than immigrants, they have typically been met with serious resistance. Although integration in this sense leaves a great deal of room for both the public and the private expression of individual and collective differences, national minorities have vehemently rejected the idea that they should view their life-chances as tied up with the societal institutions conducted in the majority's language. Immigrants, however, have historically accepted state pressure to integrate.

It's important to note that governments need not promote only one societal culture. It is possible for government policies to encourage the sustaining of two or more societal cultures within a single country; this is precisely what characterizes Canada and other 'multination' states. In the Canadian case, government policy encourages integration into one of two societal cultures, francophone and anglophone.

Thus in Canada it is a legal requirement for gaining citizenship that immigrants know either English or French (unless they are elderly), as well as some basic information about Canadian history and institutions. Similarly, it is a legal requirement under provincial education acts that the children of immigrants learn an official language and a common core curriculum. Immigrants must know an official language to gain access to government-funded job training programs, to receive professional accreditation, or to have their foreign training recognized. The most highly skilled pharmacist won't be granted a professional licence to practise pharmacy in Canada if she speaks only Portuguese. And of course knowledge of an official language is a precondition for working in the bureaucracy, or to gain government contract work. In a variety of ways, then, the Canadian government encourages, pressures—even legally requires—integration into either the anglophone or the francophone societal culture in Canada.

The adoption of these policies should not be seen purely as a matter of cultural imperialism or ethnocentric prejudice. Historically, it is true that policies aimed at integrating citizens into a common societal culture were often justified on the grounds that the cultures of ethnic minorities were backward or uncivilized. But there are a number of important and legitimate reasons for promoting a common societal culture that are not based on ethnocentric attitudes, and that remain relevant even as these prejudices fade. A modern economy requires a mobile, educated, and literate workforce, and standardized public education in a common language has often been seen as essential if all citizens are to have equal opportunity to work in such an economy. In addition, participation in a common societal culture has often been seen as essential for generating solidarity within modern democratic states. The sort of solidarity required by a welfare state requires that citizens have a strong sense of common identity and common membership, so that they will make sacrifices for each other, and this common identity is assumed to require (or at least to be facilitated by) a common language and history. Sharing a common language also makes it easier to engage in democratic deliberations with co-citizens. Promoting integration into a common societal culture has therefore been seen as essential to social equality, political cohesion, and democratic debate in modern states.

Given these legitimate goals, most Western democracies have aspired to the American or French model of a 'nation-state', in which all citizens are integrated into a common societal culture. It was seen as 'normal' and desirable for each country to have a single societal culture throughout its territory. And so all democracies have engaged in various forms of 'nation-building' to bring this about. They have promoted a common language and a sense of common membership in the social institutions based on that language.[6] Decisions regarding official languages, core educational curricula, and citizenship requirements have all been made with the express intention of diffusing a particular language and societal culture throughout society, and of promoting a particular national identity based on participation in that societal culture.

2. HOW MINORITIES RESPOND TO NATION-BUILDING

Nation-building projects are a fundamental, defining feature of modern democratic states, and as such they are an essential part of the context within which multiculturalism has to be seen. In fact, multiculturalism is a distinctive way of responding to state projects of nation-building, and we can best understand its specificity by comparing it with other ways in which minorities can respond to such projects.

As Charles Taylor notes, the process of nation-building inescapably privileges members of the majority culture:

> If a modern society has an 'official' language, in the fullest sense of the term, that is, a state-sponsored, -inculcated, and -defined language and culture, in which both economy and state function, then it is obviously an immense advantage to people if this language and culture are theirs. Speakers of other languages are at a distinct disadvantage.[7]

This means that minority cultures face a choice. If all public institutions operate in another language, minorities face the danger of being cut off from the central economic, academic, and political life of the society. To avoid perpetual marginalization, minorities must either integrate into the majority culture or seek the sorts of rights and powers of self-government needed to maintain their own societal culture—to create their own economic, political, and educational institutions in their own language.

Not all groups wish to avoid permanent marginalization; examples include the Hutterites in Canada and the Amish in the United States. But the option of accepting marginalization is likely to be attractive only to religious sects whose theology requires them to avoid all contact with the modern world. The Hutterites and the Amish are unconcerned about their marginalization from universities or legislatures, since they view such 'worldly' institutions as corrupt.

Virtually all other ethnocultural minorities, however, do want to participate in the modern world, and hence must either integrate or seek the rights of self-government needed to create and sustain their own modern institutions. Faced with this choice, national minorities and immigrant groups have responded in different ways. I will start by considering how national minorities have responded, and then consider the response of immigrant groups.

National minorities in Canada and in other Western countries have strongly resisted integration, and have instead fought for self-government. Here again, by 'national minorities' I mean historically settled, territorially concentrated, and previously self-governing cultures whose territory has become incorporated into a larger state. Such groups include the Québécois and Aboriginal peoples in Canada, the Puerto Ricans and American Indians in the United States, and the Flemish, Catalans, Saami, and Basques in Europe.

Whenever such national minorities have been subjected to pressure to integrate into the majority societal culture, they have typically responded by opposing such policies, sometimes violently, and fighting for self-government. In Canada's history, a number of abortive efforts were made to impose English on French Canada, most notably through certain provisions in the Royal Proclamation of 1763 and the Durham Report of 1839.[8] But these policies were quickly reversed once it became clear that French Canadians were implacably opposed to them.

Why do national minorities so strongly resist integration even when it is of a relatively 'thin' kind, involving only linguistic and institutional integration? I will explore this question in greater depth in Part 2 of this book, which focuses on minority nationalism. What it is important to recognize here is that, in the case of a national minority, unlike that of immigrants, the imposition of the majority language threatens a culturally distinct society that is already existing and functioning. The national minority's language and traditions are already embodied in a full set of social practices and institutions, encompassing all aspects of social life, which are now threatened by the majority's efforts to diffuse a common societal culture. Nation-building policies prevent immigrants from forming separate societies in their new country or gaining self-governing powers. But a national minority already exists as a separate society, and thus nation-building policies involve stripping it of institutions and powers that it has enjoyed for centuries, and that were adapted to its needs and identities.

It is not surprising, therefore, that a national minority will almost inevitably resist integration and seek official recognition of its language and culture. Walker Connor goes so far as to suggest that few if any recognized national groups in this century have voluntarily assimilated to another culture, even though in many cases the economic incentives and political pressures to do so have been considerable.[9]

Demands for official recognition need not take the form of a secessionist movement for a separate state. They may take the form of demands for some degree of local autonomy, perhaps through a system of federalism, with local control over education, language, and perhaps even immigration. This of course is the route taken (to date) by Quebec. But whatever the exact form, such demands typically include the sorts of legal rights and legislative powers necessary to ensure the survival of a culturally distinct society alongside the majority society.

3. WHAT DOES SEPARATISM INVOLVE?

Many people worry that multiculturalism is encouraging immigrants in Canada today to think of themselves as akin to national minorities, and hence to demand the sorts of rights and powers needed to form distinct societies alongside the majority. On the contrary, when we look at the actual substance of Canada's multiculturalism policy, as we will in the next chapter, we see that it is the expression not of a proto-nationalist desire for self-government, but rather of a desire for fairer terms of integration within the mainstream society.

First, however, it is worth thinking for a minute about what would be required for an ethnocultural minority to consolidate its own societal culture within a larger state. The idea that multiculturalism could enable immigrant groups to form and sustain their own societal cultures reflects, I believe, a failure to recognize what is actually involved in such a project. To maintain a separate societal culture in a modern state is an immensely ambitious and arduous project.

We can get a sense of what such a project involves by considering what the Québécois have had to do to maintain their societal culture. Obviously, the first demand was that their children be able to attend French-language schools. This is a crucial element in reproducing a societal culture, since it helps ensure the passing on of the language and its associated traditions and conventions to the next generation.

But ensuring that children learned the language didn't ensure that they had the opportunity to speak it in public life. In other words, it did nothing to create or sustain French-language public institutions. It is very difficult for languages to survive in modern industrialized societies unless they are used in public life—in political, economic, and academic institutions. Given high demands for literacy in people's working lives, and widespread interaction with government institutions (in courts, legislatures, welfare agencies, health services, etc.), any language that is not used in public will become so marginalized that it is likely to survive only among a small élite or in isolated rural communities, or in a ritualized form, not as a living and developing language underlying a flourishing culture.

Thus the Québécois have also fought for various substantial positive rights to use their language when dealing with government institutions. But this is not sufficient either, since most people interact with the state only intermittently. The real key to the reproduction of a societal culture is the ability to use one's language in day-to-day employment.

Hence the Québécois sought the right to use their language within government employment. It is important to remember that the government is a very large employer, and that in modern states public expenditures often account for close to 50 per cent of the economy. To survive, therefore, minority groups must have a fair share of government employment and government contracts. For example, in many countries the army is a major employer, and military service is often compulsory. If all units in the army operate in the majority language, military service becomes a crucial tool for integrating minorities. This is true in Israel, where military service is the single most important institution for integrating immigrants into a Hebrew-speaking society. The military was also a pivotal institution for integration in France. A classic study has shown that the spread of the modern French language, which was largely restricted to the Paris region at the time of the French Revolution, was primarily the result of the fact that conscripts had to learn French. The army was key, therefore, in 'turning peasants into Frenchmen'.[10]

A minority that is content to accept marginalization, as the Hutterites are, can avoid integration simply by seeking exemption from military service. If a minority wants to maintain a modern national society, however, it will insist that some army units operate in its own language. Hence the Québécois have fought for the right for French-language military training and French-language military units.

The same applies to all other areas of government employment, from food inspection to tax accounting. In every case, some part of the public business must be conducted in the minority's language. It is not enough to be able to interact with the state in one's own language: since the state is the single largest employer, minorities must also be able to work within it in their own language. On the other hand, the state is not the only large employer, and so considerable efforts have been made to ensure that French is the language of the workplace even in private firms; this is an important—and largely successful—feature of Quebec's language laws.

To make this possible, the minority must also be able to create and run its own higher education system, not simply at the elementary and secondary levels but in universities and professional schools. The group needs to be able to train the doctors, scientists, and skilled workers who will staff public institutions and private workplaces. Hence the insistence of francophones in Quebec on forming several French-language universities and community colleges.

The requirements for sustaining a national culture go further still. For example, decisions regarding immigration and naturalization also affect the viability of societal cultures. Immigration can strengthen a culture—so long as the numbers are regulated and immigrants are encouraged (or required) to learn the nation's language and history. But if immigrants integrate into the majority culture, then the minority will be increasingly outnumbered and so increasingly powerless in political life, both federally and within its own territory. A minority that seeks to sustain a distinct societal culture must therefore have some control over immigration policies. Demands for such control have been central to modern Quebec nationalism, including demands that Quebec have the right to define its own immigration criteria (which favour French-speakers), to set its own target levels (based on calculations of the absorption capacity of Quebec society), and to send its own immigration officers overseas.

Thus the historical experience of the Québécois suggests that a minority can sustain its societal culture only if it has substantial powers regarding language, education, government employment, and immigration. If the minority can be outvoted on any of these issues, its hope of sustaining its societal culture will be seriously jeopardized. But a minority can exercise these powers only if it has some forum for collective deliberation and decision-making. In other words, there must be some political body or political unit that the minority substantially controls.

This is reflected in the traditional Québécois commitment to federalism—to a system that decentralizes power to federal subunits, and whose boundaries are drawn so that francophones form a majority within one of these subunits. But just as the members of the minority fear being outvoted on specific issues relating to immigration or education, so too they fear being outvoted on changes to the federal division of powers, or the drawing of federal boundaries. This explains why the Québécois demanded that the boundaries of their province, and the powers it exercises, themselves be

constitutionally guaranteed, so that the anglophone majority cannot unilaterally reduce their self-governing powers.

This is only a brief sketch of the measures that the Québécois have
found necessary to sustain their societal culture in the face of the anglophone majority in Canada. One could list many other factors, from bilingual product labels to bilingual currency. Others argue (implausibly, I
think) that more extreme measures, from the old sign law[11] to actual separation, are needed. Nevertheless, every commentator would agree that 'la
survivance' in Quebec has depended on a number of very basic conditions:
French-language education, not only in childhood but through to higher
education; the right to use French not only when dealing with government, but also in day-to-day employment, whether in the public or the
private sector; exemption of francophone immigrants from the requirement to learn English to gain citizenship, as well as the right to select, integrate, and naturalize immigrants; and the right not only to a fair share of
political power at the federal level, but to self-government, as embodied in
a constitutionally defined federal subunit that has the power to make decisions with respect to education, employment, and immigration. Similar
conditions have proven necessary to sustain distinct societal cultures in
Puerto Rico, in Flanders, and in Catalonia. And similar conditions are
required for sustaining indigenous societies in Canada and around the
world.

It is important to reflect on how onerous these efforts at cultural reproduction have been. Sustaining a societal culture in the modern world is not
a matter of holding ethnic festivals, or having a few classes taught in one's
mother tongue as a child. It is a matter of creating and sustaining a set of
public institutions that will enable a minority group to participate in the
modern world in its own language.

To put the matter another way, it is not enough for a minority simply
to resist the majority's efforts at diffusing a single common language. The
minority must also engage in its own competing form of state-sponsored
nation-building. Nationalists in Quebec realize that to sustain their national culture, they too must seek to diffuse a common culture and language
throughout their society so as to promote equality of opportunity and political solidarity. And they use the same tools that the majority uses in its program of nation-building: standardized public education, official language
legislation (including language requirements for citizenship and government employment), and so on. The aspiration to maintain a societal culture
in the modern world is therefore an intensely political one, requiring the
use of, and control over, a variety of political powers and institutions.

4. THE IMMIGRANT RESPONSE TO NATION-BUILDING

The historical evidence, both in Canada and abroad, shows that the capacity and motivation to undertake such an ambitious nation-building project

is found only in non-immigrant national minorities. Immigrant groups have responded in a very different way to state nation-building policies. They have typically accepted the expectation that they will integrate into the dominant societal culture. They have not objected to requirements that they and their children learn an official language, and that they participate in common institutions operating in that language.

Why have immigrants historically accepted integration? One reason is that they have already voluntarily left their own cultures with the expectation of integrating into a different national society. That's just what it means to immigrate; if they found the idea of integrating into another culture repugnant, they would not have chosen to leave their homelands.[12] Moreover, since most arrive in Canada as individuals or families, rather than as entire communities, immigrants typically lack the territorial concentration or corporate institutions needed to form a linguistically distinct society alongside the mainstream society. To try to recreate such a distinct parallel society would require tremendous support from the host society—support that host governments are reluctant to offer.

In both of these respects, immigrants are very different from national minorities, for whom nation-building threatens a culturally distinct society that already exists and has functioned for generations. Historically, the nationalist option has been neither desirable nor feasible for immigrants, and in fact there are very few (if any) examples in the Western democracies of immigrant groups forming nationalist movements for self-government or secession. In short, faced with the choice between integration and fighting to maintain a distinct societal culture, immigrant groups in Canada have historically chosen the former, while national minorities have chosen the latter.

In some other countries, however, the situation is more complex. The extent to which immigrant groups have been allowed or encouraged to integrate varies considerably. Whereas in Canada it is easy for immigrants to become full citizens regardless of their race, religion, or ethnic origin, in many parts of the world, including some Western democracies, they are much less welcome, and it is far more difficult for them to acquire equal citizenship. Where immigrants are subject to severe prejudice and legal discrimination—and hence where full equality within the mainstream society is unachievable—it is possible that some may come to question the goal of integration.[13]

Similarly, the extent to which national minorities have been able to maintain separate cultures varies from country to country. National minorities that have been subject to long periods of highly coercive policies of assimilation, such as the Bretons in France, have eventually lost most or all of their institutions and traditions of self-government. As a general rule, however, in Western democracies dominant cultures have had far less success integrating national than immigrant groups. While national minorities have resisted integration into the common culture and sought to protect their separate existence by consolidating their own societal cultures, immigrants have accepted the expectation of integration.

5. Is Multiculturalism Separatist?

Is there any reason to think that multiculturalism is changing this pattern? Does it repudiate the principles and policies promoting integration, and instead treat immigrant groups as if they were national minorities? Some critics think so. According to Richard Gwyn, 'logically' the policy of multiculturalism entails that 'the doctrine of self-governing territories as applied now to native people could be extended to all identity groups'.[14] In reality, nothing could be further from the truth.

Consider any of the sorts of programs commonly associated with multiculturalism, whether curriculum reform in public schools (e.g,. revising the history and literature curricula to give greater recognition to the historical and cultural contributions of ethnocultural minorities; bilingual education programs for the children of immigrants at the primary level), or institutional adaptation (revising work schedules or dress-codes so as to accommodate the religious holidays and practices of immigrant groups; adopting workplace or school harassment codes prohibiting racist comments; guidelines from the broadcasting regulator, the Canadian Radio-television and Telecommunications Commission [CRTC], on ethnic stereotypes), or public education programs (anti-racism educational campaigns; cultural diversity training for police, social workers, or health-care professionals), or cultural development programs (funding ethnic festivals and ethnic studies programs; providing mother-tongue literacy courses for adult immigrants), or affirmative action (preferential treatment of visible minorities in access to education, training, or employment).

This list goes well beyond the confines of the federal government's official policy of multiculturalism. Many of these programs fall under the jurisdiction of other federal departments (e.g., employment equity; broadcasting guidelines), or other levels of government (school curricula), and, strictly speaking, are not part of Canada's 'multiculturalism' policy. On the other hand, since the federal policy was explicitly intended to serve as a model and catalyst for other departments and other levels of government, it is perhaps not inappropriate to consider all of these as loosely related to 'multiculturalism'.

Since each of the above programs raises its own unique issues, it would be misleading to talk about 'the impact of multiculturalism' in general, as if all of them had the same motivations and consequences. Even so, it is important to note that *none* of these programs—either individually or in combination—involves anything close to a program of nation-building, or the 'logic of self-governing territories'. None of them involves creating Spanish-language army units, or Vietnamese-language universities. And none of them involves creating new political units that would enable

Ukrainians to exercise self-governing powers in the area of government employment or immigration. Nor have any such measures been demanded by these immigrant groups. However, for the sake of argument, let's imagine that an immigrant group within Canada—say the Chinese, or the Somalis—really did want to form and maintain its own societal culture. It is worth emphasizing how much further such a group would need to go, in terms of its institutional capacities and political powers.

It is certainly possible *in theory* for the Chinese to become a national group, if they were to settle together and acquire self-governing powers. After all, this is what happened with English colonists throughout the British Empire, Spanish colonists in Puerto Rico, and French colonists in Quebec. These colonial settlers did not see themselves as 'immigrants', since they had no expectation of integrating into another culture: rather, they aimed to reproduce their original society in a new land. It is an essential feature of colonization, as distinct from individual immigration, that it aims to create an institutionally complete society, not to integrate into an existing one. It would, in principle, be possible to allow Chinese immigrants today to view themselves as colonists.

But this would require not only that children be taught Chinese in public schools, but also that there be Chinese-language universities; not only that there be Chinese-language ballots or welfare forms, but also that Chinese be the working language of the government workplace, including Chinese-language army units or hospitals; not only that Chinese not be under-represented in Parliament, but also that there be a political body within which Chinese form a majority; not only that Chinese needn't learn English or French to acquire citizenship, but also that the Chinese community be able to maintain itself over time by selecting and naturalizing future immigrants on the basis of their integration into the Chinese-speaking community.

The fact is that existing multiculturalism policies have not created *any* of the public institutions needed to create and sustain a separate societal culture for the Chinese, the Somalis, or any other immigrant group. None of the academic, political, or economic institutions that would enable an immigrant group to participate in modern life through their mother tongue have been created. If (unlike the Hutterites) Somali Canadians or Ukrainian Canadians or Vietnamese Canadians want to have access to the opportunities made available by modern society, they must do so within the economic, academic, and political institutions of either the anglophone or the francophone societal culture in Canada.

This should not be surprising, because multiculturalism has not replaced any of the broader panoply of government policies and structures that promote societal integration. It is still the case that immigrants must learn to speak one of the official languages to gain citizenship, or graduate from high school, or find government employment, or gain professional accreditation. These are the basic pillars of government-supported integration within liberal democracies, and none of them has in any way been eroded by multiculturalism policies. Nor was multiculturalism intended to erode them.

In fact, multiculturalism could not have been intended to enable or encourage immigrants to become national minorities, like the Québécois or Aboriginal peoples. Gwyn's claim that the logic of multiculturalism means that 'the doctrine of self-governing territories as applied now to native people could be extended to all identity groups' is nonsensical. It would be inherently contradictory for government to encourage immigrant groups to form their own societal cultures (via multiculturalism policies) while simultaneously insisting (via education, employment, and citizenship policies) that immigrants must learn to speak one of the official languages fluently in order to gain citizenship, graduate from school, find government employment, or acquire professional licensing or trade certification.

And even if the government had somehow adopted this contradictory set of goals, the amount of money spend on multiculturalism is so minuscule that it would have no discernible effect when weighed against all the government spending that promotes integration. The 20 million dollars spent on multiculturalism programs is a drop in the bucket compared with the billions of dollars spent on policies that directly or indirectly promote integration.

So the idea that multiculturalism policies are first steps on the road to separate public institutions is multiply bizarre. These policies have not in fact created such institutions, nor could they have been intended to do so without undermining firmly entrenched policies regarding citizenship, education, and employment; and in any event the funding they receive is so small that it could not hope to create a fraction of the institutions needed for such a separatist goal.

Of course it is still possible to fear that some leaders of ethnic groups hope multiculturalism policies will provide a springboard to a more comprehensively separatist policy. If so, however, both the hope and the fear are in vain, for they massively underestimate the sort of support needed to create and sustain a separate societal culture. It makes more sense simply to accept the obvious: there is no rational basis for the fear that multiculturalism policies will be used to enable immigrant groups to sustain their own societal cultures. This fear is a mirage, without any basis in reality. There is no evidence from any of the major Western immigrant countries that immigrants are seeking to form themselves into national minorities, or to adopt a nationalist political agenda.

6. AN ALTERNATIVE APPROACH

Once we let go of the mirage, we can look more objectively at the actual intentions and implications of multiculturalism policies. Multiculturalism involves accepting the principle of state-imposed integration, but renegotiating the terms of integration. Immigrant groups today accept the expectation that they will integrate into the larger societal culture, as they have always done. Few immigrant groups have objected to the requirement that they learn an official language as a condition of citizenship, or that their children learn an official language in school. They have accepted the assumption that their life-chances and, even more, those of their children will be bound up with participation in mainstream institutions operating in either English or French.

However, immigrants are demanding fairer terms of integration. If Canada is going to encourage immigrants to integrate into common institutions operating in either English or French, then immigrant groups understandably want to ensure that the terms of integration are fair. As I will try to show in the next chapter, the idea of 'multiculturalism within a bilingual framework' is precisely an attempt to define such fair terms of integration.

Chapter 3

Renegotiating the Terms of Integration

According to its critics, the policy of multiculturalism is intended to promote ethnocultural separatism and has led to increasing ethnic 'ghettoism' in Canada. But we can now see how bizarre such a view is. There is no evidence that 'ghettoism' is increasing; on the contrary, integration has increased since the adoption of multiculturalism in 1971. Nor is there any evidence that the policy was intended to encourage ethnocultural separatism; on the contrary, multiculturalism has not diminished any of the state-imposed pressures on immigrant groups to integrate, nor has it provided any of the institutional or political means necessary for ethnocultural groups to sustain themselves as distinct societal cultures.

What, then, is multiculturalism 'really' about? We cannot answer this question by referring to some canonical statement of its concepts or principles, for there is no such statement. Various people have tried to uncover the 'real' intentions of the decision-makers who first adopted the policy in 1971. But they have come to a dead end.[1] We now know that there was no well-developed theory underlying the original policy. It was introduced in haste, largely as a way of deflecting opposition to the apparent privileging of French and English that was implicit in the introduction of official bilingualism. Multiculturalism was introduced without any real idea of what it would mean, or any long-term strategy for its implementation. In any event, the policy has undergone dramatic changes since 1971, adapting itself, often in an ad hoc way, to new needs and new challenges. To understand the meaning of multiculturalism, therefore, we need to look at what it does *in practice*. When we do, it becomes clear that multiculturalism is a response to the pressures that Canada exerts on immigrants to integrate into common institutions. Although the policy was not originally conceptualized in this way, in practice it has developed and evolved as a framework for debating and developing the terms of integration, to ensure that they are fair.

This chapter will explore how specific multiculturalism policies work to achieve this goal. After listing the sorts of programs I have in mind (section 1), I will begin by examining the ones that aim at reforming common institutions so as to accommodate ethnic diversity (section 2). Multiculturalism instructs us to engage in a systematic exploration of the common institutions into which immigrants are pressured to integrate, to ensure that their rules and symbols do not disadvantage immigrant groups. Many multiculturalism policies can be seen as rectifying the disadvantages that have been uncovered in this process.

In section 3 I will turn to more complicated cases that involve some degree of institutional separateness. At first glance, these programs seem potentially inimical to integration. However, the sort of institutional separateness they promote is often transitional, and rests upon a recognition that integration is a long and often painful process that may take more than one generation. As a result, special institutions may be needed on a transitional basis for immigrants, and perhaps their children, to ease the process of initial integration.

Both of these sorts of policies—adapting common institutions and promoting a transitional institutional separateness—are intended to ensure that Canada is offering immigrants fair terms of integration. Of course, this does not mean that they succeed in reaching that goal. Government policies often have unintended consequences, and perhaps multiculturalism is unintentionally leading to the marginalization of ethnocultural groups. This is an important possibility to keep in mind.

But it is also important not to jump to conclusions about the likelihood of marginalization. As we saw in Chapter 1, the evidence shows that integration has improved since the adoption of multiculturalism. Policies that many critics assumed would lead to marginalization have not done so. Moreover, it is clear that most immigrant groups do not want marginalization: they do not seek to become isolated enclaves that do not participate in the larger society, and that lack the public institutions needed to form their own societal cultures. Some groups do accept permanent marginalization—groups like the Hutterites, or the Amish, or the Doukhobors. But these groups are unique in wishing to avoid the modern world. They do not want to become police officers, or doctors, or engineers, or MPs. Hence they have no interest in controlling their own political units or universities, or in ensuring their integration into majority institutions. These groups are the exceptions proving the rule that participation in the modern world requires integration into a societal culture. Most immigrant groups do want to participate in that world, and they do support multiculturalism policies that improve access to the goods and opportunities it offers.

If we examine each policy on its own merits, with an open mind, it becomes clear that most multiculturalism policies are integrative in both their intentions and their results. With any government policy there is room for improvement, and it is important to reassess multiculturalism policies periodically to ensure that they change with the times. But in general I believe that the vast majority of multiculturalism policies have been worthy, appropriate, and successful attempts to promote fairer terms of integration in Canada.

1. EXAMINING THE POLICIES

'Multiculturalism' means different things to different people, so it is important to clarify the kinds of policies and programs I am talking about. Here are thirteen policies—existing or proposed—that are often discussed under the rubric of 'multiculturalism' in the public debate:[2]

1. Affirmative action programs that seek to increase the representation of visible minorities (or women and the disabled) in major educational and economic institutions;

2. Guarantees of a certain number of seats in the Senate, or in other federal or provincial legislatures, for visible minorities (or women and the disabled);

3. Revisions to the history and literature curricula in public schools to give greater recognition to the historical and cultural contributions of ethno-cultural minorities;

4. Flexible work schedules to accommodate the religious holidays of immigrant groups (for example, some schools schedule Professional Development days on major Jewish or Muslim holidays; Jewish and Muslim businesses may be exempted from Sunday closing legislation);

5. Flexible dress-codes to accommodate the religious beliefs of immigrant groups (for example, the RCMP revised its dress code so that Sikhs can wear their turbans, and Sikhs may be exempted from mandatory motorcycle-helmet or construction-site hard-hat laws);

6. Anti-racism educational programs;

7. Workplace or school harassment codes that seek to prevent colleagues/students from making racist (or sexist/homophobic) statements;

8. Cultural diversity training for the police or health-care professionals, so that they can recognize individual needs and conflicts within immigrant families;

9. CRTC regulatory guidelines regarding ethnic stereotypes in the broadcast media;

10. Government funding of ethnic cultural festivals and ethnic studies programs;

11. Programs to help illiterate adult immigrants acquire literacy in their mother tongue, prior to or in conjunction with learning English or French;

12. Bilingual education programs for the children of immigrants, so that their earliest years of education are conducted partly in their mother tongue, as a transitional phase leading to secondary and post-secondary education in either English or French;

13. Black-focused public schools, specifically designed to serve Black students who are faring badly in racially integrated schools.

As was noted in the last chapter, many of these policies fall outside the limited range of the federal multiculturalism policy. But this list gives a fairly accurate reflection of the sorts of issues that are raised in the public debate over multiculturalism, and that have been adopted or at least seriously proposed by government parliamentary reports or royal commissions.

A number of other practices are sometimes debated under the heading of 'multiculturalism' but have not been adopted by any government, and indeed have been decisively rejected as inconsistent with government policy. They include the practice of clitoridectomy, the legal recognition of compulsorily arranged marriages and talaq divorces, and the legal enforcement of traditional Muslim family law.[3] These practices do not directly affect the societal integration of immigrant groups in terms of their participation in mainstream economic, academic, and political institutions. But they are of deep concern, because if tolerated they would jeopardize basic individual and equality rights. And it is precisely for this reason that they are prohibited in Canada. Some critics think that even if these practices are currently prohibited, the 'logic' of multiculturalism entails tolerating them. This is a grave misunderstanding of the logic of multiculturalism, which I will discuss at greater length in Chapter 4.

The next section will focus on the first ten policies listed above, all of which are aimed at accommodating diversity within common institutions. The last three, which are more complicated because they involve a degree of institutional separateness, will be discussed in section 3.

2. ACCOMMODATING DIVERSITY WITHIN COMMON INSTITUTIONS

The first two policies on the list, affirmative action policies and guarantees of group representation in Parliament, which are also two of the most controversial, are clearly integrationist in their aim. They are intended precisely to increase the numbers of immigrants who participate in mainstream institutions by guaranteeing them a certain share of the positions in various academic, economic, or political institutions. They bring members of different groups together, require them to co-operate in common tasks and common decision-making, and then require them to abide by these common decisions. They are, therefore, the very opposite of policies designed to promote ethnic separatism. (Whether they are *fair* ways to promote the integration of immigrants is a separate question, to which I will return.)

The next seven policies on the list are intended to make immigrants feel more comfortable within the mainstream societal institutions that affirmative action and group representation help them to enter. This is the purpose of demands that the curricula in public schools be revised so as to provide greater recognition for the historical contributions of immigrant groups; that public institutions recognize the religious holidays of Muslims and Jews as well as Christians; that official dress-codes for schools, work-places, and police forces be amended so that Sikh men can wear turbans, Jewish men can wear skullcaps, or Muslim women can wear the hijab; that schools and workplaces provide a welcoming environment for people of all races and religions by prohibiting hate speech; that the media avoid ethnic stereotyping and give visible representation to society's diversity in their programming; and that professionals in the police, social work, or health care be familiar with the distinctive cultural needs and practices of the peo-ple in their care.

None of these policies encourages immigrant groups to view them-selves as separate and self-governing nations with their own public institu-tions. On the contrary, all are intended precisely to make it easier for their members to participate within the mainstream institutions of the larger society. These multiculturalism policies involve revisions to the terms of integration, not a rejection of integration itself.

Prior to the 1960s, immigrants to Canada (as to Australia and the United States) were expected to shed their distinctive heritage and assim-ilate to existing cultural norms. This is known as the 'Anglo-conformity' model of immigration. Some groups were even denied entry because they were considered unassimilable; for example, Chinese immigration was restricted in Canada and the United States, and Australia had a 'white only' immigration policy. Assimilation was seen as essential for political stability, and was rationalized through ethnocentric denigration of other cultures.

However, beginning in the 1970s, under pressure from immigrant groups, all three countries rejected the assimilationist model and adopted more tolerant and pluralistic policies that not only allow but encourage immigrants to maintain various aspects of their ethnic heritage. It is now accepted that immigrants should be free to maintain some of their old cus-toms regarding food, dress, religion, and recreation, and to associate with each other for those purposes. This is no longer seen as unpatriotic or 'un-Canadian'.

The demand for multiculturalism policies was a natural extension of this change. If it is acceptable for immigrants to maintain pride in their eth-nic identity, then it is natural to expect that public institutions will be adapted to accommodate this identity. Multiculturalism allows people to identify themselves in public with their ethnic group, if they wish to do so, without fear that this will disadvantage or stigmatize them. It has made the possession of an ethnic identity an acceptable, even normal, part of life in the mainstream society.

Critics of these policies typically focus entirely on the fact that they involve public recognition and affirmation of immigrants' ethnic identi-ty—a process that is said to be inherently separatist. What they ignore is that this process of recognition and affirmation occurs *within common insti-tutions*. There is no sense in which any of these policies encourages either a Hutterite-like withdrawal from the institutions of mainstream society or a Québécois-like nationalist struggle to create and maintain separate public institutions. On the contrary, these policies stand in clear opposition to both ethnic marginalization and minority nationalism, since they encourage integration into existing academic, economic, and political institutions, and modify these institutions to make immigrants more welcome within them.[4]

Of course such policies may cause a backlash among non-immigrant groups. The demand that Sikh men be exempted from the requirement to wear ceremonial RCMP headgear was seen by many Canadians as a sign of disrespect for one of our 'national symbols'. But from the immigrants' point of view such accommodations are integrative. The fact that Sikh men wanted to be part of our national police force is strong evidence of their desire to participate in and contribute to the larger society, and the exemption they were requesting must be seen as promoting, not discouraging, their integration.

Indeed, it is the failure to adopt such policies that creates serious risks of marginalization. Without accommodation of their religious beliefs in school holidays and dress-codes, for example, immigrant groups might feel compelled to leave the public system and set up their own separate schools. And without affirmative action, fewer Blacks would feel that they have a realistic chance at succeeding within mainstream institutions. These policies can only be seen as helping to diminish potential sources of marginalization.

Some of the most virulent critiques of multiculturalism have been directed at the funding of ethnic festivals. Indeed, many people seem to equate multiculturalism with such funding, even though it accounts for only a small fraction of the overall multiculturalism budget. This is perhaps a hangover from the 1970s, when the funding of folk-culture groups played a larger role (though it was never the predominant component of multiculturalism funding). The emphasis dramatically shifted in the early 1980s, however, and today folk-culture activities make up by far the smallest program funded under the multiculturalism policy. This is one of the many changes that have taken place over the years, as Canadians have come to realize that institutional adaptation and civic participation are more important to successful integration than ethnic festivals.[5]

Still, insofar as the government does provide funding for the arts, it is important that ethnocultural minorities not be discriminated against in the allocation of funds. This happens in many countries, since a minority's forms of artistic expression are often not reflected in the categories or criteria used by traditional granting agencies. The specific targeting of a small amount of money for ethnic arts groups is one way of trying to remedy this problem. Furthermore, most of these funds go to inter-ethnic festivals, which promote contact and exchange between ethnic groups and with the larger society. They help the majority learn something about the presence of other groups in our midst, and so perhaps lead to greater recognition of the need to accommodate them. In fact, there is no reason why the government should fund folk cultural activities if they lack such an inter-ethnic dimension. I don't think the government should fund a dance festival in which exclusively Ukrainian-Canadian dancers perform for an exclusively Ukrainian-Canadian audience; this sort of cultural activity no more requires state subsidy than does a chess group or sailing club. However, cultural exhibitions and events that bring together people of different ethnic groups are often worthy of support.

To be sure, the knowledge of an immigrant group's culture that an ethnic festival provides is fairly shallow. But it is misleading to blame this sort of festival for the 'commodification' or 'Disneyfication' of ethnic cultures and ethnic history, as Neil Bissoondath and others have done.[6] A quick glance at the United States would show that this process occurs whether or not a policy of multiculturalism is in place. The commodification of ethnicity is the product of capitalism, not multiculturalism.

So far, then, I have tried to show that the rationale for the first ten multiculturalism policies is that they promote integration. But are they fair? Do they promote fairness by removing disadvantages that immigrant groups face within common institutions? Or do they give unfair benefits or undeserved privileges to people who are not actually disadvantaged? The charge of unfairness is most commonly heard in the context of affirmative action policies, and in fact there are good reasons to think that such policies, as they are currently implemented, do create unfairness. I will discuss this issue in more depth in Chapter 5, since the evaluation of affirmative action is inextricably tied up with issues of race. Here I will simply note that affirmative action is justified only under limited conditions—in particular, as a remedy for long-term discrimination and disadvantage. Unfortunately, the categories used in Canada's current affirmative action programs are over-inclusive, covering many people who cannot claim to have suffered from such long-term discrimination in Canada, including some immigrants.

Similarly, I will postpone discussion of group representation until Chapter 7. There are several models of group representation, none of which has yet been adopted in Canada, and the fairness of any particular proposal depends on the details. Here I will just say that, as with affirmative action, there are some limited conditions under which group representation can serve as an appropriate and fair remedy for the under-representation of particular groups in the political process, although it is not appropriate as a general basis for representation.

The other eight policies, however, do promote fairness. Fair terms of integration include the requirement that the common institutions into which immigrants are pressured to integrate provide the same degrees of respect and accommodation of the identities of ethnocultural minorities that have traditionally been accorded to British- and French-Canadian identities. Otherwise, the insistence that immigrants integrate into French- or English-language institutions is tantamount to privileging the interests and lifestyles of the descendants of the original British and French settlers.

Fairness therefore requires an ongoing and systematic exploration of our common social institutions to see whether their rules, structures, and symbols disadvantage immigrants. It was precisely as a result of this sort of exploration that most of the policies discussed above were developed. Multiculturalism policy has forced us to examine dress-codes, public holidays, even height and weight restrictions, to see whether they disadvantage certain immigrant groups. It has forced us to examine the portrayal of minorities in school curricula and the media to see whether they are stereotypical, or fail to recognize the contributions of ethnocultural groups to Canadian history and world culture. And so on.

It is not surprising that institutional rules and practices originally designed by and for a homogeneously British- or French-Canadian population should turn out to contain burdens and disadvantages for immigrant groups (just as it is not surprising that many institutions designed by and for men turn out to have disadvantages for women). Many of these burdens were quite unintentional: they exist as a result of rules that were adopted before these groups were even present in Canada.

For example, the fact that government offices are closed on Sunday needn't be seen as the result of a deliberate decision to promote Christianity and discriminate against other faiths. Decisions about government hours were made at a time when there was far less religious diversity, and people took it for granted that the government work-week should accommodate Christian beliefs concerning days of rest and religious observance. But these decisions can present significant disadvantages for members of other religious faiths. In order to observe their religious days of obligation, believers may have to take a day off work without pay, or close their stores when their competitors remain open—decisions that can be costly for individuals and family businesses. And having established a work-week that favours Christians, Canadians can hardly object to exemptions for Muslims or Jews on the grounds that they violate the principle of separation of state and ethnicity. These groups are simply asking that their religious needs be taken into consideration in the same way that the needs of Christians always have been.

Similar issues arise regarding police or military uniforms. Some people object to the idea that Sikhs or Orthodox Jews should be exempted from requirements regarding official headgear. Here again, though, it is important to recognize how the existing rules about government uniforms accommodate Christians. Existing dress-codes do not prohibit the wearing of a wedding ring, which is an important religious symbol for many Christians (and Jews). And it is virtually inconceivable that the framers of those codes would ever have considered preventing people from wearing wedding rings, unless this was strictly necessary for the job. There is no reason to see such a policy as a deliberate attempt to promote Christianity; it simply would have been taken for granted that uniforms should not unnecessarily conflict with Christian religious beliefs. If one accepts dress-codes that accommodate Christian needs, one can hardly object to exemptions for Sikhs and Orthodox Jews.

Similarly, many state symbols such as flags, anthems, and mottos reflect a particular ethnic or religious background; for example, our 1982 Constitution begins with the claim that Canada is founded on 'the supremacy of God'. The demand by ethnic groups for some symbolic affirmation of the value of ethnic diversity (e.g., in government declarations and documents) is simply a demand that their identity be given the same recognition as that of the original British or French settlers. Multiculturalism policy has forced us to attend systematically to these issues, and to remedy any problems as fairly as possible.

In fact, one of the most innovative features of the federal multiculturalism policy is the reporting and monitoring it mandates with respect to other federal policies and departments. While multiculturalism is itself a very small program, it has had a significant impact throughout the federal government, because other departments are required to report each year on how well their policies and programs conform to the principles of the Multiculturalism Act. It's easy for governments to talk about respecting and accommodating diversity, but multiculturalism is not just a declaration of platitudes: it is an institutionalized system for examining the impact of all government policies on the equality of ethnocultural groups in Canada.

Of course, the requirements of fairness are not always easy to identify. Consider the issue of religious holy days. It seems unfair that Christian holy days are recognized as public holidays, while those of other religions are not. But what is the fair remedy for this problem? It is not feasible to treat all religious holidays as public holidays—there are simply too many of them. Should we instead drop one of the Christian holidays (Easter, say) from the list of public holidays, and instead recognize one important holiday from each of the other two largest religions—say, Yom Kippur and Ramadan? I think there is much to be said for such a solution. It would not only reduce the burdens felt by two particular groups, and redistribute these burdens in a more equitable way, but also provide an important symbolic recognition that, like Christianity, Judaism and Islam are 'Canadian' religions.[7] Such a change might also encourage all Canadians to learn something about the beliefs and practices of other religious groups.

Or should we instead eliminate all religious holidays from the public calendar, including Easter and Christmas, and then allow everyone to take off, say, five days of their own choosing, in accordance with their own religious beliefs (or secular desires)? This might seem fairest, from a purely theoretical point of view, but it would be regrettable for just about everyone, since it would mean an end to the shared public holidays around which people can plan social events. And while it might distribute the burdens more fairly, it would not achieve the benefits that would come with a more equitable public recognition of religion in Canada. Rather than enhancing the status of Judaism and Islam, it would simply diminish the status of Christianity.

There is no single way to deal with this problem. We can lay down some general guidelines; indeed, in Canada we have developed an interesting set of precedents concerning what 'reasonable accommodation' means in this context.[8] Multiculturalism is not a formula that resolves all these questions. It simply represents a commitment to address them explicitly and fairly, accepting that people have a legitimate interest in the recognition and accommodation of their ethnocultural identities. Citizens in a free and democratic society will disagree about how to accommodate religious beliefs fairly within the public calendar. It is inevitable, and desirable, that this be a subject of vigorous debate. But we can have a sensible debate on this issue—or on the fairness of other forms of multiculturalism—only if we jettison unfounded fears of 'separatism' and 'ghettoism'.

3. INTEGRATION AND INSTITUTIONAL SEPARATENESS

The role of multiculturalism is more complicated when some form of institutional separateness is involved, as it is for the last three policies listed on p.42. Consider the issue of mother-tongue education for adult newcomers (number 11). An experimental program in Toronto that teaches illiterate newcomers how to read and write in their mother tongue reflects a significant departure from the traditional assumption that adult immigrants should focus on learning English or French as soon as they arrive. The idea of separate classes for particular ethnic groups is very worrisome to some people, as is the idea that immigrants should be encouraged to use and develop their facility in their mother tongue. Are such policies the first steps towards either marginalization or nationalism, rather than integration?

It should be obvious by now, I hope, that these policies are not inspired by any ideal of immigrant nation-building. The notion that Somalis, Cambodians, or Guatemalans who want to acquire basic literacy in their mother tongue will subsequently demand mother-tongue universities or army units in Canada is deeply implausible. But are these policies marginalizing? That depends on their long-term consequences. Critics assume that such policies prevent or discourage immigrants from learning an official language. This is a serious concern, because the evidence is clear that fluency in English or French is pivotal both to the economic prospects of most immigrants and to their more general ability to participate in social and political life.

But does teaching literacy in the immigrant's mother tongue diminish the likelihood that he or she will successfully learn English or French? There is little evidence that it does. On the contrary, there is good reason to believe that current government policy is counter-productive in this regard. The current policy assumes that immigrants should learn English as soon as possible. In fact, priority in ESL classes is given to those immigrants who have arrived most recently, so that those who have lived in Canada for a few years may find that they cannot get a place in an ESL class. This means that people who are unable or unwilling to learn a new language upon arriving in Canada are likely to be permanently marginalized. They may never be given the support they need to learn an official language later in their lives.

The idea that they should learn an official language as quickly as possible is fine for some immigrants. But for others it is totally unrealistic. There is substantial evidence that many people have great difficulty acquiring literacy in English if they are not literate in their mother tongue.[9] Under existing policies, illiterate newcomers are in effect permanently marginalized from Canadian society. Providing literacy classes in their mother tongue, therefore, may be the first step towards enabling such newcomers to become literate in English.

In other cases, people may be psychologically unprepared for learning a new language upon arrival in Canada. This is particularly true if they are refugees fleeing violence and family tragedy. It is often true of seniors. But it may also be true of other immigrants who have to struggle to survive and make a home for themselves and their families in a strange new country without any of the social supports they are accustomed to.

For newcomers who are likely to take many years to acquire English or French, the goal of integration may be best served if they have access to various services or classes in their mother tongue in the early years after their arrival. For example, mother-tongue classes could teach them about Canada's legal system and job market, or help them upgrade some of their job skills.

The issue is not whether immigrants should be encouraged to learn one of the official languages. As we have seen, failure to learn English or French is likely to lead to serious marginalization—a disadvantage that may be passed down to the next generation if parents are unable to communicate properly with their children in English or French. The real issue is much more practical: what sort of policy actually works best to enable various types of immigrants to learn English or French?

Many commentators accept that the existing policy is not working for certain groups, but argue that the problem lies in the teaching methods of ESL programs, or in a lack of adequate funding. They recommend improving the existing programs rather than experimenting with mother-tongue classes for adult immigrants. And perhaps more funding or better pedagogical techniques would help some of the immigrant groups who are currently falling through the cracks. It is also possible, however, that the current language policy is inherently inappropriate for certain groups; for these groups, temporary programs in their mother tongue may improve the chances of eventual integration.

A related issue is the question of transitional bilingualism for the children of immigrants (number 12). Here again, many people worry that such programs discourage the learning of English or French. As a general rule, the public is much more concerned about the language skills of immigrant children than of adults. Most informed commentators recognize that some adult immigrants will never acquire genuine fluency in English or French, and we do not even expect or require older immigrants to try to gain this fluency: immigrants over the age of 65 are exempted from the language requirements in the standard citizenship test. That many adult immigrants will continue to use mostly their mother tongue is expected and unavoidable.

But when it comes to children, most Canadians insist that teaching should take place exclusively in one or other of the official languages. Immigrant children should of course be free to learn their mother tongue in their own free time—and perhaps public funds and facilities should be made available for such optional extra classes—but the public-school curriculum should be taught only in English or French. To provide bilingual education using the child's mother tongue is assumed to delay, perhaps permanently, the acquisition of official-language fluency.

Yet here again the popular assumption about the impact of bilingual education may be factually incorrect. First, it is important to note that the desire for special mother-tongue education for immigrant children is nothing like the desire of Hutterites to keep their children out of public schools. In the former case, the aim is to improve immigrant children's ability to succeed in the modern world; in the latter, to ensure that Hutterite children avoid contact with the modern world. Second, it is possible that immigrant children who begin school in bilingual classes develop better language skills *both* in their mother tongue *and* in English than children who attend English-only schools. There is now a voluminous literature in the United States suggesting that Hispanic children whose parents do not speak English will learn English better over the long term if they enrol in transitional bilingual programs. Less research has been done in Canada, but a survey of existing Canadian studies concluded that

> the misgivings some educators have with respect to the educational wisdom of heritage language teaching have little basis in reality. There is no evidence of any negative effect of heritage language development on proficiency in the official languages; in fact, the trends in the research are all in the opposite direction, suggesting that the development of literacy in the heritage language may enhance aspects of students' academic performance in the two official languages.[10]

It may seem logical to think that people will integrate best if they are encouraged to participate in fully integrated institutions as quickly as possible. But whether immigrant children learn English best in English-only or in bilingual classes is not a matter of logic. It is a complicated empirical question involving questions of pedagogy, sociolinguistics, and curriculum development. To try to decide these questions without reference to the facts is unhelpful and potentially even counter-productive.

A third case involves Black-focused schools, which are currently being studied in Toronto (number 13). The aim of such schools is to reduce the drop-out rates among Black students in integrated public schools, and hence to encourage them to gain more education and job skills. This is a more complicated case because the theory of Black-focused schools emerged in the United States, where Black nationalism is a factor, and where the merits of integration are a matter of deep dispute within the African-American community. (Since this issue raises fundamental questions about race in Canada, I will discuss it in more detail in Chapter 5.)

In all of these cases, critics focus exclusively on the fact that multiculturalism policies involve some form of institutional differentiation, and so they assume that such policies encourage comprehensive and permanent ethnic separatism. It is true that the institutions themselves may be relatively permanent, especially if Canada continues to accept high levels of immigration; for example, if the bilingual Mandarin-English schools now being established in Vancouver prove successful, they will likely remain for as long as Canada accepts Chinese immigrants. But if our concern is with the integration of immigrants, we need to examine the role of these institutions on the integration of the individuals who pass through them. The fact that an institution may be permanent does not mean that the individuals who pass through it remain permanently segregated from mainstream society. On the contrary, these institutions typically serve a transitional function, facilitating greater participation in mainstream institutions.

I would argue, then, that both mother-tongue literacy and transitional bilingualism can be integrating in the long term. At the least, we should keep an open mind about the impact of these policies; there is no reason to assume in advance of the evidence that they are separatist or marginalizing.

But do they make the process of integration fairer? I believe they do. They are based on the recognition that integration does not occur overnight, but is a difficult and long-term process that may take more than one generation. This means that special accommodations are often required for immigrants on a transitional basis. For example, certain services should be available in an immigrant's mother tongue, and support should be provided for those organizations and groups within immigrant communities that assist in the settlement and integration process. Bilingual education can help children overcome the disadvantages that may arise if they do not speak English or French at home. Programs such as these are not unjust privileges, but honest attempts to cope with the distinctive problems facing particular ethnocultural groups.

In short, none of these thirteen multiculturalism policies promotes either ethnonationalism or marginalization. They simply involve renegotiating the terms of integration, in light of the specific needs of immigrant groups and the special difficulties they face.

This is not to say that there are no cases in Canada of policies that lead to marginalization. For example, educational and military exemptions are accorded to various Christian sects to enable them to live apart from the mainstream society. But these policies were adopted long before multiculturalism. In fact, many of the criticisms mistakenly directed at multiculturalism policies would be more plausibly levelled at the policies adopted early in this century to accommodate Hutterites and Doukhobors. One could argue that there is an element of racism in the way many Canadians accept the historical accommodations made for these white Christian sects—accommodations that are genuinely separatist and marginalizing—while bitterly opposing the accommodations made for more recent non-white, non-Christian immigrant groups, even though these accommodations are integrationist rather than separatist.

4. INTEGRATION AND IDENTITY

It is worth emphasizing again that I am talking about a particular kind of sociocultural integration: namely, integration into common societal institutions based on a shared language. The fact that immigrants have accepted this sort of institutional integration does not necessarily mean that they have integrated in a more purely psychological sense. That is, immigrants who accept the inevitability of participation in either the anglophone or the francophone society in Canada may still feel little sense of allegiance to these institutions, or of having embraced a new 'Canadian' identity. They may show little interest in learning about the rest of Canada, and may prefer remembering the Old World over embracing the opportunities available in the New.

The idea that multiculturalism is promoting an apartheid-like system of institutional separatism is not tenable. But is it promoting a kind of *mental* separatism? Is multiculturalism encouraging some immigrants to focus on the life they left behind, rather than the new one available here? While it is clearly possible for immigrants to integrate institutionally without identifying with these new institutions, or with Canada generally, the evidence is that most do identify with these common institutions and become deeply concerned for their health and stability. As I noted in Chapter 1, there is no evidence that the increased recognition of ethnocultural identities under the multiculturalism policy has reduced the desire of members of ethnic groups to participate in common institutions, or their valuing of Canadian political institutions, or their sense of loyalty to Canada.[11]

Nor should this be surprising. Over time, institutional integration in itself is likely to generate a sense of psychological identification. The fact that common institutions bring together members of many ethnic groups has important ramifications both personally and politically. At the personal level, it means that people meet (and sometimes fall in love with) members of other ethnic groups, promoting inter-ethnic relationships that are directly linked with their new lives here in Canada. Politically, it means that people must learn how to negotiate with members of other ethnic groups. Members of one immigrant group, for instance, might want to incorporate material about their homeland into the school curriculum; but since public schools are common institutions, they will have to persuade other groups of the value of this material. The inevitable result is that immigrants must focus on contributing to life in Canada, rather than dwell on the society they left behind.[12]

Still, there is no reason to leave this sort of psychological integration to chance, and it is worth examining specific policies to see whether they can be improved in this respect. In assessing the funding of ethnic studies programs or ethnic presses, for example, it is right and proper that the government encourage immigrant groups to focus primarily (though not necessarily exclusively) on their contributions to Canada, rather than on the accomplishments of the society they have left behind. Similarly, government-funded bilingual education programs for children, or mother-tongue literacy programs for adults, should be used primarily as vehicles for teaching immigrants about Canada, not the history of the Old World.

Of course, even if these policies are integrationist from the point of view of immigrants, they may create ethnic tensions and lead to a backlash on the part of native-born Canadians that may inhibit integration. Indeed, reading between the lines, I think this may be Gwyn's real concern. His explicit argument is that multicultural groups are putting up 'cultural walls' and retreating into 'monocultural' ghettos. As we've seen, this is not true: immigrants are knocking on the door of mainstream society, asking to be let in as full and equal participants. It may be true, however, that some native-born Canadians are putting up cultural walls in a backlash against multiculturalism. They may be feeling a certain cultural insecurity, feeling like 'strangers in their own cities'. They express this fear in charges of ghettoism against immigrants, but these charges may really represent a reaction against the extent to which immigrants are entering mainstream society and renegotiating its rules and practices. In other words, the problem may be less that multiculturalism is leading immigrants to ghettoize than that multiculturalism is leading British Canadians to feel estranged from mainstream institutions that are becoming increasing pluralistic. According to Gwyn, middle-class British Canadians feel that they are being 'pushed out' of common institutions by aggressive ethnic groups who seek to reform these institutions, and so they 'withdraw from the centre'.[13]

If true, this is a serious problem. But it could be true only if the rest of Gwyn's analysis is wrong, for it presupposes precisely the sort of institutional integration that he elsewhere says is not occurring. Still, the possibility of alienation is worrisome. Increasing the integration of immigrants into common institutions will be of limited benefit if native-born

Canadians become increasingly alienated from those institutions. Gwyn is surely right that the 'Anglo-Celtic' population (as he calls it) is still a vital part of Canadian life, and that the country cannot survive if it becomes increasingly alienated. Nor is this problem easy to overcome. Demonstrating that charges of ghettoism are factually incorrect is unlikely to assuage the deep-seated anxieties about cultural change that give rise to those charges.

This is not a new problem, however. Much of the fear that native-born Canadians express today regarding the integration of Muslims, for example, is virtually identical to the fear expressed a century ago regarding the integration of Catholics. Catholics were perceived as undemocratic and unpatriotic because their allegiance was to the Pope, and as separatist because they demanded their own schools. The fear that Catholics would not integrate took many years to disappear; yet today they are seen as a vital component of the mainstream society into which Muslims are allegedly not integrating. It may take many years, but I believe that one day Muslims too will be seen as constituent components of the mainstream society into which future immigrants will be expected to integrate. Every new wave of immigration brings its own stresses, conflicts, fears, and misunderstandings between immigrants and native-born Canadians. It takes time to overcome these misunderstandings, but there is no reason to think that the long-term prospects for overcoming backlash against new waves of immigrants will be any different than for previous generations.

Such backlash, then and now, is rooted in the belief that immigrants are seeking unjust privileges from society while simultaneously refusing to integrate into it. This belief fades with the growing recognition that immigrants are only seeking fair terms of integration, and in time the backlash dissipates. Unfortunately, misinformed critiques of multiculturalism may be prolonging the process.

5. THE SYMBOLIC VALUE OF MULTICULTURALISM

So far I have tried to point to some of the tangible ways in which multiculturalism involves renegotiating and improving the terms of integration. I hope that most readers will sense the basic fairness of these policies, or rather the unfairness of pressuring immigrants to integrate without these sorts of specific accommodations. But multiculturalism promotes fair integration in another, more symbolic, way as well.

To see this, we need to recall the connection between multiculturalism and bilingualism. The federal multiculturalism policy was adopted only two years after the Official Languages Act of 1969, which strengthened the equality of French and English as Canada's two official languages. In fact, the policy was referred to as 'multiculturalism within a bilingual framework', to emphasize the connection between the two policies. But what exactly is that connection?

As Prime Minister Trudeau noted, Canada's adoption of multiculturalism was intended to emphasize that the 'official language' status of English
and French was not meant to privilege either the lifestyles or the interests
of the descendants of the original English and French colonists. In adopting English as an official language, the government wasn't promoting the
Church of England, cricket, and tea. Similarly, recognizing French as an
official language wasn't intended to promote the sorts of religious and
recreational practices, or patterns of leisure and consumption, favoured by
the ethnic French. To make this clear, the multiculturalism policy contained
two symbolic claims: (a) it explicitly rejected the previous history of assim-
ilationism, which required that immigrants not only learn English but also
assimilate as completely as possible to the culture of English Canada; and
(b) it explicitly affirmed that immigrants—those who were not descended
from the original British or French colonists—had made a vital contribution to Canadian life, and that their distinctive identities were a defining
feature of Canadian society that must be reasonably accommodated.

In other words, the adoption of multiculturalism was a way of accepting the need for official languages—something that all countries have,
implicitly or explicitly—but then of rigorously separating languages from
lifestyle on the one hand, and from ethnic descent on the other. It was a
way of insisting that while the languages of public life in Canada are determined by the historical fact that Canada was colonized by France and
Britain, this does not mean that the interests or lifestyles of those Canadians
descended from the original colonists are to be privileged over the interests and lifestyles of other Canadians.

Canada was the first country to adopt multiculturalism as an official
government policy, but Australia and New Zealand subsequently adopted
similar policies, explicitly modelled on Canada's. In all three countries,
'multiculturalism' involves the same basic message. While upholding the
necessity of official languages, and while expecting immigrants to learn an
official language, 'multiculturalism' makes explicit the principle that the
interests and lifestyles of immigrants are as worthy of respect (and accommodation) as those of the people descended from the country's original
colonists. It insists that immigrants are not any less 'Canadian' or
'Australian' for having and cherishing ethnocultural identities that differ
from those cherished by descendants of the original colonists.

Moves towards multiculturalism are taking place in almost all democratic countries with significant levels of immigration—even in some that
explicitly reject the term, like France. The basic task of multiculturalism is
one that all immigrant-accepting democracies must confront, since in all of
them the government upholds and promotes one or more official languages, languages that invariably reflect the historical dominance of particular ethnonational groups. In the past, the state's promotion of these
languages went hand in hand with the privileging of the particular lifestyles
associated with these historically dominant groups: the dominant group's

religion determined the schedule of public holidays, its history dominated the school curriculum, and immigrants were often judged by how able or willing they were to assimilate to the majority's cultural practices.

All of these countries, therefore, are now discussing how to separate the continued dominance of these common languages (and no state has become less eager for immigrants to learn the common language) from the historical privileging of the interests or lifestyles of the people descended from the historically dominant groups. This task is just as important, and just as difficult, in France as it is in Canada or Australia, as the '*foulard* affair' (the debate over whether to allow Muslim girls to wear headscarves to school) shows. France may reject the term 'multiculturalism', but it cannot avoid the need for multiculturalism in practice. Canada and Australia have simply dealt with the issue in a more explicit and open, and more successful, way.

Having an explicit multiculturalism policy not only provides a framework within which these issues can be debated: it also has an important symbolic value, particularly in countries like Canada that have had a history of racial or ethnocentric bias in the selection of immigrants (which is to say, in virtually all countries). Adopting multiculturalism is a way for Canadians to say that never again will we view Canada as a 'white' country (and hence deny entry to Asians or Africans, as both Canada and Australia did earlier this century); never again will we view Canada as a 'British' country (and hence compel non-British immigrants to relinquish or hide their ethnic identity, as both Canada and Australia used to do). It is a way for Canadians to explicitly denounce those historical practices, and to renounce forever the option of returning to them.

Instead, we have recognized and affirmed the fact that Canada is a multiracial, polyethnic country, in which full citizenship does not depend on how close one's ethnic descent or cultural lifestyle is to that of the historically dominant group. This may seem of merely symbolic value, but the symbolism is very important, and is genuinely appreciated by those immigrant groups that historically have been the object of racial exclusion and cultural oppression.[14]

'Multiculturalism' in this sense is not only necessary and important, but also generally successful. Countries like Canada and Australia really have achieved a high degree of separation of language from lifestyle and descent, thereby making full citizenship possible for people from very different ethnocultural backgrounds.

6. Conclusion

This may seem an overly rosy picture of multiculturalism in Canada, and indeed there are many important problems that remain unresolved. For example, some critics argue that multiculturalism has really worked only for white (non-British) ethnics. On this view, Catholic Italians and

Orthodox Greeks are now seen as no less 'Canadian' (or 'Australian') than British Protestants, but Lebanese Muslims or Black Jamaicans are still not fully accepted; I will discuss this question in Chapter 5. Others worry that multiculturalism is being used, or misused, to justify inequality and mistreatment within immigrant communities, particularly with respect to girls and women. On this view, multiculturalism sets no limits on the sorts of cultural practices that we must tolerate in the name of respecting cultural diversity; I will discuss this question in Chapter 4.

These are serious issues. In general, however, multiculturalism must be seen as a success. It has provided a useful organizing principle around which to debate the changing terms of integration of immigrant groups. It affirms a few clear principles regarding the renunciation of both racial exclusion and coercive assimilation, and focuses attention on an important set of issues regarding the kinds of mutual adaptations involved in immigration. It helps us debate what we can expect from immigrants in terms of their integration into mainstream society, and what immigrants can expect from us in terms of accommodation of their ethnocultural identities.

Almost everything that is done under the heading of multiculturalism policy, not only at the federal, provincial, and municipal levels but in school boards and private companies, can be defended as promoting fairer terms of integration. Moreover, as we saw in Chapter 1, all the evidence suggests that multiculturalism has had good results. The integration of ethnic groups in Canada is going better now than it has in the past, and is going better here than it is in any country that rejects multiculturalism.

I have not tried to prove that all of these policies are effective or morally required. Some are clearly experimental, and it is too early to judge their efficacy. It is also true that the requirements of fairness are not always obvious, particularly in the context of voluntary immigrants, people who have chosen to enter the country knowing that a certain amount of adaptation will be expected of them. What I have argued is that the debate on these policies has been derailed by misinformed and hysterical claims about 'separatism', 'ghettoism', and 'apartheid'—claims that are empirically false and conceptually incoherent. Once we situate multiculturalism in the context of the full range of government policies, we can see that it is a rather modest attempt to renegotiate the terms of integration, and has operated in a way that is generally both fair and effective.

Of course, to point this out may simply raise an entirely different line of criticism. There are many people who accept that multiculturalism has not diminished the rate of integration into either anglophone or francophone society in Canada, but who view this as proof that multiculturalism is a myth. If immigrants are integrating, in what sense do we really live in a 'multicultural' society? In Christopher McAll's view, the reality of integration makes a 'mockery' of multiculturalism's premise of diversity.[15]

This argument misses the point. The purpose of multiculturalism is not to prevent or impede integration, but to renegotiate the terms of integration. This is the crux of the issue, but it has been almost entirely lost in the crossfire between those who view multiculturalism as a failure because it impedes integration and those who view it as a myth because it hasn't impeded integration. There is a third option that neither side has considered: namely, that multiculturalism has succeeded in renegotiating of the terms of integration.

Perhaps the term 'multiculturalism' itself is partly to blame here, since it can be read as implying that immigrant groups should not integrate into the French or English societal cultures, but should be able to develop their own institutionally complete cultures alongside the French and English. The full title of the policy, 'multiculturalism within a bilingual framework', is less misleading, and keeping the larger framework of official bilingualism in mind helps to clarify the goals of the policy. But it would have been more accurate, sociologically, to describe the policy as supporting 'poly-ethnicity'—that is, recognizing and accommodating immigrant ethnicity within the public institutions of the English and French societal cultures. As Jean Burnet noted shortly after the introduction of the policy, a societal culture and its language

> can only be maintained and developed when it is employed in all areas of life. So far as this is so, it cannot have been the intention of the policy to promote multiculturalism: that there was to be a bilingual—English and French—framework makes this evident. Rather, the policy makers wished to endorse polyethnicity.[16]

Unfortunately, the names of policies are chosen for political reasons, not for their sociological accuracy, and so we are stuck with 'multiculturalism'. The term is now too deeply entrenched in public discourse in Canada to change, and it has become an established part of the discourse in other immigrant countries as well. But we shouldn't let the word 'multiculturalism' obscure the reality of the policies developed in its name, which aim to promote fair terms of integration and have largely succeeded in that task.

Chapter 4

> ► *The Limits of Tolerance* ◄

I have argued that anxieties about the impact of multiculturalism on the integration of ethnic groups are misplaced. But integration is not the only important question raised by multiculturalism. For many people, multiculturalism also raises the question of the limits of tolerance. Does multiculturalism require that we tolerate the traditional practices of other cultures, even if these violate the principles of individual rights and sexual equality guaranteed in Canada's Constitution? Should ethnic groups be allowed to perform clitoridectomy on young girls? Should compulsorily arranged marriages or talaq divorces be legally recognized? Should husbands be allowed to cite 'culture' as a defence when charged with beating their wives? Each of these practices is permitted in some parts of the world, and may even be viewed as an honoured tradition.

Most Canadians are unwilling to tolerate such practices, and in fact none of them is permitted in Canada. They have never been sanctioned by Canada's multiculturalism policy. But many Canadians worry that the logic of multiculturalism will lead to acceptance of such practices. As Neil Bissoondath puts it, since 'the Multiculturalism Act suggests no limits to the accommodations offered to distinct cultural practices', why doesn't the logic of multiculturalism extend to accommodating clitoridectomy?[1] Richard Gwyn makes the same point: 'To put the problem at its starkest, if female genital mutilation is a genuinely distinctive cultural practice, as it is among Somalis and others, then since official multiculturalism's purpose is to "preserve" and "enhance" the values and habits of all multicultural groups, why should this practice be disallowed in Canada any more than singing "O Sole Mio" or Highland dancing?'[2]

Defenders of multiculturalism have, in general, failed to answer this question clearly. Some have talked in a vague way about the need to 'balance' individual rights and the rights of ethnic groups, as if it were all right to violate individual rights a little bit, just not too much. Many other defenders have ignored the question entirely, and have sometimes implied that only prejudiced people would even raise it. But Canadians have a right to ask the question, and they deserve a proper answer.

To be sure, part of the explanation for the fear of a limitless multiculturalism derives from xenophobia, racism, and prejudice. Some Canadians see immigrants as dangerous 'others' whose differences are an inherent threat to 'our' way of life, particularly if they are non–white and non–Christian. But this is only part of the explanation. There is also some good-faith uncertainty among many Canadians about the limitations on multiculturalism. Many Canadians support the general principle of multi-culturalism—and welcome the sort of diversity that immigrants bring—so long as it works within certain clearly demarcated bounds. The increased questioning of multiculturalism is not the product solely of xenophobia (the real xenophobes never supported multiculturalism in any case), but of a good-faith concern that the policy may get out of control and lead to violation of our most basic principles of individual freedom and equality.

So long as Canadians have this sense of insecurity about the limits of multiculturalism, no amount of data on the beneficial effects of multicul-turalism will change the public debate. Publicizing statistics on the impact of multiculturalism is essential to set the record straight. But what many Canadians really worry about is the future of multiculturalism—in partic-ular, whether it has put us on a slippery slope leading away from social and political integration and towards acceptance of any form of 'cultural dif-ference', regardless of its impact on Canadian institutions and principles.

Legal and political theorists often discuss the issue of tolerance in terms of the relationship between 'group rights' and 'individual rights'. For exam-ple, they ask how the rights of ethnocultural groups fit into a constitution that is committed to the firm protection of individual rights, and what we should do when the claims of groups conflict with the rights of individu-als. But casting the debate in terms of 'group rights versus individual rights' is not necessarily helpful; it can obscure as much as it reveals about the real issues at stake. This chapter will try to clarify the relationship between mul-ticulturalism and individual rights. I will begin by exploring some confu-sions in the language of 'group rights'; in particular, I will distinguish two kinds of group rights—one of which is consistent with liberal–democratic values, and one of which is not (section 1)—and show why multicultural-ism falls into the former category (section 2). I will then discuss how and why these limits should be made more explicit (section 3) and included in the public debate over multiculturalism (section 4).

1. Individual and Group Rights

Group rights have tended to be controversial in political systems, like Canada's, that are founded on liberal–democratic values, in particular the ideals of individual freedom and social equality. A liberal democracy aspires to be a 'society of free and equal citizens', as John Rawls, the most promi-nent contemporary liberal philosopher, has put it.[3] Traditionally, liberals have assumed that the best way to achieve such a society is by guarantee-ing each citizen an identical set of individual civil, political, and economic rights—the common rights of citizenship.

But ethnic groups today, like many other previously disadvantaged groups (women, gays, people with disabilities), are demanding something more than these familiar individual rights. They want not just the common rights accorded to all citizens, but also specific rights that recognize and accommodate their particular ethnocultural practices and identities. These demands are often described, by both defenders and critics, in the language of 'group rights'. Defenders, however, typically see group rights as *supplementing* individual rights, and hence as enriching and extending traditional liberal-democratic principles to deal with new challenges, whereas critics tend to see group rights as *restricting* individual rights, and hence as threatening basic democratic values.

To understand the relationship between group rights and individual rights we need to distinguish two kinds of rights that a group might claim. The first involves the right of a group against its own members; the second involves the right of a group against the larger society. Both kinds of group rights can be seen as protecting the stability of national, ethnic, or religious groups. But they respond to different sources of instability. The first kind is intended to protect the group from the destabilizing impact of *internal* dissent (e.g., decisions by individual members not to follow traditional practices or customs), whereas the second is intended to protect the group from the impact of *external* pressures (e.g., economic or political decisions made by the larger society). To distinguish these two kinds of group rights, I will call the first 'internal restrictions' and the second 'external protections'. Internal restrictions regulate *intra*-group relations, whereas external protections regulate *inter*-group relations.

Internal restrictions are clearly inconsistent with liberal-democratic values. Such group rights are invoked in many parts of the world where groups seek the right to legally restrict the freedom of their own members in the name of group solidarity or cultural purity; this is especially common in theocratic and patriarchal cultures where women are oppressed and religious orthodoxy is enforced. This type of group right, then, raises the danger of individual oppression.

Of course, all forms of government restrict the liberty of citizens in certain ways (e.g., requiring payment of taxes, jury duty, or military service). Even the most liberal democracies impose such restrictions in order to uphold individual rights and democratic institutions. It is when groups within those democracies seek to impose much greater restrictions not in order to maintain liberal institutions, but to protect religious orthodoxy or cultural tradition, that problems arise. Such internal restrictions are widely opposed in Western democracies, including Canada. Groups are free to impose certain restrictions as conditions for membership in voluntary associations, but it is considered unjust to use legal coercion, or the distribution of public benefits, to restrict the liberty of members.

External protections, by contrast, do not raise problems of individual oppression. Here the aim is to protect a group's distinct identity not by restricting the freedom of individual members, but by limiting the group's vulnerability to the political decisions and economic power of the larger society. For example, guaranteeing representation for a minority on an advisory or legislative body can reduce the chances that the group will be outvoted on decisions that affect the community; financial subsidies can help provide goods and services to members of a minority that they could not afford in a market dominated by majority preferences; and revising dress-codes and work-schedules can help ensure that decisions originally made by and for the dominant group are sufficiently flexible to accommodate new ethnic groups. These sorts of external protections are not inconsistent with liberal-democratic principles, and may actually promote justice. They may help put the different groups in a society on a more equal footing, by reducing the extent to which minorities are vulnerable to the larger society.

Some claims for external protections are unjust. Perhaps the clearest example is the apartheid formerly practised in South Africa, where whites, who constituted less than 20 per cent of the population, owned 87 per cent of the land mass of the country, monopolized all the political power, and imposed their language on other groups. But the South African case is atypical. Most ethnocultural minorities in Western democracies do not have the ability or the desire to dominate larger groups. The external protections they seek would not deprive other groups of their fair share of economic resources, political power, or language rights. As a rule, minorities simply seek to ensure that the majority cannot use its superior numbers and wealth in ways that disadvantage them. And that, most people would agree, is a legitimate goal. Whereas internal restrictions are almost inherently in conflict with liberal-democratic norms, external protections are not—so long as they promote equality between groups, rather than allow one group to dominate or oppress another.

2. MULTICULTURALISM AND INDIVIDUAL RIGHTS

It is important to determine whether multiculturalism involves internal restrictions or external protections. In the case of the thirteen policies listed on page 42, it is clear, I think, that they all involve external protections. All of them attempt to deal with the impact on immigrant groups of the institutional rules of the larger society, and are intended to help redress disadvantages that can arise as a result of those rules. They are not intended to police the extent to which members of ethnic groups engage in unorthodox or non-traditional behaviour. In fact, not one of these policies gives groups the power to restrict the liberty of their own members.

Thus multiculturalism policies increase the access of immigrants to mainstream institutions (e.g., affirmative action), prohibit discriminatory or prejudiced conduct within these institutions (harassment codes, media guidelines), improve the sensitivity of these institutions to cultural differences (training for police and health-care workers), and provide services that the minority could not otherwise afford (funding of bilingual classes, ethnic media). All of these policies have to do with inter-group relations: they regulate how the minority is treated by and within the larger society, and are intended to promote fairness between groups.

Here again we see the profound difference between the sorts of demands made by immigrant groups and those made by national minorities. Both the Québécois and Aboriginal peoples have demanded the sort of self-government power that could be used to restrict the liberty of their own members. They have their own legislatures, and their own courts and legal codes, which can be used to limit individual rights. In fact, Aboriginal peoples have sought qualification of, or exemption from, the Canadian Charter of Rights and Freedoms in the name of self-government. These limits on the application of the constitutional bill of rights create the possibility that individuals or subgroups within Indian communities could be oppressed in the name of group solidarity or cultural purity.

Whether there is a real danger of intra-group oppression within Indian (or Québécois) societies is open to considerable debate, although I suspect any such danger is overstated.[4] But there is no comparable issue in the case of immigrant groups. They simply do not have any legal powers over their own members, and, as we saw in Chapter 3, multiculturalism does not grant such self-governing powers. What multiculturalism does provide is a set of external protections for immigrant groups dealing with the rules and institutions of the larger society.

The particular external protections provided by multiculturalism are fully compatible with liberal values. None of the thirteen policies will put ethnic groups in a position to dominate the majority, as in apartheid. On the contrary, as we saw in Chapter 3, they can be seen as putting the various groups on a more equal footing vis-à-vis each other. Thus multiculturalism in Canada involves external protections, not internal restrictions. And this has been understood and accepted by immigrant groups themselves: there has been no support among any of the major immigrant organizations for the imposition of internal restrictions within their communities.[5]

Of course, Gwyn and Bissoondath are aware that immigrant groups are not permitted to restrict the civil liberties or equality rights of their members, and that oppressive practices are not permitted in Canada. Their concern is that the 'logic' of multiculturalism requires us to tolerate these practices as well. Imagine, then, that one day an immigrant group does invoke multiculturalism as a pretext for imposing traditional patriarchal practices on women and children. Perhaps a group will demand the right to stop their children (particularly girls) from receiving a proper education, so as to reduce the chances that the children will leave the community; or the right to continue traditional customs such as clitoridectomy or compulsory arranged marriages; or the right to invoke culture as a defence against charges of wife-beating.

Do we have any grounds for rejecting such demands, or do they simply reflect multiculturalism 'taken to its logical extreme'?[6] According to Gwyn, a demand that 'culture' be accepted as a defence for criminal conduct would simply be a 'variation' on the demand of Sikhs for revisions to the RCMP dress-code, or the demand of Blacks for Black-focused schools— implying that accepting these demands entails accepting the former.[7] Similarly, Bissoondath argues that a 'truly multicultural society', to be consistent, would permit clitoridectomy and enforce Muslim family law.[8] They both imply that the limits we now draw in accommodating diversity are arbitrary and ad hoc, and that the 'logic' of multiculturalism will drive us towards accepting such illiberal practices.

This is not true. Such oppressive practices are not the 'logical' extension of current multiculturalism policies. Existing policies are intended to enable immigrants to express their ethnic identity, if they so desire, and to reduce some of the external pressures on them to assimilate. It is perfectly logical to accept that aim while denying that groups are entitled to continue practices that violate individual rights, or to impose practices on members who do not wish to maintain them. The model of multiculturalism in Canada supports the ability of immigrants to choose for themselves whether to maintain their ethnic identity. There is no suggestion that ethnic groups should have the power to impose a conception of cultural tradition or cultural purity on their members, or to regulate the freedom of individual members to accept or reject their ethnic identity.

The line that has been drawn in Canada—rejecting internal restrictions while accepting some external protections—is neither arbitrary nor ad hoc. It is just what one would expect in a liberal democracy. We have accepted demands for external protections that are consistent with liberal-democratic values and that promote fairness between groups, but rejected demands for internal restrictions that are inconsistent with liberal-democratic values and that restrict the freedom of individuals within groups.

3. MAKING THE LIMITS EXPLICIT

Why, then, do some Canadians believe that multiculturalism has no limits? Mainly, I think, because these limits have never been made explicit in government policy documents, or in the public debate. This is a shortcoming that must be rectified.

It is not quite true to say, as Bissoondath does, that 'the Multiculturalism Act suggests no limits to the accommodations offered to distinct cultural practices'.[9] On the contrary, the preamble to the Multiculturalism Act emphasizes human rights, individual freedom, and sexual equality. And its specific provisions stipulate that the aims of multiculturalism are to promote individual freedom, and to do so in a way that respects sexual equality. (For excerpts from the Act, see p.184.) In any event, the Act must comply with the Canadian Charter of Rights and Freedoms, and would be struck down if it imposed any restrictions on individual rights that were not 'demonstrably justified in a free and democratic society'.

However, it is fair to say that the federal government has never really explained the limits to accommodation. (This is part of its more general failure to explain how multiculturalism fits into the larger context of government laws and policies.) In this respect Australia has done a better job than Canada. After laying out the principles and goals of multiculturalism, including the right of immigrants to 'be able to develop and share their cultural heritage', and the responsibility of institutions to 'acknowledge, reflect and respond to the cultural diversity of the Australian community', the policy statement immediately goes on to emphasize that 'there are also limits to Australian multiculturalism', which it summarizes as follows:

- multicultural policies require all Australians to accept the basic structures and principles of Australian society—the Constitution and the rule of law, tolerance and equality, Parliamentary democracy, freedom of speech and religion, English as the national language, and equality of the sexes;
- multicultural policies impose obligations as well as conferring rights; the right to express one's own culture and beliefs involves a reciprocal responsibility to accept the right of others to express their views and values;
- multicultural policies are based upon the premise that all Australians should have an overriding and unifying commitment to Australia, to its interests and future first and foremost.[10]

This is the kind of explicit statement of limits that we need in Canada. I find the third limit troublesome, however, at least in its present form, which overstates the sort of allegiance that states can rightfully demand from their citizens. We are citizens of Canada, but also citizens of the world, and sometimes the interests of others can—and should—take precedence over our national interests. A Canadian who commits some of her time and resources to helping people in developing countries, or in her country of origin, or who pushes Canada to increase its foreign-aid budget, may not be putting Canada's interests 'first and foremost', but she is not doing anything wrong.

A better way to make the point underlying this third limit is to say that we all have an obligation to do our fair share to uphold the basic institutions of Canadian life, and to tackle the problems that the country faces. The public institutions of Canadian life provide most citizens with remarkable benefits of peace, prosperity, and individual freedom, and we all have a responsibility to do our share to ensure both that these institutions endure and function, and that all Canadians enjoy these benefits, whatever their race, religion, gender, or ethnicity. This is an obligation of democratic citizenship that the state should promote, and that sets a limit to multiculturalism. It does not, however, require that every Canadian put the interests of Canada 'first and foremost'.

Perhaps an even better model of how to make explicit the limits to multiculturalism can be found closer to home in the Quebec government's policy towards ethnocultural groups, which is sometimes called 'interculturalism'. As we saw in Chapter 2, Quebec has demanded and gained, as part of its nation-building program, substantial control over immigration. And it exercises this power actively, since Quebec now has the lowest birth rate in Canada, and immigrants are needed to build the 'distinct society' that Quebec nationalists desire. As a result, Quebec now faces the same question that the federal government faced in the 1970s and 1980s: what are fair terms of integration?

The answer it has developed is similar to the federal multiculturalism policy in affirming and accommodating ethnocultural identities and practices within common institutions. But the Quebec policy makes it explicit that this 'interculturalism' operates within three important limits:

- recognition of French as the language of public life;
- respect for liberal-democratic values, including civil and political rights and equality of opportunity; and
- respect for pluralism, including openness to and tolerance of others' differences.

These three principles form the bedrock of the 'moral contract' between Quebec and immigrants that specifies the terms of integration.[11]

It may seem paradoxical to cite Quebec as a model of multiculturalism, since many commentators (including both Gwyn and Bissoondath) think that Quebec's 'interculturalism' policy is the very opposite of the federal government's multiculturalism policy, particularly in its active promotion of societal and political integration. Thus Bissoondath argues that

> In English Canada, the prevailing attitude seemed to be 'Come as you are— Do as you please'. The society had few expectations beyond adherence to the basic rule of law. Quebec, however, was more demanding. The prevailing attitude was 'Come as you are, but be prepared to engage with a French-speaking society'. This meant that advancement would depend on your ability to work in French, it meant that your children would attend French schools.[12]

Similarly, Gwyn argues that Quebec followed 'an entirely different route' from the federal government, one aimed at 'cultural convergence' rather than ethnic separatism, so that newcomers must either integrate into the national culture 'or remain forever on the society's margins'.[13]

But this is yet another misunderstanding. The actual substance of the Quebec policy, and the limits it is subject to, are virtually identical to the federal policy (although the federal policy, of course, defines both English and French as the languages of public life, and hence of schooling and advancement). The federal government policy is subject to the same three limits: it upholds the supremacy of our two official languages as the languages of public life and public institutions; it insists on respect for norms of democracy, individual rights, and equal opportunity; and it encourages openness to and tolerance of each other's differences.

The main difference is simply that the Quebec government is more explicit about these limits.[14] The same limits are implicit in the Multiculturalism Act, which says that multiculturalism policy should 'strengthen the status and use' of the official languages; should 'ensure that Canadians of all origins have an equal opportunity'; and should promote 'interaction between individuals and communities of different origins'. These limits are also implicit in the fact that the Multiculturalism Act is subordinate to both the Charter and the Canadian Human Rights Act, which guarantee basic individual civil and political rights for all Canadians, including gender equality rights and equal opportunity.

Thus the federal policy has limits similar to those of the Quebec policy: (a) it works within the framework of official bilingualism, and insists that immigrants learn and accept English or French as the languages of public life in Canada; (b) it works within the constraints of respect for liberal-democratic norms, including the Charter and the Human Rights Act, and insists on respect for individual rights and sexual equality; and (c) it encourages openness to and interaction with people of different origins, rather than promoting segregated and inward-looking ethnic ghettos. Multiculturalism in Canada, like interculturalism in Quebec, represents the commitment that within the constraints of these three principles, the government has a positive obligation to respect and accommodate diversity.

Unfortunately, the federal policy contains no explicit statement of these limits comparable to the statements in the Australian or Quebec policies. The time has come to fill this gap.

4. THE NEED FOR A PUBLIC DEBATE

Given the failure of the government to address the issue directly, it is understandable that many Canadians feel confused about the limits of multiculturalism. Worse, many feel unable even to raise the issue in public forums, for fear of being labelled racist or prejudiced. This is one instance in which I agree with Gwyn, who says that when ordinary Canadians asked about the limits of multiculturalism, political élites 'had no answer other than guilt-tripping'.[15]

Canadians want to know that being a Canadian citizen entails certain 'non-negotiable' requirements, including respect for human rights and democratic values; yet debate on this issue has been suppressed by political élites, who suggest that anyone who criticizes multiculturalism is prejudiced. This attempt to stifle debate over the limits of multiculturalism is counter-productive. Instead of promoting understanding or acceptance, it leads to silent resentment of the policy.[16]

Of course, any attempt to promote a public debate over the limits of multiculturalism is bound to stir up feelings of prejudice. We can reliably predict that any public debate will be painful at times, as some people out of fear and ignorance label other cultures as barbaric or undemocratic. But the result would be worth the temporary costs.

Consider, as an example, the debate over the hijab in Quebec schools. When this issue first arose, many Quebecers automatically assumed that all Muslims were fundamentalists opposed to sexual equality; or that all Muslims who supported the hijab also supported clitoridectomy and talaq divorces, and perhaps even supported Iranian terrorism and the death sentence against Salman Rushdie. These stereotypes about Muslims were all present in the back of many people's minds, and the debate over the hijab provided an opportunity for them to emerge. The result, in the early stages of the debate, was almost certainly harmful and painful to Muslims, who must have felt they were destined to be permanent outsiders, defined as the ultimate 'other' to Quebec's modern, pluralist, secular society.

But the debate progressed, and the final result was actually to challenge these stereotypes. Quebecers learned not to equate Islam with fundamentalism. They learned that not all Muslims support keeping women locked up in the house; not all Muslims support talaq divorces and clitoridectomy; not all Muslims support killing authors who criticize Islam. In fact, they learned that very few Muslims in Quebec endorse any of these practices. In the end, they learned that the enemy was not Islam as such, but rather certain forms of extremism that can be found in many different cultures, including 'our own'. The result was a more profound understanding and acceptance of Islam than existed before.

This was a painful process, certainly, but it was an essential one. People needed an opportunity to disentangle the various ideas that were conflated in their minds. They had legitimate objections to certain practices that are clearly worth fighting against. Before they were able and willing to accommodate the hijab in schools, therefore, they had to be convinced that accepting the hijab was not going to mean accepting those other practices. They were willing to embrace the accommodation of diversity, but only once they were clear about the limits of such accommodation. Debating the limits of diversity made possible the greater acceptance of diversity within those limits, and Quebec society today is better off for having had that debate.

In fact, it is often ethnic groups themselves that want to clarify the terms of integration and the limits of accommodation. As Tariq Modood notes, the greatest psychological and political need for clarity about a common framework and national symbols comes from the minorities. For clarity about what makes us willingly bound into a single country relieves the pressure on minorities, especially new minorities whose presence within the country is not fully accepted, to have to conform in all areas of social life, or in arbitrarily chosen areas, in order to rebut the charge of disloyalty.[17]

What many newcomers most desire from Canada is a clear understanding of the criteria for social and political acceptance, and a debate over the limits of multiculturalism would help to provide that.

It is also possible that a more general debate over the limits of multiculturalism in Canada would not have such a positive outcome. Perhaps it would never get beyond the stage of expressing stereotypes; perhaps the initial heated debate would lead to a backlash against multiculturalism. There are no guarantees in politics. I am optimistic that the debate would, in the end, be productive, but in any event we have little choice. Unless Canadians are reassured about the limits of multiculturalism, no amount of statistical evidence about integration will allay their fears or dispel their opposition.

5. CONCLUSION

The 'logic' of multiculturalism, then, is not to undermine respect for liberal-democratic values, any more than it is to undermine institutional integration. On the contrary, multiculturalism takes these political values as given and assumes that immigrants will accept them, just as it takes integration into mainstream francophone or anglophone institutions as given. Multiculturalism simply specifies *how* this sort of political and social integration should occur—in a way that respects and accommodates diversity. Within the constraints of liberal-democratic values, and of linguistic/institutional integration, governments must seek to recognize and accommodate our increasing ethnocultural diversity.

Critics of multiculturalism sometimes say that group rights are inherently incompatible with individual rights and social equality. But in fact group rights can promote liberal-democratic values, under two conditions: they must uphold or promote equality between groups, rather than allow one group to oppress other groups; and they must respect the freedom of individuals within each group, rather than allow a group to oppress its own members by limiting their basic civil and political rights.

Multiculturalism passes both of these tests. The external protections it provides help to ensure equality between immigrants and the larger society by providing fair terms of integration; and it protects individual freedom by enabling individuals to express their ethnic identity within mainstream institutions, if they so choose, while firmly rejecting any internal restrictions by ethnic groups on their own members.

Not only is this a consistent liberal-democratic approach to ethnocultural diversity; it is arguably the only approach that is truly consistent with liberal-democratic values. This helps to explain why multiculturalism has been adopted not only in Canada but in other Western democracies as well.

Chapter 5

▶ *A Crossroads in Race Relations* ◀

I have argued that multiculturalism policies in Canada have not undermined the historical tendency for immigrant groups to integrate. Many people worry, however, that these integrationist trends apply only to white immigrant groups, not to non-white groups. Others worry that while some non-white groups appear to be integrating—particularly Latin American, Asian, Arab, and East Indian groups—Blacks are not.

This chapter will look more closely at the status of racial minorities in Canada.[1] I will begin by briefly comparing race relations in the United States (section 1) and Canada (section 2). In each case there are concerns about the lack of integration of racial minorities and the creation of a racially defined underclass whose members are in a state of more-or-less permanent alienation from, and opposition to, the mainstream society. But many of the factors that explain the societal segregation and subordinate status of African Americans do not apply to racial minorities in Canada. The situation of racial minorities in Canada is such, I believe, that integration remains a realistic policy goal.

However, there is no denying that Blacks, particularly immigrants from the Caribbean, face many distinctive barriers to integration (section 3). While their situation is very different from that of historically oppressed African Americans, Blacks in Canada see themselves as the victims of racial bias in the schools, courts, and economy, and have sought to avoid this racism by partially separating themselves from the mainstream society. As a result, the potential for the creation of a separatist Black subculture is real, and some disturbing signs of this trend can already be seen. I will conclude by considering some of the factors that may be particularly important in promoting societal integration for Blacks in Canada (section 4).

1. RACE IN THE UNITED STATES: THE CASE OF AFRICAN AMERICANS

The historical treatment of racial groups in North America provides a stark reminder that integration is always a two-way street. On the one hand, it requires a willingness on the part of the minority group to adapt to certain features of the mainstream society—learning the official language, participating in certain common institutions. But it equally requires a willingness on the part of the majority to accept the minority as equal citizens—a willingness to extend the full range of rights and opportunities to the minority, to live and work co-operatively alongside members of the minority, and to adapt mainstream institutions where necessary to accommodate the distinctive needs and identities of the minority.

The historical record shows that, in many instances, the majority has lacked the sort of openness that makes it possible for ethnic groups to integrate. In the case of African Americans this sort of openness has been almost entirely absent. African Americans arrived as slaves, not immigrants, and have been subject to discrimination ever since. Many commentators argue that the systemic discrimination faced by African Americans has made integration virtually impossible, or at least much more difficult than for immigrant groups.

I believe that this is true, but it is important to clarify exactly how the barriers confronting African Americans differ from those confronting immigrant groups. It goes without saying that African Americans have faced great prejudice and discrimination from the moment they arrived in the United States. But that in itself is not the crucial factor. After all, most American immigrant groups historically have faced discrimination and prejudice, from the Irish in the 1840s to the Japanese in the 1940s; Kenneth Karst notes, 'virtually every cultural minority in America has had to face exclusion, forced conformity, and subordination.'[2]

It would be misleading, therefore, to say that integration requires that immigrants be 'welcomed'. There are relatively few cases where (non-British) immigrants have been warmly welcomed; most have been viewed with fear and apprehension. Even when the American government has been committed to encouraging immigration, and to encouraging immigrants once landed to acquire citizenship, this official policy has rarely been fully reflected in everyday public attitudes. Large elements of the American public have always viewed immigrants as a threat to their culture, or to their jobs, or to political stability. Throughout their history, many Americans have believed that the health and stability of American society depends on maintaining the hegemony of its original British Protestant cultural traditions, and hence is threatened by widespread immigration from non-British, non-Protestant, and non-white countries. This nativist streak has been reflected not only in various attempts to implement restrictive and discriminatory immigration policies, but also in widespread discrimination (in housing, employment, banking, education, private clubs, etc.), and in the prejudicial stereotypes that were accepted and disseminated in the media.

For example, there were laws against the teaching of immigrant languages—a prohibition aimed primarily at German immigrants; there were laws prohibiting the employment of Asians in certain professions; quotas limiting the numbers of Jews in universities; restrictive covenants that prevented non-whites from buying houses in particular neighbourhoods; literacy tests that were used to prevent Hispanics and other non-Anglos from voting; and, at a more general level, widespread prejudice made it very difficult for members of any of these groups to gain elected public office. These restrictions were justified on the grounds that 'aliens' were stupid, lazy, irresponsible, deceitful, unclean, undemocratic, unpatriotic, and so on. Such stereotypes were often justified by reference to pseudo-scientific arguments about 'racial' differences. (It is important to remember that until well into the twentieth century, Eastern and Southern Europeans were viewed as separate 'races', sometimes even as 'Black'. The idea that all Europeans belong to a single 'white' race is comparatively new.) Yet most immigrant groups have gradually overcome these barriers. The long history of virulent prejudice and discrimination against immigrant groups—whether Irish Catholics, Jews, Germans, Japanese, or Hispanics—deferred, but did not ultimately prevent, their integration.

Why then has the integration of African Americans proven so difficult? The explanation lies not in discrimination and prejudice per se, but rather in the *kind* of discrimination they faced. With most immigrant groups, discriminatory policies were intended to keep them in a subordinate status, but this was still subordination *within the larger society*. They were treated as second-class citizens, but they were still seen as members of the mainstream society. There was never any intention of allowing or encouraging Jews or Germans to form a society apart from the mainstream.

Since immigrant groups were included in the larger society, albeit as second-class citizens, their struggles took the form of demanding more equal inclusion within the mainstream society. Moreover, as we saw in Chapter 2, the whole idea of building a separate society is an enormous undertaking, one that is simply beyond the reach of immigrant groups even in an avowedly 'multicultural' society. Hence if immigrants were to succeed in their new 'land of opportunity', it could only be through greater inclusion, not through building a separate society.

In fact, if we examine the period of highest immigration, in the early part of this century, much of the prejudice and discrimination that immigrant groups faced was aimed at inhibiting any public expression of their ethnic identity, and at coercively assimilating them into the dominant 'Anglo-conformity' mould. If immigrants faced discrimination within mainstream institutions, they faced even greater hostility when they were perceived as trying to build separate ethnic enclaves. Ethnic separatism was seen as proof of 'un-American' sentiments, and was ruthlessly suppressed. As Karst put it, immigrants faced 'forced conformity and subordination': they were forcibly Americanized, yet were allowed to become only second-class Americans.

In short, while immigrant groups in the United States often faced virulent prejudice and systemic discrimination, these restrictions operated alongside a kind of societal integration. Immigrants were shunted into subordinate positions within the mainstream society, and were often prevented from occupying the élite positions within mainstream institutions, but they were also prevented from creating separate societies.

By contrast, African Americans were discouraged—indeed legally prevented—from integrating into the societal institutions of the mainstream. Prior to the Civil War they were not even seen as persons, let alone equal citizens. As slaves they were denied all civil and political rights, and even after the Civil War they faced a system of total institutional segregation—not just in public parks and residential neighbourhoods, but in buses and trains, in bars and restaurants, in workplaces and unions, in washrooms and at drinking fountains. Segregation extended into government services and employment (e.g., schools, hospitals, army units), and in many states there were laws against miscegenation, so as to prevent any mingling of races.

Given this total institutional segregation, African Americans had no choice but to develop their own separate society. They created their own schools and universities, hospitals and businesses, churches and recreational associations. This was particularly true in the south, but even in cities like Chicago, Black urban neighbourhoods functioned in effect as institutionally complete societies.[3]

In this respect, African Americans are closer to the 'national minority' pattern than the 'immigrant' pattern. Like Aboriginal people, Québécois, or Puerto Ricans, African Americans formed an institutionally complete society alongside the dominant society. Yet it would be misleading to equate the institutional segregation of African Americans with that of national minorities. In the case of national minorities, a culturally distinct society, settled for centuries in its historic homeland, seeks to defend its pre-existing institutional separateness out of a desire to maintain its existence as a separate society, and to preserve its language and culture.

African Americans, however, did not choose to separate themselves from mainstream institutions: they were forcibly excluded. Furthermore, the slaves brought from Africa did not have a common language, culture, or national identity. They came from a variety of African cultures, with different languages, and no attempt was made to keep together those with a common ethnic background. In fact, people from the same culture (even from the same family) were often split up once in America. And even if they shared the same African language, slaves were forbidden to speak it, because slave-owners feared that such speech could be used to foment rebellion.[4] Insofar as they had a common national identity, therefore, it was as anglophone 'Americans', and when slavery was abolished, most wanted to integrate into the mainstream society. Yet because they were coercively prevented from integrating, they had no choice but to build their own separate institutions.

It is important to emphasize this point. The reason that African Americans were excluded from mainstream institutions was not to encourage or enable them to maintain an already existing culture. On the contrary, their exclusion went hand in hand with systematic efforts by whites to prevent the maintenance of any previous African languages, cultures, or national identities. In terms of their uprootedness, then, African Americans are much closer to immigrants and refugees than to national minorities. Over time they have developed a high degree of institutional separateness, like national minorities; yet like immigrants and refugees they have been uprooted, physically and culturally, from their homeland. In fact, their physical and cultural uprooting was much more violent and radical than that of any immigrant group in North America. Thus their subsequent institutional separateness was not a way of maintaining an existing culture on a historic homeland, but simply one component in a larger system of racial oppression.

Nonetheless, the history of almost total institutional segregation helps to explain why Black nationalism has at times been a potent force within the African-American community. The fact is that after the Civil War, Blacks did create a viable, functioning, and highly developed separate society, with its own economy, press, schools, hospitals, churches, sports leagues, music halls, and so on. These separate institutions provided avenues for meaningful accomplishments, upward mobility, and social recognition. Because their institutional segregation was complete, there were Blacks in virtually all professions and class categories; there were Black professors, lawyers, doctors, journalists, librarians, authors, scientists, musicians, engineers, etc. And there were Black newspapers that recognized their accomplishments.

The impact of desegregation, therefore, has been viewed with considerable ambivalence in the African-American community. Although it has meant the gradual loss of these Black-focused institutions, the history of racism and economic disadvantage is such that Blacks lack equal opportunity in the mainstream society, and have become overwhelmingly concentrated in the lower classes. In fact, many Blacks now believe that the opportunities to move into professional occupations were greater under the old segregated system than within today's 'integrated' institutions. At the same time, the accomplishments of Black people have become almost invisible within the mainstream news media, where (except in the fields of sports and entertainment), Blacks are portrayed primarily as criminals and drug addicts.[5]

The feeling among Blacks that they face insuperable obstacles within the mainstream society has sometimes been heightened by the apparent success of immigrant groups. It's important to note that the success of these groups is not viewed by most African Americans as evidence that non-whites can succeed in America. On the contrary, it is seen as proof of how much the odds are stacked against them. Anglo-Saxon whites who have resolutely avoided genuine educational or residential integration with Blacks have nonetheless accepted and eventually welcomed Jews, Irish, Italians, Asians, and to a lesser extent Arabs and Latinos into their schools, workplaces, and homes. Many Blacks believe that the success of these groups has come at their expense, and they deeply resent it. This feeling is reflected in the conflict between Blacks and Hispanics in Miami, Blacks and Asians in Los Angeles, Blacks and Jews in New York, Blacks and Irish in Boston.

As a result of all these factors, many Blacks have come to look with some nostalgia at the era of separate institutions, and believe that Black success in America can be achieved only by creating a self-governing nation within the United States. Over the years, various attempts have been made to redefine African Americans as a national minority. Some African Americans, sceptical about the possibility of integration, have adopted the language of nationalism and sought a form of territorial self-government; the idea of creating a 'Black state' in the south had some support in the 1930s (it was even endorsed by the American Communist Party), and resurfaced briefly in the 1960s. But that idea was never realistic, not only because Blacks and whites are intermingled throughout the south, but also because African Americans are no longer concentrated there, having migrated throughout the country. As a result, there is no state where African Americans form a majority. In any event, most Blacks do not have or want a distinct national identity. They see themselves as entitled to full membership in the American nation, even if whites deny them that birthright, and so have fought for full and equal participation within the mainstream society.

Accordingly, many Americans have hoped that the immigrant model of integration can be made to work for African Americans. Thus John Ogbu wants to 'help [African Americans] understand and adopt the immigrant minorities' model'.[6] Nathan Glazer expresses the hope that if anti-discrimination laws were firmly enforced, Blacks could become 'the same kind of group that the European ethnic groups have become':

> with proper public policies to stamp out discrimination and inferior status and to encourage acculturation and assimilation, [Blacks] will become not very different from the European and Asian ethnic groups, the ghost nations, bound by nostalgia and sentiment and only occasionally coalescing around distinct interests.[7]

Similarly, Michael Walzer writes that separatism would not be tempting if Blacks had the 'same opportunities for group organization and cultural expression' available to white immigrant groups. He too hopes that this model of integration, 'adapted to the needs of immigrant communities', can 'be extended to the racial minorities now asserting their own group claims'.[8]

This was the underlying premise of the American civil rights movement in the 1960s: greater protection against discrimination would make it possible for Blacks to follow the immigrant path to integration and economic success. But this hope too has proven unrealistic, given the profound historical differences between immigrants and African Americans, and it is increasingly accepted that some new model of integration will have to be worked out. African Americans must be seen as a highly distinctive group, with needs and aspirations that do not match those of either immigrant groups or national minorities. Indeed, part of the tragedy of the African-American experience is the fact that there is no clear theory or model for understanding or meeting the needs of African Americans. Neither the nation-building nor the immigrant model is helpful here.

It's interesting to note, however, that the immigrant model has worked for many Blacks who really are immigrants to the United States: recent immigrants from the Caribbean have done quite well, and second-generation Caribbean Americans do better than average on many criteria.[9] But these immigrant Blacks see themselves (and are seen by other Americans, both white and Black) as separate from the historical African-American community, and their relative success has not eased the burdens of the latter.

3. VISIBLE MINORITIES IN CANADA

It should be clear that the experience of visible minorities in Canada does not really match that of African Americans, although there are some important similarities. Slavery was practised in Canada from 1689 to 1834, both under French rule and after the British conquest. It primarily involved Indian people, but commentators have estimated that up to 1,000 slaves in Canada in this period were of African descent. There was even a time when slavery was legal in Canada but illegal in the northern United States, and some slaves fled south to gain their freedom. Moreover, as in the US, the abolition of slavery led not to racial equality but to a system of segregated institutions (the last segregated school in Ontario did not close until 1965).[10] These facts are useful reminders of the depth of racism in Canada's past. However, they are not really the root of Canada's current race relations problems, since these long-settled Blacks make up only a fraction of the visible minorities who live in Canada today. Indeed, they form only a small minority of those who define themselves as 'Black'.

The Black community in Canada in the nineteenth century—the descendants of former slaves and Black United Empire Loyalists—was never very large compared with the African-American population in the United States, and it shrank dramatically between 1870 and 1930 as Blacks moved back to the United States. There were several waves of emigration, first between 1870 and 1902, and then again in the 1920s and 1930s as Blacks pursued greater opportunities to the south. In fact, the overall population of Blacks in Canada decreased by two-thirds over this period.[11]

As a result, the largest group of Blacks in Canada today are recent immigrants from the Caribbean. In Montreal, 80 per cent of Blacks are from the Caribbean—primarily Haiti, but also various British Caribbean islands, particularly Jamaica and Trinidad; descendants of long-settled Blacks form only a small minority, under 20 per cent.[12] The same general trend is found in Toronto, although there the largest group are Jamaicans rather than Haitians. The only major Canadian city where the long-settled Black population still outnumbers recent Caribbean immigrants is Halifax. Thus the history of slavery and segregation in Canada, while more similar to the US experience than most Canadians realize, is not the source of contemporary race-relations problems. The numbers of Blacks who experienced these conditions were relatively small, and their descendants are now massively outnumbered by immigrants from the Caribbean or Africa.

This pattern has two important consequences. First, the idea of Black nationalism has never taken hold in Canada. Because the Black community was small during the period of official segregation and discrimination (before the 1960s), it never developed the same degree of institutional completeness as in the United States. As Dorothy Williams puts it:

> Widespread discrimination in the United States had created two parallel societies. American Blacks lived in a fully segregated society from top to bottom, that had its own Black universities, businesses, lawyers, newspapers, hospitals, tradesmen and labourers. But in Canada, where opportunities were purported to be equal, most Blacks, regardless of skills, tended to fit into one level of society—*the bottom*.[13]

There were a few avenues for Black mobility and achievement (for example, in journalism). And it is possible to find some Blacks who express mild nostalgia for these segregated institutions.[14] But the Black community was so small, and so widely dispersed, that the idea of developing a complete and separate Black society was never seriously contemplated. The only viable way for Blacks to participate in modern life in Canada was through inclusion in the mainstream society.

Second, whereas in the United States the success of Jews, Greeks, and Asians is perceived as having come at the expense of Blacks, in Canada the fact that most Blacks today are recent immigrants means that they can build on the success of earlier non-British immigrants. One could even argue that the obstacles facing many visible minorities in Canada today are comparable to those faced by immigrant groups in the past. Visible minorities today face enormous prejudice and discrimination, but so did earlier immigrants. Current stereotypes about violence and criminality among Jamaicans are not very different from historical stereotypes about the Irish; current misperceptions about the 'clannish' and 'ghettoized' nature of the Chinese community are not very different from earlier misperceptions about Italians and Ukrainians; current fears about the dangers of religious extremism among Muslims and Sikhs are not very different from earlier fears about the dangers of Catholicism and Judaism.

There is reason to believe that visible minorities today can overcome these barriers to integration, just as earlier immigrant groups have done.

Certainly it is premature to conclude otherwise. After all, most visible minorities have arrived in Canada in the last thirty years. It often took non-British immigrants three or more generations to integrate fully, and we simply do not yet know how the grandchildren of Jamaican or Vietnamese immigrants will fare. Even today, however, we can see evidence that some visible minorities are doing quite well in Canada; for example, 1986 Census statistics show that Arab Canadians have higher per capita incomes than British Canadians, and that South Asian Canadians have a higher average income than either South European or French Canadians.[15]

Similarly, many non-white immigrant groups in the United States are integrating well. This is particularly true of some Asian-American groups, who have moved 'from pariahs to paragons', as one recent commentator put it.[16] But it is also true to some extent of newer Black groups in the US, including Caribbean immigrants. As I noted earlier, they too are following the general immigrant pattern of integration, though only by deliberately distancing themselves, physically and culturally, from African Americans. It would seem, therefore, that African Americans constitute a very special case, and that the difficulties they have faced do not presage the future of other non-white minorities in Canada or the United States.

4. Towards a Multiracial Society

If it is too early to conclude that racial minorities will not successfully integrate, however, we should not be complacent about the level of racism in our society. In particular, there are serious concerns about the future of the Black community in Canada. As Stephen Lewis noted in his controversial 1992 *Report on Race Relations in Ontario*, Blacks in Canada face obstacles that other non-white groups do not:

> What we are dealing with, at root, and fundamentally, is anti-Black racism. While it is obviously true that every visible minority community experiences the indignities and wounds of systemic discrimination throughout Southwestern Ontario, it is the Black community which is the focus. It is Blacks who are being shot, it is Black youth who are unemployed in excessive numbers, it is Black students who are being inappropriately streamed in schools, it is Black kids who are disproportionately dropping-out, it is housing communities with large concentrations of Black residents where the sense of vulnerability and disadvantage is most acute, it is Black employees, professional and non-professional, on whom the doors of upward equity slam shut.[17]

Defining and measuring racism is a difficult task, but there appears to be ample scientific and anecdotal evidence that Blacks are subject to particularly harsh prejudice compared with other visible minorities. This is reflected in statistics on housing and job discrimination;[18] in the negative portrayal of Blacks in the media;[19] in the way Blacks are punished more severely for breaking the rules in schools or in jails;[20] and in surveys asking how comfortable Canadians feel around different ethnic groups, in which Blacks are ranked well below Chinese or Japanese.[21]

More subtly, it is also reflected in the way many people assume that a particular crime is likely to have been committed by a Black person; or in the way many people criticize Blacks for trying to understand their African heritage, or for giving their children African names, yet smile when Irish Canadians celebrate their ethnic heritage.[22] Even more subtly, anti-Black racism is reflected in the widespread assumption that all Blacks must be recent immigrants, which ignores the long history and many contributions of Blacks in Canada.[23] It is important to note that none of these forms of prejudice need involve what Jean Elliot and Augie Fleras call 'red-necked racism'—the explicitly avowed belief that one race is genetically superior to another. Nor need they involve 'polite racism', the kind practised by people who believe in racial superiority but avoid saying so in public. Rather, such prejudices can be seen as examples of what Elliot and Fleras call 'subliminal racism'. This sort of racism is found in people who genuinely accept egalitarian values, but who nonetheless, often unconsciously, invoke double standards when evaluating or predicting the actions of different racial groups. This sort of racism is particularly difficult to identify, or to eliminate, since it is found in people who consciously and sincerely reject all racist doctrines.[24]

This observation raises an important point about racial dynamics in Canada. As I noted earlier, there has been considerable historical variation in people's perceptions of who is 'white' and who is 'Black'. For example, the idea that all Europeans are white is relatively recent, and the same dynamic is at work today in South Africa, where the (mixed-race) 'Coloureds', who used to be considered Black, are increasingly seen as (almost) white. Such shifts in the colour line have made it possible for various visible minorities to gain equality with whites in North America. It may even be possible to measure a group's success at integrating by examining how it has moved on the colour line. I think that Latin Americans are increasingly seen as white by many Canadians. Perhaps some day the Japanese and Chinese will be seen as white as well.

The problem is that each of these groups have 'become white' precisely by gaining some distance from 'Blacks'. They have come to be seen as 'respectable', like whites, in contrast to 'unruly' Blacks,[25] as decent, hardworking, and law-abiding citizens, as opposed to promiscuous, lazy, and criminal Blacks. This raises questions about the very term 'visible minorities'. The adoption of this term in the 1970s was premised on the assumption that the fundamental divide in Canada was between whites and non-whites. Although that probably was true thirty years ago, it is increasingly misleading today. Our society remains racially divided, but now the fundamental divide is less white/non-white than white/Black. Where do groups that are neither white nor Black—Latinos, Asians, Pacific Islanders, Arabs—fit in this new racial dichotomy? The term 'visible minorities' presupposes that, for sociological and public policy purposes, these non-white groups are closer to the 'Black' side than the 'white'. But in reality many of these groups are coming to be seen as (almost) white. The term 'visible minorities' may be blinding us to this important trend.

The extent of this phenomenon shouldn't be overstated. For example, while Latinos and East Asians (e.g., Chinese, Japanese) are now reaching the same levels of acceptance as white ethnic groups, Arabs and South Asian Muslims (e.g. Indo-Pakistanis) face greater resistance, with levels of acceptance closer to those of West Indian Blacks.[26] However, these results may reflect religious as much as racial prejudice. Perhaps Canadians mistrust Arabs and South Asians on the assumption that they are Muslims or Sikhs—groups often seen as prone to violence and fundamentalism—whereas they have no such qualms about followers of East Asian religions. It would be interesting to know whether the acceptance of Lebanese Christians is closer to that of whites or Blacks. (So far as I know, such a question has not been asked in the recent surveys of Canadians' ethnic attitudes.) My guess is that Arabs are increasingly seen as 'white', racially, even if they remain subject to religious prejudice.

It is difficult to know exactly how we should understand this phenomenon. Are Asians and Arabs in Canada (or Coloureds in South Africa) in fact being perceived as 'white'? Or is it rather that whites continue to see 'brown' people as non-white, but now draw finer distinctions among different kinds of non-white groups, emphasizing the difference between brown and Black? In other words, is the fundamental racial divide between whites and non-whites, so that social acceptance in Canada requires being seen as white? Or is the fundamental divide between Blacks and non-Blacks, so that acceptance does not depend on 'whiteness'—a person could be brown, yellow, or red and still be one of 'us'—so long as one is not Black?

If the latter is true, it has potentially profound and disturbing implications for the integration of Blacks in Canada. Although there is much reason for optimism about the status of some visible minorities in Canada, it may be that their increasing acceptance is not opening the door for Blacks. If visible minorities gain acceptance only to the extent that they come to be seen as 'white', then perhaps very little has really changed in the racial psyche of Canadians. (I don't mean to suggest that all these groups have deliberately sought to distance themselves from Blacks, although some have. It is more a matter of how whites perceive the distinctions between these various groups.) In this case, even if the category of 'Black' shrinks, it seems likely that prejudice against 'Blacks' will prove very difficult to dispel.

The existence of this anti-Black racism creates a serious potential for racial conflict in Canada. If Blacks are driven to adopt an oppositional stance towards the mainstream society, a separatist subculture may develop in which the very idea of pursuing success in mainstream institutions is viewed as 'acting white'. There is some evidence that this is already happening among Caribbean students in some Toronto high schools, as it has among many African-American students in the United States,[27] leading to unusually high drop-out rates.[28]

An even more disturbing trend is the emergence of almost conspiracy-like fears about the police and the courts among some Blacks in Canada. This too is imported from the United States, and seems to be influenced as much by American events (Rodney King, O.J. Simpson) as by events here. Whatever the reality of discrimination by police and courts—and it does exist—clearly some Blacks have exaggerated its scope, drawing on African-American rhetoric about 'white justice' and 'government plots'. Andrew Hacker argues that such fears are pivotal in explaining the existence and persistence of a separatist and oppositional subculture among Blacks in the United States, and Cecil Foster worries that a similar phenomenon is developing in Canada.[29] If these perceptions of injustice and fears about conspiracy are not addressed, Canada is in danger of falling into the American pattern of race relations.

Yet it is unclear how widespread this tendency towards adopting an oppositional subculture is. It seems most prevalent among Blacks from the Caribbean, rather than immigrants from Africa (who remain a relatively small percentage of the overall Black population). It is also unclear whether this tendency is being passed on to native-born Blacks. There is some evidence that native-born Blacks are less likely to adopt this oppositional stance.[30] And other commentators stress the extent to which Black students are still committed to the idea that success in mainstream institutions is possible and worth pursuing.[31]

It seems that we are at a turning point in the history of race relations in Canada. With meaningful reforms, Caribbean Blacks could overcome the barriers of racism and follow the historical pattern of immigrant integration. But if nothing is done, the drift towards an American-style oppositional subculture could snowball. The history of race relations in the United States and Great Britain suggests that once such a subculture is created, it is very difficult to break out of. The costs of allowing such a subculture to arise are enormous, both for Blacks themselves, who are increasingly condemned to lives of poverty, marginalization, and violence, and for society at large, in terms of the waste of human potential and the escalation of racial conflict.

Given these costs, it would seem imperative that we adopt whatever reforms are needed to prevent such a situation. Although I do not have the expertise to assess all the policies that have been suggested, I would like to briefly consider two issues of current concern: Black-focused schools and affirmative action programs. My aim is not to defend either unconditionally, but simply to emphasize the need to think seriously, and with an open mind, about possible strategies for dealing with an urgent situation.

Black-focused schools

Some Black groups in Toronto have supported the establishment of Black-focused schools, which would be open to students of all races but designed with the educational needs of Blacks in mind. Many Canadians fear that this would be the first step towards a more comprehensive Black separatism and nationalism. This concern makes some sense in the American context, where, as we saw above, the idea of Black nationalism has some historical and sociological relevance. The promotion of 'Afrocentric' public schools could be seen as part of a larger project for building a separate society, which would include reviving or creating segregated Black universities, businesses, media, and so on. In the United States, the idea of a separate Black societal culture is coherent, if ultimately unrealistic, and defenders of Black-focused schools there will inevitably be asked if their proposals are part of a more comprehensive goal of Black separatism.

However, the idea that Black-focused schools could lead to comprehensive Black separatism is clearly off-base in the Canadian context. Unlike the United States, Canada has no history of Black universities, and no one has proposed creating them. Demands for Black-focused public schools, therefore, are like the demand for bilingual classes for immigrant children discussed in Chapter 3. They can only be seen as a transitional step aimed at reducing drop-out rates and thereby enabling more Blacks to acquire the skills and credentials needed to succeed in mainstream educational, economic and political institutions in Canada.[32] In fact, this is often the aim of Afrocentric schools in the US as well. Far from promoting separatism, Black-focused schools may actually be the last, best chance for avoiding the creation of a separatist Black subculture. A series of studies has consistently concluded that integrated schools in Toronto are inhospitable for Caribbean Black students because of the low numbers of Black teachers and guidance counsellors, the invisibility of Black authors and history in the curriculum, the failure of school authorities to crack down on the use of racial epithets by fellow students, double standards in disciplinary decisions, and the disproportionate streaming of Blacks into dead-end non-academic classes.[33] Among the consequences are rising drop-out rates and reinforcement of the feeling that success in 'white society' is impossible.[34]

Some of these problems can and should be resolved by aggressively attacking racism within the integrated schools. Yet two decades of studies and reforms have apparently had little effect in improving Black students' performance, and it is worth considering the possibility that Black-focused schools can help as a transitional step towards long-term integration. One area where they might be particularly effective is in dealing with the difficult issue of Caribbean dialects.[35] Studies show that many Caribbean students suffer in schools because of their English. Students realize this, and know that they need to learn Canadian English in order to succeed in Canadian society. However, they feel deeply insulted by the way their dialects are treated within the school system. They are often told that they do not speak or write 'properly', as if Jamaican English were an inferior or less accurate form of English. They understandably resent this perception, which they see as reflecting a subtle form of racism, and some even refuse to speak in class lest they face ridicule for their language.

Most school administrators now accept that teachers should not describe Jamaican English as an inferior or inaccurate form of English. It is simply a different form—one of many world Englishes—and no better or worse than Canadian. Caribbean students need to learn Canadian English not because it is superior, but because it is the form of English used in Canadian society. In this respect, Jamaicans are in the same boat as any other immigrants who do not speak Canadian English: they must learn English as a second language. Hence they are sometimes encouraged to take ESL classes.

The problem is that most Caribbean students do not like being lumped in with non-English-speaking immigrants in the same ESL class. After all, English is their language, and the immigration system awards them points for their mastery of it. Insisting that they take ESL classes is perceived as denigrating their language. Even when schools create special 'English as a second dialect' classes to remedy this problem, Caribbean Blacks perceive (not unreasonably) that their dialect is treated with less respect, and is accorded less status, than dialects from, say, Newfoundland or India.

This may seem a trivial point. But in fact there is widespread evidence that while immigrants want to learn (Canadian) English, they also bitterly resent any implication that their mother tongue is inferior. And denigrating an immigrant's mother tongue (in the hope of encouraging the learning of Canadian English) has proven to be counter-productive. Immigrants learn English best when they believe that their native tongue is respected within the larger society, and when their attachment to it is accepted as valid.

School administrators have tried to promote the view that Jamaican English should be treated with respect. But the very fact that Jamaican English is so close to Canadian English makes this balancing act much more difficult than for other immigrant groups. Correcting the English usage of a Vietnamese person will not be seen as a reflection on the value of her mother tongue; but 'correcting' the English of a Jamaican may be seen that way. To date, we have few models of how public schools should respond to the issue of non-Canadian English dialects. A Black-focused school might have the flexibility required to come up with innovative solutions to this problem.

Whether Black-focused schools would improve long-term integration is an empirical question. But we need to avoid the simplistic assumption that they necessarily promote separation, or that integrated schools necessarily promote integration. Black-focused schools are no more *inherently* separatist than girls-only classes in mathematics or science. Whether such classes encourage more girls to study science in university is a complicated question, but clearly it is this kind of long-term integration that they are intended to promote, rather than any kind of comprehensive gender separatism. Everyone expects that the girls who attend girls-only science classes will go on to work alongside men, and in most cases to live with men in their personal lives. In the same way, there is no reason to assume that the students who attend Black-focused schools will not go on to work and live with whites. These schools are intended precisely to make it easier for Blacks to succeed in the mainstream.

Their success in achieving that goal would depend on many factors, including the details of their organization and curriculum. The decision to attend such a school would have to be freely made, and the pedagogical materials used would have to meet appropriate provincial standards. In particular, it would be important to ensure that such schools did not simply import the materials used in American 'Afrocentric' schools. Indeed, one vital purpose of the project would be to provide accurate information about Blacks in Canada, so that students wouldn't rely so heavily on American media for their vocabulary and models of race relations as they do now.

Needless to say, these schools could never be a complete solution to the issue of racism in schooling. For one thing, many Black parents would not want their children to attend such schools. And in many parts of Canada Blacks are too dispersed to form the numbers needed to sustain such schools. So it is not a question of choosing *either* to create Black-focused schools or to fight racism within integrated schools. Whether or not Black-focused schools are adopted, reforming integrated schools remains an essential task.

And if we do succeed in eliminating racism in integrated schools, we can safely predict that the demand for Black-focused schools will diminish. As in the United States, most Black parents want their children to attend integrated schools, just as they want to live in integrated neighbourhoods, so long as they believe they are safe from racism. But racism in schools seems peculiarly stubborn, and in the meantime we should take seriously proposals for Black-focused schools.

Affirmative action

Another policy that is intended to promote the integration of Blacks is affirmative action. Yet this too is currently under attack in various parts of Canada, particularly Ontario, on the grounds that it is unfair and divisive. It is certainly true that affirmative action for Blacks in Canada, unlike in the United States, cannot be defended on grounds of 'compensation' for historical injustices. Since most Blacks in Canada are members of immigrant communities, historical injustice is not generally relevant except in places like Halifax, where there is a serious debate about compensation for the unjust resettlement of the historic Africville community.

But compensation is not the only basis for affirmative action. Its primary justification in the Canadian context is that it can help to undermine the belief that everything is stacked against Black Canadians. Affirmative action has enormous symbolic value in the Black community precisely for this reason. It is seen as one of the few signs that whites have a genuine, good-faith commitment to equality, and one of the few cases where whites have put their money where their mouth is, backing up their pronouncements about equality with tangible action. It shows that whites are willing to pay a price—albeit a small one—to promote racial equality. As Stephen Lewis put it, affirmative action 'is a kind of cause célèbre of visible minority communities everywhere. They see it as the consummate affirmation of opportunity and access.'[36]

But the value of affirmative action is not just symbolic. Studies show that a crucial element in the emergence of a racial underclass is the fact that many families of Caribbean origin in Canada are headed by single parents. Teenage girls from the Caribbean have a disproportionate tendency to get pregnant, drop out of school, and remain unmarried. These families tend to be very poor. The precise causes for the phenomenon are complex, but there is reason to believe that the poor economic prospects of Black men in Canada are a factor.[37] If a young woman could expect that her partner would be able to help support a family one day, she might delay having children until he had a steady job. In the meantime, the young woman herself would be improving her education and job skills. This is not to suggest that teenage girls consciously choose to get pregnant. Teenage pregnancies are almost always unplanned, and so the immediate explanation is usually the lack of adequate sex education and birth control. At another level, though, the poor economic prospects of Black men may partly explain why out-of-wedlock teenage pregnancies have come to some extent to be accepted and expected as normal—an expectation that surely influences the decisions girls make about schooling, and about birth control. This means that fighting poverty within the Caribbean community requires improving the job prospects of Black men. And affirmative action is one of the few policies in place which can promote that goal. To eliminate affirmative action could simply deepen the sense that Blacks have little or no economic prospects, and so perpetuate the cycle of poor, single-parent families.

However, if Blacks face barriers to integration that other visible minorities do not face, then we should consider revising the target groups of our affirmative action programs. There seems to be no pressing need or valid justification for including all 'visible minorities' in such programs. If, say, Arab Canadians have a higher average income than British Canadians, it is not clear that they need preferential access to jobs. Much the same could be said about recent immigrants from Hong Kong. These groups cannot claim compensation for historical injustice; they do not suffer from a cycle of poverty in Canada; and there is no danger that they will adopt an oppositional subculture. In fact, it seems quite unfair that the child of highly educated and wealthy Asian immigrants living in Vancouver should have preferential access to jobs over the child of poor and uneducated whites living in Newfoundland.[38] This is one case where multiculturalism has indeed gone beyond the requirements of fair integration, to give at least some immigrants an unjust privilege. I don't mean to trivialize the reality of ongoing prejudice against Asians or Arabs in Canada. But we can think of the glass as either half-full or half-empty. Prejudice against Asians and Arabs is real, but not all that different from the sort of prejudice faced by Irish, Jews, or Poles when they arrived in Canada. Prejudice against Blacks, on the other hand, seems more deeply rooted.

In any event, even if all visible minorities continue to be included in affirmative action programs, we should make sure that Blacks form their own category, with their own targets. According to a widely circulated story, when the federal affirmative action program was announced, banks hired enough Asians to meet their quotas of 'visible minorities', thereby avoiding the need to hire any Blacks. This story is probably apocryphal, but it points to a genuine issue. Insofar as we view affirmative action as a way of helping the least advantaged members of our society, and of overcoming racial exclusion and separatism, we must make sure that it is actually helping the group most in need. And among Canada's visible minorities, that is surely Blacks.

We should not exaggerate the benefits that affirmative action offers for poor Blacks in Canada. In the end, relatively few people benefit from such programs, and we know that the beneficiaries tend to be those members of the target group (whether women or visible minorities) who are already comparatively well-off.[39] Thus affirmative action should be only a modest part of a much larger strategy for addressing societal inequalities, one that would include race-neutral anti-poverty programs. Nevertheless, affirmative action is important for its symbolic value. It is a concrete manifestation of Canadians' commitment to ensure equal opportunity for Blacks, and a tangible refutation of the 'conspiracy' fears that generate an oppositional subculture.

I realize that many people will remain deeply sceptical about affirmative action programs, or Black-focused schools. But if we reject these ideas, what are the alternative strategies for dealing with the worrisome prospect of the emergence of an oppositional subculture among Caribbean Blacks in Canada? It is easy to point out limitations and drawbacks, but unless we have some coherent alternatives ready to put in place, the refusal to even consider these proposals is tantamount to putting our heads in the sand.

5. CONCLUSION

In this chapter I have tried to present a somewhat optimistic picture of race relations in Canada. The hope that visible minorities can follow the same pattern of integration as earlier immigrant groups is not an unreasonable one. The extent of prejudice and discrimination in Canada is significant, but there is no reason to think that it creates an insurmountable barrier for visible minorities. However, success is by no means assured, and concerted efforts are needed to improve the prospects for Blacks in particular. Moreover, there are reasons to think that time is running out. For one thing, the power of the American media in Canada means that race relations in the US have a great influence on Canada, despite the very different historical circumstances of the two countries. The frustrations expressed by African Americans could easily spill over and inflame tensions here.

In addition, immigrants today are less patient than their counterparts earlier in this century. They are not willing to put up with discrimination and prejudice for decades in the hope that things will be better for their children or grandchildren. In the words of a government report on visible minorities, they want *Equality now!*[40] And rightly so. The idea that immigrants should keep quiet and be grateful in the face of discrimination and prejudice is inconsistent with the spirit and the letter of our own principles of equality and human rights.

That immigrants—who may themselves have come from societies with institutionalized inequalities and traditions of deference to authority—have quickly adopted Canadian constitutional principles is in itself a sign of how much they desire integration. But it means that the stakes in race relations are higher now than before. Government failure to address discrimination is no longer grudgingly accepted: it is immediately seen as a violation of justice and fundamental rights. As a result, we simply have less time to tackle discrimination, or to prove our good-will.

Race relations have in fact become an increasingly important goal of the federal multiculturalism policy, a shift that started in the 1980s and continues today, reflected most recently in the establishment of a Canadian Race Relations Foundation in October 1996. This is another example of how the policy has shifted to meet new conditions and needs, and to identify areas where fair terms of integration are most lacking. But the problems of racism cannot be solved by the meagre resources of the federal multiculturalism policy alone. It will require a commitment on the part of all governments in Canada, and of all Canadians.

Chapter 6

Can Multiculturalism Be Extended to Non-Ethnic Groups?

Critics argue that multiculturalism has been a failure and should be scrapped. Since, in reality, ethnocultural relations in Canada have improved since the adoption of multiculturalism, scrapping the policy now would make no sense. A more pertinent question is whether it should be extended to non-ethnic groups.

The demands of ethnic groups for multiculturalism are part of a broader movement towards a 'politics of identity', in which a wide range of previously disadvantaged groups seek public recognition of their distinctive identities and needs. Among these groups are women, gays and lesbians, religious minorities, and people with disabilities. All these groups seek not only the common rights of Canadian citizenship, but also certain forms of group-specific rights. They want not only freedom from discrimination in the exercise of their common rights, but also group-specific forms of recognition, affirmation, and political participation.

There are obvious similarities between the struggle for multiculturalism and these other movements. In fact, in the United States the term 'multiculturalism' typically includes all forms of identity politics. It encompasses any social group that has been excluded or marginalized from mainstream society. Can the multiculturalism model of integration be extended from immigrants to these non-ethnic groups?

In this chapter I will consider the similarities between ethnocultural groups and other identity groups, particularly gays and lesbians and people with disabilities. There are important commonalities between these groups in the ways they conceive of their differences from the larger society. Both gays/lesbians and the Deaf are increasingly moving towards quasi-'cultural' conceptions of their group identity, and quasi-'ethnic' models of group organization. They often compare themselves to ethnic groups, and some gay groups have even adopted the language of ethnic separatism and minority nationalism (section 1).

The demands of identity groups thus raise many of the same concerns about divisiveness and the 'fragmentation' of Canadian society as do the demands of ethnocultural groups. However, I will argue that despite the occasional adoption of the rhetoric of nationalism, these identity groups are in fact much closer to immigrant groups than to national minorities in their relations with the larger society. As with immigrant groups, the separatist option is neither desirable nor feasible for gays/lesbians or people with disabilities (section 2).

The challenge, therefore, is to find models of inclusiveness and tolerance that recognize and affirm these diverse forms of group identities and cultural differences. The existing practice of multiculturalism in Canada, based on the needs and aspirations of immigrant groups, is not sufficient for these other identity groups. Nevertheless, many of the lessons we've learned through experience with immigrant groups should help us in grappling with these broader debates (section 3).

1. NEW SOCIAL MOVEMENTS AS IDENTITY GROUPS

In Canada, the status of ethnocultural groups is usually discussed quite separately from that of other identity groups, such as gays/lesbians and the disabled. In particular, the language of 'multiculturalism'—and the official government agencies and policies relating to it—is almost entirely focused on ethnocultural groups. While people often talk about a gay 'community' or a Deaf 'subculture', these groups fall outside the multiculturalism rubric, and are served by separate government policies and administrative agencies.

Yet these non-ethnic identity groups share a number of important features with ethnocultural groups, and the two sorts of groups have tended to converge in recent years in the way they describe themselves. In particular, both have increasingly defined themselves in 'cultural' terms. On the one hand, groups like gays/lesbians and the Deaf increasingly view themselves in quasi-'ethnic' or 'cultural' terms—that is, as sharing not only a medical condition or biological disposition, but also a common 'identity', 'community', 'history', and 'way of life'. On the other hand, ethnic groups have increasingly come to define themselves in terms of culture rather than race or descent. Membership in an ethnic group is not something fixed at birth by one's genes: it is a matter of socialization into, and identification with, a way of life—a sense of membership and belonging in a historical community. And in both cases, groups are increasingly demanding some form of recognition for their community and cultural identity.

It is worth exploring this convergence in more depth, starting with the non-ethnic identity groups such as gays and people with disabilities. These groups are often described as 'new social movements' (along with peace groups, environmental groups, human rights groups, etc.). What makes these social movements 'new'—what distinguishes them from traditional left-wing or farmer-based political movements—is the fact that they are rooted not in a 'common interest' but in a 'common identity'.[1] Traditional class-based political movements emerge when people who share a prior material interest, based on a common class or regional economic position, mobilize to protect their interests. They are defined, therefore, in terms of common material interests, a common social-democratic ideology, and a commitment to achieving electoral success.

New social movements, by contrast, are not defined in terms of any pre-existing interest. Rather, these groups emerge because they provide a way for people to define their sense of self and to shape a new way of life and identity. They see themselves primarily as 'instances of cultural and political praxis through which new identities are formed, new ways of life are tested, and new forms of community are prefigured'.[2] And while these new social movements make demands on the state, they do not, individually or collectively, seek to form a governing party.

This emphasis on identity is true of most 'new social movements', including peace and environmental groups. But it is especially true of gays/lesbians and people with disabilities. The case of gays is particularly interesting, since the changes that have taken place in recent years in both social understandings and self-understandings of homosexuality have been dramatic.[3] Today we take for granted the idea of a gay identity and gay community, and yet this is in many ways a historical novelty. As Michel Foucault noted, while sodomy has always been a sin within the Judaeo-Christian tradition, it was seen as a temptation, like adultery, that everyone was subject to. There were homosexual acts, but it was not until the nineteenth century that commentators started talking about 'homosexuals' as a separate group 'oriented' exclusively to same-sex sexual relations. As Foucault puts it, 'The sodomite has been a temporary aberration; the homosexual was now a species.'[4]

But while homosexuals were increasingly seen as a group, they were not yet seen as a 'community', let alone a 'culture'. They were seen as simply a statistical group—the random proportion of individuals affected by the medical 'condition' or biological 'orientation' of homosexuality. This condition itself was viewed as an affliction or disease; in fact, homosexuality was officially defined as an illness by the American Psychiatric Association until 1972, and by the American Psychological Association until 1975.

As homosexual enclaves developed in major cities, however, gays began to see themselves not just as a statistical group but as members of a community, with their own separate institutions and hence their own culture.[5] And in looking for a model to describe their new-found identity as a cultural group, they naturally looked to ethnic groups. As Stephen Epstein puts it,

> gays in the 1970s increasingly came to conceptualize themselves as a legitimate minority group, having a certain quasi-'ethnic' status, and deserving the same protections against discrimination that are claimed by other groups in our society. To be gay, then, became something like being Italian, black or

Jewish. . . . This 'ethnic' self-characterization by gays and lesbians has a clear
political utility, for it has permitted a form of group organizing that is particularly suited to the American experience, with its history of civil-rights
struggles and ethnic-based, interest-group competition.[6]

Indications of this 'ethnic' self-identity can be traced back to the 1950s,
but only in the late 1970s did it truly seem to correspond to the reality of
the burgeoning gay male communities. Gays increasingly formed self-
contained 'cities-within-cities' or 'ghettos' in major cities like New York
and San Francisco.[7] In Toronto the levels of residential concentration and
institutional completeness of the gay community equal or exceed those of
most immigrant groups,[8] and in San Francisco those levels are greater
still.[9] In addition, gays, like ethnic groups, are developing a sense of communal history, and a separate literature.[10]

In short, gays claim that they are as much a 'cultural' group as many ethnic groups. This shift from a 'medical' to a 'cultural' definition is reflected
in the way gays distinguish (cultural) 'gayness' from (behavioural) 'homosexuality'. Not all people who engage in homosexual acts participate in the
gay community and culture; many homosexuals and bisexuals view their
sexual behaviour as totally separate from the rest of their social and cultural lives. Thus many commentators distinguish between 'homosexual doing'
and 'gay being'.[11] As Gilbert Herdt and Andrew Boxer put it:

> A hundred homosexuals do not, say we, a gay make. . . . 'Gay', in other
> words, represents more than a sexual act, as 'homosexual' once did . . . it
> signifies identity and role, of course, but also a distinctive system of rules,
> norms, attitudes, and, yes, beliefs from which the culture of gay men is made,
> a culture which sustains the social relations of same-sex desire.[12]

A similar shift from a medical category to a cultural identity has
occurred among the Deaf. Until recently, most people viewed the Deaf
simply as a statistical category, defined by a common medical condition
affecting a random percentage of individuals. And this condition, like
homosexuality, was viewed as an affliction or a disease. Today, however,
commentators increasingly see the Deaf 'in a new "ethnic" light, as a people with a distinctive language, sensibility, and culture of their own'.[13] In
fact, the claim of the Deaf to be a distinct quasi-ethnic culture is in some
ways even greater than for gays, since the Deaf have their own separate language or, more accurately, languages—the family of sign languages, most
prominently American Sign Language (ASL).[14] The shift from a 'medical' to
a 'cultural' definition of deafness is reflected in the way commentators distinguish 'the Deaf' (as members of a linguistic/cultural group) from 'the
deaf' (as people with a medical condition that prevents them from hearing)—a distinction that parallels the one between 'gays' and 'homosexuals'.[15]

Moreover, the historical treatment of sign language closely parallels the treatment of other minority languages. Sign language was first formalized in France in the 1770s, and was used as the language of instruction for Deaf children for over a century in France and the United States. However, after the Milan conference of professional educators of the Deaf in 1880, a concerted effort was made to suppress the use of Sign and force Deaf children to try to speak. Hence Deaf children were put into 'oral' schools, and were made to learn to talk as much as possible like other children. The use of Sign was seen as interfering with the acquisition of speech and lip-reading skills, and hence as inhibiting the integration of the Deaf into the larger society. Providing schooling in Sign was seen 'as perverse, as conducive to isolation and a set-apart people'.[16] Sign language itself was seen as 'primitive', incapable of expressing sophisticated thoughts or artistic creativity.

This argument was precisely the same one used to deny education to national minorities in their mother tongue.[17] As Oliver Sacks notes, the suppression of Sign in the nineteenth century was part of a general 'Victorian oppressiveness and conformism, intolerance of minorities, and minority usages, of every kind: religious, linguistic, ethnic. Thus it was at this time that the "little nations" and "little languages" of the world (for example, Wales and Welsh) found themselves under pressure to assimilate and conform.'[18] The consequences for Deaf children were generally pernicious. It is extraordinarily difficult for Deaf children to learn how to speak, and as a result the average educational attainment of Deaf children deteriorated dramatically following the elimination of Sign as the language of instruction.

But while professional educators (and the general public) denigrated Sign, the Deaf themselves always retained a deep commitment to it. Like most national minorities, they resent being forced to use a language that is not their own. Sign remained the primary means of communication among Deaf people and served as the vehicle for transmitting 'the knowledge, beliefs and practices that make up the culture of Deaf people'. Residential schools were pivotal in passing on and developing the Deaf language and culture, since they exposed Deaf children both to each other and to adult signers. As Padden and Humphries put it, 'this knowledge of Deaf people is not simply a camaraderie with others who share a similar physical condition, but is, like many other historical cultures, historically created and actively transmitted across generations.'[19] More recently, the Deaf have begun to demand greater recognition and use of Sign in schools and government institutions. They have been supported by recent studies confirming that ASL is a full-fledged language, capable of expressing thought whether abstract or concrete, poetic or rigorous, as effectively and grammatically as speech.[20]

Hence, as with gays, there has been a shift from a medical to 'a "cultural" view of the Deaf as forming a community with a complete language and culture of its own'.[21] And, as with gays, there has been a gradual institutional elaboration of this community and culture. There are Deaf schools and clubs, theatre groups and service agencies. Deaf communities are pri-marily found in big cities (as with gays), or near the residential schools established for Deaf children. As Sacks puts it, the experience of Deaf res-idential schools helped create the sense that 'they were no longer just indi-viduals, with an individual's plights or triumphs; they were a *people*, with their own culture, likes the Jews or the Welsh'.[22]

However, to say that the Deaf themselves have shifted from a medical to cultural self-identity would be incorrect, for they never saw themselves as 'disabled'. To the Deaf, the term 'disabled' refers to people with physical handicaps, not to themselves. As Padden and Humphries note, 'knowing well the special benefits, economic and otherwise, of calling themselves disabled, Deaf people have a history, albeit an uneasy one, of alignment with other disabled groups.' But this is not their primary self-identification:

> When Deaf people discuss their deafness, they use terms deeply related to their language, their past, and their community. Their enduring concerns have been the preservation of their language, policies for educating deaf children, and maintenance of their social and political organizations. The modern language of 'access' and 'civil rights', as unfamiliar as it is to Deaf people, has been used by Deaf leaders because the public understands these concerns more readily than ones specific to the Deaf community.[23]

Not all people who are hard of hearing participate in the Deaf communi-ty and culture, or use the Deaf language (Sign). This is particularly true of people who lose their hearing as adults because of illness, trauma, or old age. Having been raised and educated entirely in a hearing world, these people often do view themselves as 'disabled'. Their primary concern is not to learn Sign and join the Deaf culture, but rather to re-establish their con-nection to the larger society through medical treatment, hearing aids, or learning to lip-read.[24] For the Deaf as a cultural group, however, Sign is not only their mother tongue: it is also what unites them as a culture.

In both of the above cases, then, a non-ethnic group has increasingly adopted a quasi-ethnic model of group identity and group organization. These are not just 'lifestyle enclaves' defined by a 'narcissism of similarity' in patterns of leisure and consumption.[25] They are genuine subcultures, with significant degrees of residential concentration, institutional com-plexity, and cultural distinctiveness, as well as a sense of history.[26]

2. SHOULD MULTICULTURALISM INCLUDE ALL CULTURAL GROUPS?

So far I have tried to show that certain identity groups are similar in important respects to ethnocultural groups. They are not 'ethnic', strictly speaking, since they are not defined by a common ethnic descent, but they are certainly 'cultural'. Should our multiculturalism ideals and policies therefore be extended to them?

This question has become more pressing because of the way multiculturalism policies are typically defended today. As Brian Walker notes, there has been a trend within liberal thought to justify greater accommodation for ethnocultural groups (Walker calls this 'liberal culturalism'). But the basis for this defence of ethnocultural groups has almost invariably been the fact that members of these groups share a common *culture*, not that they share a common *ethnic descent*. The reason ethnocultural groups deserve recognition, liberal culturalists argue, is not that blood and descent are important, but rather that culture provides people with meaningful options, and with a sense of belonging and identity that helps them negotiate the modern world. As Walker notes, this view marks a significant shift from earlier accounts of nationalism. Prior to the Second World War, defenders of nationalism often appealed to the 'social–Darwinist picture of a struggle among races for scarce living space'. Since the war, however, this 'racialist' defence of nationalism has given way to a 'culturalist' defence 'based on the need to protect fragile cultures'.[27]

The extent of this shift from race to culture varies from group to group. In the case of Quebec, for example, until quite recently only the descendants of the original French colonists were considered 'true Québécois'. Yet today the overwhelming majority of the province's people, and all its main political parties, endorse a non-ethnic definition of 'Québécois' that accepts (indeed encourages) immigrants and their children to integrate into the francophone society and to think of themselves as Québécois.[28] As Jacques Parizeau's famous comments after the October 1995 referendum indicate, the older ethnic definitions of Québécois identity remain near the surface, and sometimes come out in moments of anger or frustration. But the shift to a cultural definition appears to be irreversible, reflecting both the liberalization of Quebec society and the increasing numbers of immigrants within the population. Throughout this book, then, I have used 'Québécois' in the cultural sense, to refer to anyone who participates in the French-language society in Quebec, regardless of ethnic descent.

Among Aboriginal peoples, the adoption of 'blood quantum' membership rules by some bands is a notable exception to the trend towards cultural definitions. In fact, such rules are controversial within Aboriginal communities, and are widely seen as violating Aboriginal people's own understandings of themselves as peoples and cultures rather than races. The use of blood quantum rules was also strongly criticized by the recent Royal Commission on Aboriginal Peoples, which argued that it violated not only human rights but traditional Indian practices, and was actually counterproductive with respect to ensuring cultural survival.[29]

According to Walker, the shift from racialism to culturalism is an obvious moral improvement, and helps to explain why the demands of ethnocultural groups are not necessarily inconsistent with liberal-democratic principles. But it raises the question of why proponents of multiculturalism continue to focus on groups that are defined by a shared ethnic descent. If ethnocultural groups are worthy of recognition because they provide people with valuable cultural practices and group identities, and not because they are united by shared blood, then why not also include non-ethnic groups that have developed a common culture, like gays or the Deaf?[30]

This is a legitimate point. However, as we have seen, ethnocultural group themselves take two very different forms: immigrant groups and national minorities. Insofar as identity groups are becoming more like ethnocultural groups, are they more akin to immigrants or to nations?

Some commentators argue that gays/lesbians are adopting a distinctly 'national' identity. They have adopted nationalist labels ('Queer Nation') and a nationalist agenda of separatist self-government. For example, Dennis Altman argues that

> the past decade and a half has seen the creation of a gay and lesbian 'nation', much as nineteenth-century Europe saw the creation of Czech and Romanian 'nations'. To be gay has taken on meanings that go far beyond sexual and affectional preference, binding us through a whole set of communal, religious, political and social activities with other gays.[31]

Moreover, this 'nation' has often been seen as having a territorial dimension focused on the gay ghettos, particularly in San Francisco. As Stephen Epstein puts it, even though the majority of self-identified gays did not live in these communities, in the 1970s

> many of them did make their pilgrimages to the 'Gay Mecca', or were exposed to it through the media. And beyond that, to use a different religious metaphor, San Francisco came to symbolize for gays around the United States what Israel represents for Jews around the world: a focal point for cultural identity that functions even for those who are not firmly integrated into the culture.[32]

This nationalist agenda is increasingly seen as neither feasible nor attractive. According to Larry Kramer, 'For a while, San Francisco was the gays' Israel. For decades, gays migrated there, and in time they attained great power in the political structure of that city.' But the option of moving to San Francisco was never really available to more than a small minority of America's gays, and the idea of making San Francisco a gay nation was seriously undermined by AIDS. Kramer concludes that whereas Zionism represented 'a hopeful haven from the world's hatred', such escape is not a realistic option for gays.[33] Gays have no choice but to form a 'community that is dispersed throughout society, fighting homophobia wherever it occurs'.[34]

The problem is not simply the lack of a shared territory or historic homeland for the 'gay nation'. A deeper problem is intergenerational continuity. Most gays are born to heterosexual parents, and gay parents usually have heterosexual children. Even if there were inducements for gays to move to a gay community, one could maintain a gay-majority town only by expelling the heterosexual children of gay parents. A related problem with the nationalist conception is the fact that gays don't generally enter the gay community until their twenties or thirties, after they have already been socialized into a national community. As Epstein notes, national identification is a form of 'primary socialization' that is 'conferred at birth and transmitted through the family', whereas entry into a gay community constitutes a 'secondary socialization' occurring later in life. Secondary socialization is typically less formative than primary socialization, because it must deal with an already formed self. Individuals being socialized into a gay community 'will already possess a variety of cross-cutting identities'—ethnic, racial, class, gender, religious, occupational, and so on—and these 'may claim much greater allegiance and inhibit the secondary socialization process'.[35] For these reasons, gay identity cannot really be seen as analogous to the sort of cultural membership and national identity provided by a national culture. Francophone gays in Quebec, for example, are born and raised to think of themselves as Québécois, and to think of their life-chances as tied up with participation in Quebec societal institutions. Entering the gay community in later life is unlikely to change this deeply rooted sense of national identity, or the desire to continue to live and work in one's original national language and culture.

For this reason, the aim of most gays is not to relinquish their original national membership, but rather to make their national community more inclusive of gays. In this respect, gays are much closer to immigrant groups. As Epstein puts it, political mobilization around 'gay ethnicity', like the mobilization of immigrant ethnicity, does not aim at separatist nationalism, but rather involves 'influencing state policy and securing social rewards on behalf of the group' to assist in societal integration and acceptance. The adoption of a 'neo-ethnic' form of identity and organization, together with a civil-rights political strategy, 'implies that gays are asserting their differences partly as a way of gaining entry into the system. By consolidating as a group, they are essentially following the rules of the modern American pluralist myth, which portrays a harmonious competition among distinct social groups.'[36]

Like immigrant groups, most gay groups aim to show that their members are good citizens who are willing to participate in the larger society and seek only fair accommodations within mainstream institutions for their distinctive needs and identities. However, some gay activists and theorists have concluded that the level of homophobia in the larger society is so great that the 'ethnic model' of integration is unrealistic. As Cathy Cohen notes, surveys consistently show that despite our many attempts at normality, service to our country, and good citizenship, gays and lesbians remain one of the most hated and despised groups within this society. The fact is that gays and lesbians, unlike purely white ethnic groups (Irish, Germans), encounter a level of hatred and exclusion that is more consistent with the experiences of racial groups, in particular African Americans.[37]

Like African Americans, gays and lesbians face systematic attempts by dominant groups and individuals to deny them 'informal equality, even when formal inclusion has been won'. Rights may be secured in legal documents, but these formal guarantees are always 'up for grabs in the social, political, and economic interactions between individuals'. This raises the question of whether integration is a worthwhile or realistic goal. As Cohen puts it, 'If we know that even when we are allowed formal inclusion it provides only minimal protection against the daily decisions of individuals who have the localized power to decide whether our rights will be respected, then why expend political resources on such demands?' Given this resistance to real equality, gays may have to acknowledge that 'no matter how normal they attempt to be, they hold a permanent position on the outside.'[38] There is some truth in this critique of the 'ethnic model' of inclusion.[39] As we saw in Chapter 5, it is far from clear that the path to integration taken by white ethnic groups is available to African Americans. And insofar as gays/lesbians face comparable barriers and prejudice, the ethnic model may not be sufficient for them either.

Yet what is the alternative? Gay separatism is not viable. There are gay ghettos in large cities, but most gays do not live in them, and despite the impressive institutional elaboration of gay communities in recent years, gay culture remains far from institutionally complete. There are no gay universities or governments, and gays lack the territorial concentration to create such institutions. Gays who want to become doctors, lawyers, police officers, teachers, or politicians, can do so only by entering mainstream schools and institutions. There is no evidence that gays are willing to give up these life-chances in order to live in a gay ghetto.[40] In this respect, the institutional completeness of the gay community is much less than that of the Québécois.

Moreover, most gays do not wish to give up their birthright in the larger society. For them, separatism is not the first option—it is simply a defensive response to the hostility and prejudice that faces gays who have 'come out' in the larger society. As Mark Blasius puts it:

All laws, forms of culture (rituals, symbols etc) and the most mundane social expectations make one an alien in the world. It is for this reason that the 'gay ghetto' exists. Gay and lesbian commercial establishments, social institutions, neighbourhoods, resorts, and cruising areas [etc.] constitute a 'liberated zone' where lesbians and gay men can feel at home in and at peace with the world. . . . the ghetto exists because lesbians and gay men, to the extent that they come out, have been forced by societal rejection to find other means of livelihood, other sources of emotional sustenance, and other institutional frameworks within which to pursue their life objectives; the gay ghetto is significantly a manifestation of forced ghettoization.[41]

Gays who come out do not wish to sever relations with their friends, family, and colleagues in order to move to a gay ghetto. Indeed, most gays are unwilling to sever these connections, and those who do move do so only as a last resort, in the face of intolerable prejudice. Here again the situation is very different from that of national minorities. The reason Québécois want to live and work in their own language and culture is not that they have been rejected by anglophones. They cherish their separate culture simply because it is the one they were born and raised in. By contrast, gay separatism would involve cutting oneself off from the culture one was raised in, and relinquishing one's sense of national identity and cultural membership. Thus gay nationalism is neither feasible nor desirable for most gays. The task, therefore, must be to fight homophobia within the larger society, to gain recognition and acceptance for gays and lesbians within its schools, media, courts, businesses, and so on.

In thinking about models of gay inclusion, it is important—as with models of immigrant inclusion—to distinguish integration from assimilation. Some early homosexual rights groups in the 1950s adopted an assimilationist agenda. They sought the decriminalization of homosexuality, and protection from job and housing discrimination, but in return they were prepared to hide their homosexuality—to treat it as a purely 'private' matter. For public purposes, homosexuals would be invisible, and heterosexuality would remain the sole publicly recognized form of sexual identity.

This is unacceptable to most gays today, who demand not only protection from discrimination but public affirmation of their identity through, for example, recognition of gay marriages and positive portrayals of gay lives in school texts.[42] Like immigrants, gays today want a change in public attitudes so as to accommodate new ways of being a 'good Canadian' and new ways of belonging to and participating in Canadian society.[43] For both gays and immigrants, therefore, integration will involve both a strong sense of identity and an affective bond with their subgroup, together with concerted efforts to reform institutions and public perceptions within the larger society.

The situation of Deaf people is rather different. For many Deaf children, their primary socialization is into the Deaf culture and sign language. Unlike gays, many Deaf children are born and raised in a Deaf culture, and so they exhibit the same tenacious commitment to their first language that other national minorities do. Even for those who have entered the Deaf community later in life, after learning to speak (the 'postlingually Deaf'), the fact is that they can interact with the hearing world only through translators, or via lip-reading, which works only for a limited range of social circumstances. Insofar as they wish to participate in the social world, it will largely be through Sign. For this reason, the Deaf have attempted to create an institutionally complete societal culture based on signing. Although they have rarely adopted the rhetoric of nationalism, there is an important sense in which they are genuinely separatist. As Oliver Sacks notes, 'the deaf world feels self-sufficient, not isolated—it has no wish to assimilate or be assimilated; on the contrary, it cherishes its own language and images, and wishes to protect them.'[44] In the nineteenth century, this sense of self-sufficiency even led to a 'Deaf Zionism'—dreams of creating territorially based Deaf townships or states. Deaf people, it was argued, 'need to be not only one another's friends but one another's neighbours, to create together not only a culture but a society'.[45] But these dreams were not realistic. For one thing, Deaf people are too few in numbers, and territorially too dispersed, to develop the necessary critical mass in a particular region.[46] For another, any such community would immediately face the same problem of intergenerational continuity faced by gays: most Deaf children are born to hearing parents, and Deaf parents usually have hearing children. Even if there were inducements for Deaf children to move to the community, a Deaf majority could be maintained only by expelling the hearing children of Deaf parents.

Nevertheless, for a Deaf culture to survive requires some degree of territorial concentration and institutional elaboration. Thus concerted efforts have been made to establish and support the residential schools that sustain a genuine Deaf community. These schools were initially limited to elementary and secondary levels, but in the 1850s a Deaf college was created. This college—today known as Gallaudet University—is one of several offering college courses in Sign language.[47] And around these residential schools and colleges a larger Deaf community has arisen, with Deaf cafés, clubs, and so on.

Unfortunately, recent 'mainstreaming' laws in the United States are encouraging Deaf children to attend local rather than residential schools. As a result, Deaf children meet few other Deaf children or adult signers, and so gain only a limited competence in Sign. This not only reduces their access to Deaf culture but retards their overall intellectual development, since they are now marginalized from both the Deaf and hearing cultures. As Padden and Humphries note, 'the new social order of "mainstreaming", instead of introducing new worlds to deaf children, may well lead to a new kind of isolationism.'[48]

This points to a profound difference in self-identity and group life between the Deaf and other people with disabilities, most of whom seek integration into the larger mainstream society in which they were born and raised, and do not want their participation in their societal culture to be impaired by their disability. Thus the DisAbled Women's Network (DAWN), for example, works for 'full equality and integration' into the mainstream of Canadian society, while also fostering 'a sense of identity and pride'.[49] Such disability groups are pushing for 'mainstreaming' in schools, and rightly so, since it helps break down their sociocultural marginalization and isolation. For the Deaf, however, their 'disability' is not a source of sociocultural isolation, but a defining feature of their own separate societal culture. And so in their case the aim of political mobilization is not primarily to gain access to the mainstream society, but to protect and enhance their separate institutions.

There are also important differences between gays and the Deaf. The latter are much closer to a genuinely 'national' form of cultural separateness, whereas the former are closer to the immigrant model of integration. The reason for this difference is not that nationalism is more feasible for the Deaf than for gays; on the contrary, the Deaf are fewer in number than gays. The reason is that Deaf people were raised in a Deaf culture, and indeed this is the only culture they are effectively able to participate in. To pursue integration, therefore, would mean abandoning their original language and primary cultural identity. For gays, on the other hand, it is separatism that would require abandoning the national identity and cultural membership they acquired as children.

The Deaf can never become a genuinely 'national' minority. They will always remain at best a quasi-national group, and will have a difficult time developing and maintaining a complete societal culture. And yet the cultural nationalist aspirations of the Deaf must be respected, and accommodated as far as possible, not only because this is the language and culture they cherish, but also because the obstacles to integration in the mainstream are enormous—much greater than for immigrant groups, or even for more traditional 'national' minorities.

4. CONCLUSION

In this chapter I have tried to show that certain identity groups have developed forms of group identity and group culture similar to those of ethnocultural groups. Hence they have the same need for recognition as ethnic groups, and pose many of the same challenges for multiculturalism regarding the balance between affirming group differences and promoting societal integration. And while the existing multiculturalism policy does not provide a magic formula for these other groups, it does offer helpful insights and lessons about the requirements of, and obstacles to, social integration.

The similarities in demands between these identity groups and ethnic groups should help dispel the myth that multiculturalism is simply a passing fad, or the artificial product of 'ethnic entrepreneurs' trying to milk the government for money. The fundamental issue raised by multiculturalism—defining fair terms of integration into mainstream society for newly arriving or previously disadvantaged groups—is a ubiquitous and enduring one for all liberal democracies.

Should official multiculturalism policies therefore be amended to include these identity groups? Not necessarily. There may be good administrative and jurisdictional reasons why gays and the Deaf should continue to be served by different government agencies and policies. In addition, to extend the notion of multiculturalism to include all issues of identity and cultural difference might create unnecessary confusion. Multiculturalism in Canada has, to date, provided a more or less coherent framework for debate over the fair terms of integration for immigrant groups. Extending this debate to include all issues of diversity and pluralism might simply invite misunderstandings and false analogies. We can see this problem in the American literature on 'multiculturalism'. Because in the United States all issues of pluralism—not just questions concerning immigrants and national minorities, but even feminism and gay rights—are discussed under the heading of 'multiculturalism', the latter has ceased to have any coherent meaning. It has become a vague label for a vast range of disparate issues, with the result that important differences among groups are often ignored or downplayed in the American debate.[50]

However, even if multiculturalism in Canada remains focused on immigrant integration, it is important to ensure that the language used to explain it also promotes recognition of the wider range of groups that have a legitimate claim for greater public recognition and acceptance of their cultural identities and practices. Multiculturalism should be seen as one part of a larger struggle to build a more tolerant and inclusive society, working together with policies to promote the integration of gays and people with disabilities.

Chapter 7

► *Towards a More Representative Democracy* ◄

Multiculturalism is a policy in continuous evolution, involving an ongoing renegotiation of the terms of integration in Canada. Some of this renegotiation occurs on the street, as it were, in particular schools and workplaces. But in the end this renegotiation is overseen and regulated by the democratic political process. It is our elected political officials who define the legislative and policy framework within which more specific issues of multiculturalism are settled on a day-to-day basis. The continuing evolution of multiculturalism in Canada must therefore be determined politically, by good-faith negotiations and the give and take of democratic politics. If the resulting decisions are to be seen as fair, the political process itself must be seen as open and inclusive. This requires, among other things, that the interests and perspectives of all groups be listened to and taken into account.

Yet increasing numbers of Canadians today consider the political process 'unrepresentative' in that it fails to reflect the diversity of the population. A vivid illustration was the process of constitutional negotiation leading up to the Meech Lake and Charlottetown Accords, in which the fundamental terms of Canadian political life were being decided by eleven middle-class, able-bodied, white men.[1] A more representative process, many said, would have included women, members of ethnic and racial minorities, the poor, and people with disabilities.

The constitutional negotiations were a specific and perhaps extreme case, but under-representation of women, visible minorities, and other groups is a much more general phenomenon. The 1991 Royal Commission on Electoral Reform examined statistics from the 34th Parliament (elected in 1988) and noted that although women constituted more than 50 per cent of the population, they made up just 13 per cent of federal MPs; that is, women had only one-quarter of the seats they would have had if their representation were proportionate to their demographic weight. Visible minorities constituted 6 per cent of the population but only 2 per cent of federal MPs (one-third). Aboriginal people constituted 3.5 per cent of the population but only 1 per cent of federal MPs (less than one-third). People

with disabilities and the economically disadvantaged were also significantly under-represented.[2] Studies of the two most recent parliaments
(elected in 1993 and 1997) show the same general trends, although the
representation of visible minorities is slowly improving (they now make
up about 10 per cent of the Canadian population and approximately 6 per
cent of MPs).[3]

These studies have led to several proposals for addressing the problem
of under-representation. For example, political parties could be made more
inclusive by reducing the barriers that inhibit women, ethnic minorities, or
the poor from becoming party candidates or party leaders. This route was
the focus of the recent Royal Commission, which studied options such as
caps on nomination campaign expenses; public funding of nomination
campaign expenses, either directly or through tax deductions for campaign
contributions; the establishment of formal search committees within each
party to help identify and nominate potential candidates from disadvantaged groups; and financial incentives to parties that nominate or elect
members of disadvantaged groups.[4]

Another approach would be to adopt the sort of electoral system that is
common in Europe: namely, a 'party list' system. In its simplest form, each
political party offers a single list of candidates, and the number of seats each
wins depends on its percentage of the popular vote nation-wide. A party
with 25 per cent of the popular vote would gain 25 per cent of the seats:
thus in a 200-seat legislature, the first 50 names on its list would be elected.

This system was intended to ensure fairer representation of smaller
political parties, but it has historically been associated with greater inclusiveness of candidates as well. As Lisa Young notes,[5] under our current system of single-member constituencies and first-past-the-post elections, each
party's local riding association can nominate only one candidate.
Nomination campaigns, therefore, are zero-sum: selecting a woman (or a
member of a visible minority) means rejecting a man (or a white). A party
list system, by contrast, allows for and encourages 'ticket-balancing'—making sure that the party list includes both men and women, whites and visible minorities. It also makes under-representation in the nomination
process more visible, and thus makes parties more accountable. Under the
current system, if nine of ten local constituencies choose a white male, this
may well be the unintended result of ten independent decisions, none of
which was necessarily intentionally discriminatory or exclusionary. Under
a party list system, however, if a party puts forward a list of ten people for
election with only one woman or visible minority, its decision not to field
a more representative slate of candidates is clearly deliberate. For these and
other reasons, it is likely that a party list system would lead to a more representative House of Commons than the current system permits.

Versions of these proposals for campaign finance reform and a party list
system have been tried in many countries. While they have helped, they
have not entirely succeeded in eliminating the problems of under-repre-

sentation.[6] So a third, more radical, proposal is increasingly made: namely, that a certain number of seats in Parliament be reserved for members of disadvantaged or marginalized groups. During the Charlottetown debate, for example, a number of recommendations for guaranteed representation were made. The National Action Committee on the Status of Women (NAC) recommended that 50 per cent of Senate seats be reserved for women, and that proportionate representation of ethnic minorities also be guaranteed; the Francophone Association of Alberta recommended that at least one of the proposed six senators elected from each province represent the official language minority of that province; and various government commissions have advocated Aboriginal-only districts in either the House of Commons or the Senate.[7] More recently, when the constitution for the new territory of Nunavut was being drawn up, serious consideration was given to reserving 50 per cent of the seats in the territorial assembly for women.[8] Similar proposals to guarantee seats for women, Blacks, and other groups have been made in the United States and in Britain, and in some other countries such provisions are already in place.

Unfortunately, many Canadians have a knee-jerk reaction to the idea of group representation, seeing it as further evidence of 'apartheid' and 'separatism'. In this chapter I will try to show that, on the contrary, proposals for group representation are serious attempts to deal with a serious problem, and to do so in a way consistent with principles of liberal democracy and social integration. Here again, my aim is not to defend or criticize any particular proposal, but rather to underline the importance of examining the idea of group representation with an open mind. At a time when Canadians are becoming increasingly dissatisfied with their role as citizens—as participants in the process of democratic self-government—major changes are required in the political process; without them, the legitimacy and stability of our democratic institutions may well erode.

2. WHAT'S NEW ABOUT GROUP REPRESENTATION?

Some people believe that group representation is a radical departure from our existing conception of representative democracy, one that threatens to undermine the cherished liberal-democratic norms of individual rights and responsible citizenship. Others believe that group representation is the logical extension of existing principles and mechanisms of representation, and is consistent with the long-standing aim of Canadian political culture to balance individual and collective rights. There is a certain amount of truth in both views. On the one hand, group representation is a radical departure from our existing system of single-member, geographically defined constituencies. And it does pose a profound challenge to our traditional notion of representation, which could have dramatic implications for Canadian politics; I will discuss some of these implications in the next section.

But it is also true that group representation is consistent with certain long-standing features of the electoral process in Canada. For example, it can be seen as an extension of the familiar practice of drawing the boundaries of local constituencies so as to correspond to 'communities of interest'. While constituencies in Canada are supposed to be of roughly equal size, they are not intended to be random collections of equal numbers of citizens. Rather, constituency boundaries are drawn so far as possible in such a way that the people within the constituency will share certain interests—economic, ethnic, religious, environmental, historical, or other—that can then be represented in Parliament.

In both Canada and the United States, district boundaries have been drawn so as to create predominantly rural ridings; in an increasingly urbanized society, rural and agricultural interests might not otherwise be heard. The practice of promoting the representation of communities of interest is not only widely accepted, but required by law under the Electoral Boundaries Readjustment Act (1964) and the Representation Act (1985). It was affirmed by the Royal Commission on Electoral Reform in 1991:

> When a community of interest is dispersed across two or more constituencies, its voters' capacity to promote their collective interest is diminished accordingly. Their incentive to participate is likewise reduced because the outcome has a lesser relevance to their community of interest. When this occurs, especially if it could have been avoided, the legitimacy of the electoral system is undermined.[9]

In this passage the commissioners had in mind territorially concentrated communities of interest, and of course these are the very groups for which boundary-drawing techniques can work. But their argument here would seem to apply equally to non-territorial communities of interest. If special measures should be taken to ensure the representation of communities dispersed across two constituencies, why not take measures to ensure the representation of communities of interest that are dispersed across the entire country, like women, people with disabilities, visible minorities, or the poor?[10] Would such measures not be similarly justified by the goals of representation, efficacy, and legitimacy?

The commitment to representing communities of interest shows that politics in Canada has never been based on a purely individualistic conception of the franchise or of representation. On the individualistic view, all that matters is that each individual has an equal vote within equal constituencies. This is all that is required to conform to the principle that each individual has an equal right to vote, and it should be a matter of indifference how these boundaries are drawn, so long as constituencies are of equal size. But this position ignores the reality that Canadians vote as members of communities of interest, and wish to be represented on that basis. As the Commission's report put it:

neither the franchise nor representation is merely an individualistic phenomenon; both also take expression through collective or community functions. The individualistic perspective is based upon a partial and incomplete understanding of the electoral process and representation. In advancing the ideal of equally weighted votes, it does promote a critical constitutional right. But in ignoring the community dimension, this perspective is unrealistic at best; at worst it ignores the legitimate claims of minority groups.[11]

Even the United States, often viewed as the epitome of an individualistic polity, accepts the need to deviate from a strictly individualized franchise in order to represent communities of interest. And in both countries the underlying logic of these practices can be extended to defend the principle of (non-territorial) group representation.[12]

Similarly, demands for group representation by disadvantaged groups can be seen as an extension of long-standing demands by smaller regions for increased Senate representation. Many people in Atlantic Canada and the West have sought to reform the Senate and use it as a forum for increased regional representation at the federal level. They have demanded an American-style 'Triple-E Senate', in which each province would elect an equal number of senators regardless of its population. The intent is to ensure effective representation for smaller provinces that might be neglected in the House of Commons, where the majority of members come from the two most populous provinces, Ontario and Quebec.

Some Canadians have come to believe that if marginalized regions need special representation, then so do disadvantaged or marginalized groups such as women or the poor. Historical evidence suggests that these groups, even more than smaller provinces, are likely to be under-represented in Parliament and ignored in political decision-making. And so while groups like the National Action Committee on the Status of Women have not opposed the idea of increased Senate representation for smaller provinces, they have argued that similar measures are needed to ensure increased Senate representation for disadvantaged and marginalized groups, particularly women and visible minorities.[13]

Some long-time proponents of increased regional representation have resented this attempt to broaden the Senate reform debate to include group representation; they accused NAC and other proponents of group representation of 'hijacking' the Calgary constitutional conference in January 1992 and displacing the intended topic of debate—namely, how to improve regional representation in the Senate.[14] In fact, though, we might well ask whether the two topics can be severed, or whether the proponents of regional representation aren't compelled, by the logic of their arguments, to accept group representation.

The traditional argument for increased regional representation—made repeatedly by the Canada West Foundation, for example—assumes that (a) the significant economic and cultural differences between Canada's regions leads to different and sometimes conflicting interests; (b) the interests of smaller or poorer regions may not be effectively represented under a pure system of majority rule; and (c) majority rule is legitimate only 'in a set of governmental structures that ensure adequate sensitivity to the concerns of minorities'.[15] But each of these claims can also be made for non-territorial groups: the diverse conditions and experiences of men and women, whites and Blacks, able-bodied and disabled, rich and poor give rise to different and sometimes conflicting interests; and the interests of smaller or poorer groups may not be represented under a system of majority rule.

There are, then, important aspects of political life in Canada that lend support to the idea of group representation. This suggests that the demands for such representation that surfaced during the most recent round of negotiations on constitutional reform should not be dismissed as momentary aberrations.

In the end, of course, the Charlottetown Accord rejected most proposals to guarantee Senate representation for women or other social groups, and instead focused on increased regional representation. The one exception was a proposal for guaranteed Aboriginal seats. However, the Accord allowed each province to decide how its senators would be elected, and three of the ten provincial premiers immediately said they would pass provincial legislation requiring that 50 per cent of the Senate seats from their province be reserved for women. Although the Accord was defeated, it seems likely that any future proposal for Senate reform will have to address group as well as regional representation.

3. WHY GROUP REPRESENTATION?

The idea that the existing political system is 'unrepresentative' is widespread. But what exactly does this mean? While the eleven white men who negotiated Charlottetown were not *demographically* representative of the population at large, they were the *elected* representatives of the population at large, and in many cases had broad electoral support from minority and disadvantaged groups. The claim that minority groups were not represented in the negotiations, therefore, seems to presuppose that people can be fully 'represented' only by someone who shares their gender, class, ethnicity, language, etc.

This idea is sometimes referred to as 'mirror representation': a legislature is said to be representative of the general public if it mirrors the ethnic, gender, and class characteristics of the public. Or, to put it another way, a group of citizens is represented in a legislature if one or more of the assembly's members are the same sort of people as the citizens.[16] This idea contrasts with the more familiar principle that defines representation in terms of the procedure by which office-holders are elected, rather than their personal attributes. On this traditional view, a group of citizens is represented in the legislature if they participated in the election of one or more members of the assembly, even if the elected members are very different from them in their personal characteristics.

Why are the personal characteristics of representatives so important? Some commentators argue that people must share certain experiences or characteristics in order to truly understand each other's needs and interests. On this view, a man simply cannot know what is in the interests of a woman: 'no amount of thought or sympathy, no matter how careful or honest, can jump the barriers of experience.'[17] This is a radical claim about the limits of representation, and I will dispute it below. Nevertheless, it's important to understand why questions about the personal characteristics of representatives are so much more common now than in earlier left-wing movements. This issue did not arise for traditional left parties, which focused on material interests or social-democratic ideology. To members of these parties, it did not seem very important that working-class people themselves serve as representatives of the movement. The relevant question was simply who could best articulate the movement's ideology and defend its interests. Not surprisingly, highly educated academics, lawyers, clergy, and social workers have tended to dominate the leadership of traditional labour-based political parties.

Identity groups, however, are not based on material interests or political ideologies. Rather, as we have seen, both ethnic and non-ethnic identity groups define themselves in terms of culture, and emphasize community and identity. This helps explains why the personal characteristics of representatives are so relevant in today's social movements. When groups define themselves in terms of a common sense of 'identity' and 'community', and organize around the public recognition of this identity, then it seems more plausible to say that only people who are actually members of the group should speak on its behalf. On this view, to understand why certain policies are, or are not, acceptable to a group, it is not enough to understand economic theories or political ideologies; one must understand the lived experiences of the group—the indignities it has suffered and the hopes it clings to. This need for group-based representation leads to what Anne Phillips calls the 'politics of presence', as distinct from an earlier 'politics of interests' or 'politics of ideas'.[18]

Another argument for focusing on the personal characteristics of representatives it that even if white men can understand the interests of Blacks or women, they cannot be trusted to promote those interests. For example, Christine Boyle argues that because men's interests differ from women's in terms of income, discrimination, legal rights, and child care, 'it seems reasonable to conclude that it is impossible for men to represent women.' The reason is not necessarily that men don't understand women's interests, but rather that 'at some point members of one group feel that someone belonging to another group has such a conflict of interest that representation is impossible, or at least unlikely.'[19] The same argument has been made in the context of white representation of African Americans.[20]

There is some truth to both these arguments; our ability to put ourselves in other people's shoes is limited, however sincerely we try—and most of us are not willing to try terribly hard. Nonetheless, the idea of mirror representation is seriously flawed, and few proponents of group representation defend it as a general theory of representation.

For one thing, the idea that the legislature should mirror the general population, taken to its logical conclusion, leads away from electoral politics entirely towards selection of representatives by lottery or random sampling. As Hanna Pitkin notes, 'selection by lot, or a controlled random sample, would be best calculated to produce the microcosm of the whole body of the people.'[21] Yet most proponents of group representation would see such a system as abandoning the democratic principle that representatives should be authorized by, and accountable to, the public.

Second, the claim that men cannot understand the needs and interests of women, or that whites cannot understand the needs of Blacks, can easily become an excuse for white men not to try to understand or represent the needs of others. This is precisely what critics say has happened in New Zealand, where the Maori have been guaranteed certain seats in the Parliament and non-Maoris have interpreted this guarantee as absolving them of any responsibility to take an interest in Maori affairs.[22]

Third, the claim that men cannot understand the interests of women cuts both ways—implying that women cannot understand and therefore represent men. This idea (with which some men may agree) carries with it the unattractive suggestion that men were right, historically, to resist representation by women, and, more generally, that people can speak only for their own group. Some proponents of group representation are willing to accept this result; according to Beverley Baines, 'if the truth be known, women [are not] particularly interested in representing men.'[23] Still, most proponents of group representation do not favour 'the kind of politics in which people [are] elected only to speak for their own group identity or interests'.[24]

These objections do not prove that the members of one group can in fact understand and therefore represent the interests of the members of other groups who have significantly different experiences or characteristics. But the claim that members of one group cannot represent members of other groups is surely too strong, for it must apply within groups as well as between them. Every group has subgroups, each with its own distinctive experiences and characteristics. If men cannot represent women, can white women represent women of colour? And within the category of women of colour, can Asian women represent African-Caribbean women?[25] Can middle-class heterosexual able-bodied Asian women represent poor, lesbian, or disabled Asian women? Taken to its logical conclusion, the principle of mirror representation seems to undermine the very possibility of representation itself. If 'no amount of thought or sympathy, no matter how careful or honest, can jump the barriers of experience',[26] how can anyone represent anyone else?

These difficulties suggest that the idea of mirror representation should be avoided as a general theory of representation. No doubt there are limits to the extent to which people are able and willing to 'jump the barriers of experience'. But the solution is not to accept those limits. Rather we should fight against them, in order to create a political culture in which people are more able and more willing to put themselves in other people's shoes and truly understand (and therefore become able to represent) their needs and interests. This is no easy task. It would require changes to our education system, to the media portrayal of various groups, and to the political process. And even then there would still be no guarantee that the members of one group would understand the needs of another. But to renounce the possibility of cross-group representation is to renounce the possibility of a society in which citizens are committed to addressing each other's needs and sharing each other's fate.

Thus few proponents of group representation endorse the idea of mirror representation as a general theory of representation. Instead, group representation is defended on more contextual grounds, as an appropriate mechanism for representing certain groups under certain conditions. In the Canadian debate, these contextual arguments for group representation fall into two major categories: systemic discrimination and self-government.

Group representation rights are often defended as a response to some systemic disadvantage or barrier in the political process that makes it impossible for the group's views and interests to be effectively represented. For example, Iris Young, writing in the American context, argues that special representation rights should be extended to 'oppressed groups':

> In a society where some groups are privileged while others are oppressed, insisting that as citizens persons should leave behind their particular affiliations and experiences to adopt a general point of view serves only to reinforce the privilege; for the perspective and interests of the privileged will tend to dominate this unified public, marginalizing or silencing those of other groups.[27]

According to Young, oppressed groups are at a disadvantage in the political process, and 'the solution lies at least in part in providing institutionalized means for the explicit recognition and representation of oppressed groups.'[28] These measures would include public funds for advocacy groups, guaranteed representation in political bodies, and veto rights over specific policies that affect a group directly. The point here is not that the legislature should mirror society, but rather that the historical domination of some groups by others has left a trail of barriers and prejudices that makes it difficult for historically disadvantaged groups to participate effectively in the political process.[29]

A version of this argument for the group representation of women in Canada was made by Christine Boyle in 1983. She argued that the 65 years of experience since women obtained the vote have shown that 'the inclusion of women into a system that was developed by men for use by men' does not provide adequate representation for women's interests.[30] Because the system was 'developed by men for use by men', women are at a disadvantage with respect to their ability to participate (e.g., because of their family responsibilities) and to get their perspectives taken seriously (e.g., because of sexist prejudice and stereotypes). Guaranteed seats for women would lead to real 'power-sharing' between men and women. This in turn would lead to various systemic reforms, so that one day the system could be seen as one developed by both men and women for use by both men and women.

Insofar as guarantees of group representation are adopted as a response to oppression or systemic disadvantage, they are most plausibly seen as temporary measures on the way to a society where the need for special representation would no longer exist—as a form of political 'affirmative action'. Society should seek to remove the oppression and disadvantage, thereby eliminating the need for these guarantees. In Canada, however, the issue is complicated by the fact that special representation for groups is sometimes defended not on grounds of overcoming systemic discrimination, but as a corollary of the right to self-government. As I noted in the introduction, the term 'self-government rights' refers to demands by Aboriginal peoples and the Québécois to govern themselves in certain key matters so as to ensure the full and free development of their cultures in the best interests of their people. Self-government would set limits on the authority of the central government over Quebec or Aboriginal reserves. And as we will see in Part 2, these limits might be asymmetrical: that is, full recognition of rights to self-government might mean that some federal laws that apply elsewhere in Canada would not apply to Quebec or to Aboriginal communities. Such limits on federal authority are not seen as a temporary measure, nor as a remedy for a form of oppression that we might (and ought) someday to eliminate. On the contrary, the right of self-government is often described as 'inherent', and thus permanent (which is one reason why supporters of self-government seek to have recognition entrenched at the constitutional level).

I will explore the logic and dynamics of self-government claims in Chapters 9 to 13. The question here, however, is the relationship between self-government and guaranteed representation. This connection is quite complicated, and adds a new dimension to the more familiar debate over group representation as a remedy for discrimination. On the one hand, insofar as it would reduce the jurisdiction of the federal government over Quebec or Aboriginal reserves, self-government seems to entail reduced influence (at least on certain issues) at the federal level for the self-governing group. For example, if self-government for the Québécois leads to the asymmetrical transfer of powers from Ottawa to Quebec, so that the federal government would be passing laws that would not apply to Quebec, it seems only fair that Quebecers not have a vote on such legislation (particularly if they could cast the deciding vote). It would seem unfair for Quebec MPs to decide federal legislation on immigration if the legislation does not apply to Quebec. The same principle would apply to any Aboriginal MPs elected by specially created Aboriginal districts voting on legislation from which Aboriginal people would be exempt.

On the other hand, the right to self-government does entail the right to guaranteed representation on any body that can interpret or modify these powers of self-government. It would seem to be a corollary of self-government that Quebec, for example, be guaranteed representation on the Supreme Court, since the Supreme Court resolves conflicts over the division of powers between the federal government and Quebec. And indeed Quebec is guaranteed three of the nine seats on the Court. Similarly, Aboriginal people insist that they be represented on any judicial bodies (e.g., land claims courts) that resolve disputes over their self-government rights.[31]

To oversimplify, then, self-government entails guaranteed representation on *judicial* or *inter-governmental* bodies that negotiate, interpret, or modify the division of powers, but reduced representation on federal bodies that legislate in areas of purely federal jurisdiction.[32] It is a mistake, therefore, to argue (as the Beaudoin-Dobbie Commission did) that 'guaranteed aboriginal representation in the Canadian Senate will be a logical extension of aboriginal self-government.'[33] If anything, the logical consequence of self-government is reduced representation. The right to self-government is a right against the authority of the federal government, not a right to special influence in the exercise of that authority. It is for this reason that some Indians who support self-government oppose guaranteed representation in the Commons, since this might give the central government the idea that it has the right to govern Indian communities.[34]

Of course, Aboriginals may also claim special representation in the federal legislature on grounds of systemic disadvantage. Claims of an inherent right to self-government do not preclude claims based on temporary disadvantage. However, it is important to know which claim is being made, since they apply with different force to different governmental bodies, over different time-frames, and to different subgroups within Aboriginal communities.[35] Since the claims of self-government are seen as inherent and permanent, so too are the guarantees of representation that follow from that self-government, whereas claims based on disadvantage are in principle temporary.

4. EVALUATING GROUP REPRESENTATION

I have tried to show that the idea of group representation cannot be dismissed. It has important continuities with existing practices of representation in Canada, and while the general principle of mirror representation is untenable, there are two contextual arguments that can justify certain limited forms of group representation under certain circumstances: namely, overcoming systemic disadvantage and securing self-government. These arguments provide grounds for thinking that group representation can play an important, if limited, role within the system of representative democracy in Canada. However, any proposal for group-based representation must answer a number of difficult questions. In this final section, I will simply flag some of these questions, to indicate the sorts of issues that need to be addressed when developing or evaluating any specific proposal for group representation.

Which groups should be represented?

How do we decide which groups, if any, should be entitled to group-based representation? Many critics of group representation believe that this is an unanswerable question—or rather, that any answer to it will be arbitrary and unprincipled. But the arguments above suggest that there are ways of drawing principled distinctions between various groups. A group has a claim to representation if it meets one of two criteria: either (a) its members are subject to systemic disadvantage in the political process or (b) its members have a claim to self-government.

Of these two criteria, self-government is the easier to apply. In Canada, only Aboriginal peoples and the Québécois formed self-governing nations prior to their incorporation into Canada. The criterion of systemic disadvantage is more complicated. Many groups claim to be disadvantaged in some respect, even though they may be privileged in others, and it is not clear how we can measure overall levels of disadvantage. According to Iris Young, 'Once we are clear that the principle of group representation refers only to oppressed social groups, then the fear of an unworkable proliferation of group representation should dissipate.'[36] However, her list of 'oppressed groups' in the United States appears to include four-fifths of the population. As she puts it elsewhere, 'in the United States today, at least the following groups are oppressed in one or more of these ways: women, blacks, Native Americans, Chicanos, Puerto Ricans and other Spanish-speaking Americans, Asian Americans, gay men, lesbians, working-class people, poor people, old people, and mentally and physically disabled people'[37]—in short, everyone but relatively well-off, relatively young, able-bodied, heterosexual white males.

Even if the list of oppressed groups were shorter, it is hard to see how Young's criterion would avoid an 'unworkable proliferation', since each of these groups has subgroups that might claim their own rights. In the case of Britain, the category of 'Black' people obscures deep divisions between the Asian and Afro-Caribbean communities, each of which in turn can be broken down into finer distinctions between many different ethnic groups. Given the almost endless capacity for fragmentation, we might ask, with Phillips, 'What in this context then counts as "adequate" ethnic representation?'[38]

On the other hand, as Young notes, many political parties and trade unions have allowed for special group representation without entering a spiral of increasing (and increasingly fragmented) demands.[39] In addition, we already have some experience with this issue in the context of affirmative action programs,[40] and the Supreme Court already faces the task of developing criteria for identifying historically disadvantaged groups in interpreting section 15(2) of the Charter of Rights and Freedoms.[41] The problem is formidable—and certainly none of the proposals for group representation to date has addressed it in a satisfactory way—but it is not unique to issues of political representation, and it may not be avoidable in a country with Canada's political and legal commitment to redressing injustice.

Generally speaking, white ethnic groups have shown little interest in group representation. They prefer to work within existing political parties to make them more inclusive, rather than try to get guaranteed seats in legislation.[42] This is not surprising, since statistics show that they are not in fact disadvantaged in the political process. Visible minorities, however, who are clearly under-represented in Parliament, have expressed interest in the idea of group representation.

How many seats should a group have?

If certain groups do need special group-based representation, how many seats should they have? There are two common answers to this question that are often conflated but should be kept distinct, since they lead in different directions. One view is that a group should be represented in proportion to its numbers in the population at large. For example, NAC proposed that women be guaranteed 50 per cent of Senate seats (women made up 50.7 per cent of the population in the 1991 Census). The second view is that there should be a threshold number of representatives, sufficient to ensure that the group's views and interests are effectively expressed.

The first view follows naturally from a commitment to the general principle of mirror representation; but, as we've seen, most proponents of group representation do not embrace that principle. And once we drop the idea of mirror representation in general, there seem to be no grounds for demanding exactly proportional representation rather than a threshold level. For example, Anne Phillips rejects the underlying premise of mirror representation that one has to be a member of a particular group in order to understand or represent that group's interests. However, she goes on to say that 'in querying the notion that only the members of particular disadvantaged groups can understand or represent their interests [one] might usefully turn this question round and ask whether such understanding or representation is possible without the presence of any members of the disadvantaged groups'.[43] Her argument is that without a threshold number of seats, others will not be able to understand, and so be able to represent, the interests of a disadvantaged group.

In practice, the rule of a threshold number of seats may lead to results quite different from exact proportional electoral representation. In the case of women, the threshold number of seats necessary to effectively present women's views is arguably less than the proportional number of seats. The president of NAC defended the guarantee of 50 per cent Senate seats for women on the ground that this would ensure women a 'place at the table'[44]; that is, she demanded proportional representation, but defended it in terms of the need for threshold representation. But does having a place at the table require having half of all the places?

In other cases, however, the threshold number of seats necessary for effective representation may be greater than the proportional number. Evidence suggests that if there are only one or two members from a marginalized or disadvantaged group in a legislative assembly or committee, they are likely to be excluded, and their voices ignored.[45] Thus proportional representation for some disadvantaged groups, such as Aboriginal people or visible minorities, is likely to amount to only such token representation. The number of seats necessary for effective presentation of their views, therefore, may exceed the number of seats required for proportional electoral representation. Given these possible divergences between the two goals of threshold and fully proportional representation, proponents of group representation must decide which is truly important.[46]

How are group representatives held accountable?

What accountability mechanisms can be put in place to ensure that the MPs or senators who hold reserved seats in fact serve the interests of the groups they are supposed to represent? How do we ensure that group 'representatives' are in fact accountable to the group? Here again we need to distinguish two very different answers. Recent proposals for guaranteed Aboriginal representation, based on the Maori model in New Zealand, involve setting up a separate electoral list for Aboriginal people, so that some MPs or senators are elected solely by Aboriginal voters.[47] This model of group representation does not try to specify the characteristics of the candidate; it is possible, if unlikely, that Aboriginal voters would elect a white MP. What matters here is not who is elected, but how: an MP elected by Aboriginal people would be accountable to them.

Such proposals recall the practice, discussed earlier, of drawing constituency boundaries so that they largely coincide with a 'community of interest'. It is safe to assume that these communities will tend to use their electoral strength to elect 'one of their own'. But they can, and sometimes do, elect someone who is not a member of their group. This does not undermine the value of accommodating communities of interest, because the justification for the practice is not mirror representation (which could be secured by a lottery or random sample). Rather, the justification is to promote the representation of the group's interests by making an MP accountable to the community. In the US, some defenders of 'affirmative gerrymandering'—a process used to create districts with a Black or

Hispanic majority—insist that they are more interested in accountability than mirror representation:

> affirmative gerrymandering is, in my view, misconceived if it is seen as a mechanism to guarantee that blacks will be represented by blacks, Hispanics by Hispanics, and whites by whites; rather, the proper use of affirmative gerrymandering is to guarantee that important groups in the population will not be substantially impaired in their ability to elect representatives *of their choice*.[48]

The Maori model attempts to provide the same sort of accountability for smaller or more territorially dispersed groups.

In most proposals for group representation, however, there are no separate electoral lists. Most proposals focus entirely on the characteristics of the candidates rather than the characteristics of the electorate. For example, while the NAC proposal required that 50 per cent of senators be women, they would be chosen by the general electorate, which contains as many men as women. And while the NAC proposal would guarantee a proportional number of seats for visible minorities, these senators too would be chosen by the general electorate, which is predominantly white.

In this model, group representation means having MPs or senators who belong to a particular group, even though they are not elected by that group. It is unclear, however, in what sense this is a form of *representation*, for there are no mechanisms in this model for establishing what each group wants, or for ensuring that the 'representatives' of the group act in accordance with what the group wants. The representative is not accountable to the group, and so may simply ignore its views. Indeed, given that the group's 'representatives' are chosen by the general electorate, it might be unwise for representatives to act in ways that displease dominant groups. As Phillips puts it, 'Accountability is always the other side of representation, and, in the absence of procedures for establishing what any group wants or thinks, we cannot usefully talk of their political representation.'[49]

In other words, guaranteed seats would not ensure that women's interests or needs or perspectives were 'represented'. The idea that the presence of women senators would *by itself* ensure the representation of women's interests, even in the absence of any electoral accountability, makes sense only if one thinks that there is 'some fundamental unity between women, some essential set of experiences and interests that can be represented by any interchangeable combination of women'.[50] This is implausible, not only in the case of women, but also in the case of ethnic, national, or racial minorities, given the heterogeneity of interests and perspectives within each of these groups.

So here again we have conflicting models based on conflicting ideals. The Aboriginal model guarantees that some representatives would be accountable solely to Aboriginal voters, although it does not guarantee that the representatives themselves would be Aboriginal—that the representative would 'mirror' the electorate. The NAC model guarantees that representatives would mirror important groups in the electorate, but it does not guarantee that the representatives would be accountable to the group they mirror. Of course, many proponents of guaranteed representation for women firmly believe in the need for accountability, and would like to find some way of making sure that women representatives are accountable to women. To date, however, the ideals of mirror representation and democratic accountability have not yet been adequately integrated.

Even if these problems can be solved, critics of group representation will object that institutionalizing group differences, and ascribing political salience to them, would have serious implications for Canadian unity. They believe it would encourage a 'politics of grievance', or a 'mosaic madness', and inhibit the development of a shared sense of citizenship and national purpose. Critics have claimed that group representation would be a source of disunity that could lead to the dissolution of the country, or, less drastically, to a reduced willingness to make the mutual sacrifices and accommodations necessary for a functioning democracy.

However, we need to keep in mind the distinction between the two grounds for special representation: systemic disadvantage and self-government. Generally speaking, the demand for representation rights by disadvantaged groups is a demand for *inclusion*. Groups that feel excluded want to be included in the larger political process, and group representation is intended to facilitate this. As we've seen, this sort of special representation can be considered an extension of the long-standing practice of defining geographic constituencies in such a way as to ensure representation of 'communities of interest'. It can also be seen as an extension of the tradition of giving smaller regions extra seats in the Senate. These practices are not seen as threats to national unity. On the contrary, they are rightly seen as promoting civic participation and political legitimacy, and as alleviating the 'sense of injustice' that arises when communities and regions lack effective representation.[51] Why then should guaranteed representation for non-territorial communities of interest be regarded as a threat to unity, rather than as evidence of a desire for integration?

Claims based on self-government, by contrast, are not aimed at integration, but rather at preserving a separate and culturally distinct society. Whereas demands for representation by disadvantaged groups seek greater inclusion into the larger political community, demands for self-government reflect a desire to weaken the bonds with the larger community, and to assert the primacy and inherence of the minority's national rights.

But while claims of self-government raise deep problems for social unity, which I will discuss at length in Part 2, it appears that the particular aspect of self-government we are considering here—guaranteed representation at the federal or inter-governmental level—clearly serves a unifying function. The existence of such group representation helps reduce the threat of self-government, by reconnecting the self-governing community to the larger federation. It is a form of connection that remains, and can be drawn upon, when other connections are being weakened. This is true, I think, of Quebec's representation on the Supreme Court, and of proposals for Aboriginal representation in the Senate.

5. CONCLUSION

Any proposal for group representation must answer the difficult questions of how to identify the truly disadvantaged groups and how to hold their 'representatives' accountable. The debate in Canada has barely begun to address these questions, but they need to be examined seriously because demands for group representation will not go away. Proponents of group representation appeal to some of the most basic practices and principles of Canadian representative democracy to defend their proposals, and some forms of group representation may be able to play an important, if limited, role within the Canadian political system.

Of course, issues of representation cannot be reduced to the composition of the legislature. Representation in the House of Commons or Senate needs to be situated within the context of other mechanisms for representing the views or interests of a group, such as legal challenges to unfavourable legislation in the courts and interest-group advocacy. Any assessment of the need for group representation must take these alternative routes to representation into account. Yet many of the barriers that affect women, visible minorities, and other disadvantaged groups in the electoral process also affect their access to these alternative mechanisms of representation. Moreover, Parliament has a special symbolic role in representing the citizens of the country. Citizens who do not see themselves reflected in Parliament may become alienated from the political process and question its legitimacy.[52] If not the only route to representation, legislative representation is a uniquely important one.

That is a rather vague conclusion, I'm afraid, and I have not tried to define or defend any specific model of group representation. Indeed, it may not be possible to say much more at the general level. Democracy involves a commitment to the principle of political equality, but it is not possible to deduce the single best system of representation from that abstract principle.[53] There are many ways of achieving political equality, and the results of particular electoral mechanisms are notoriously context-specific. All I have tried to show in this chapter is that group representation is not inherently illiberal or undemocratic. It is a plausible extension of our existing democratic traditions, and there may be some circumstances in which it is the most appropriate way to ensure an adequate voice for minority interests and perspectives. Since it is vital that minorities have a fair hearing in the political process, proposals for group representation themselves deserve a fair hearing.

Chapter 8

A Truce in the Multiculturalism Wars?

The preceding chapters have covered a lot of ground. If there is a single theme that unites them, however, it is that neither side in the debate over multiculturalism as it is currently being conducted has helped us to understand the real issues.

On the one hand, increasing number of critics argue that official multiculturalism is encouraging 'ghettoism' and 'apartheid' among ethnic groups in Canada, and impeding their integration into mainstream society. As we've seen, there is no evidence to support this claim. And once we situate multiculturalism within the larger context of government policies that influence ethnocultural relations, we can see that the claim is not just factually incorrect, but wrong in principle.

Why then have critics dismissed these policies so quickly, without examining the evidence? The answer appears to be that they simply assume from the start that defenders of multiculturalism are motivated by what Neil Bissoondath calls a 'psychology of divisiveness without limits',[1] or what Richard Gwyn calls 'the new cultural creeds' of 'moral absolutism and cultural apartheid'.[2] If one assumes that such divisiveness is the real motivation behind multiculturalism policies, then there is no need to check the evidence about their actual results: one can simply assume that such policies are by nature incapable of promoting integration.

Both these assumptions, of course, are unfounded. There is no evidence that Canadians today are motivated by a psychology of divisiveness without limits or a creed of cultural apartheid. And there is positive evidence that ethnic groups are more thoroughly integrated into Canadian society today, in terms of participation in common societal institutions and adherence to common political values of democracy and individual rights, than they were before the adoption of multiculturalism in 1971. Demands for multicultural accommodations, or proposals for new multiculturalism programs, are not manifestations of an irrational virus of 'identity politics' or what Gwyn calls 'identity anger'.[3] They are serious attempts to deal with serious issues: What are fair terms of integration? How can we counteract the trend towards an oppositional subculture among Blacks? How can we make our democracy more representative? Not all of the proposals I've discussed are feasible or desirable; I have tried to point out the limitations and uncertainties involved. But they are worthy of genuine consideration as thoughtful attempts to deal with real problems in ways that are consistent with social integration, individual rights, and democratic justice.

On the other hand, the defenders of multiculturalism have been strangely inarticulate in explaining or justifying the policy. They have not explained the limits of multiculturalism, in terms either of social integration or of respect for individual rights. Even worse, they have responded to critics of multiculturalism by accusing them of intolerance, perhaps even racism. Such accusations are equally unfounded. Indeed, to say that critics of multiculturalism are motivated by intolerance is just as absurd as to say that defenders of multiculturalism are motivated by a psychology of divisiveness. The fact is that most Canadians, including most critics of multiculturalism, believe in tolerance and racial equality. But as Canadian citizens they have the right—and the responsibility—to ask hard questions about the limits of diversity, and about the impact of multiculturalism on common values and institutions. And too often their valid questions have been ignored or dismissed.

Thus we have a debate in which misinformed critics and inarticulate defenders simply exchange equally unfounded accusations. Needless to say, it is impossible to make any progress when the debate is conducted in such terms, and nothing can be learned from it—except perhaps that Canadians have trouble listening to each other.

I would like, therefore, to propose a truce in the war over multiculturalism. What we need is a new debate, on new terms. In particular, I would suggest the following. First, we should assume (until shown otherwise) that participants in the debate, on both sides, are reasonable. We should assume that Canadians share basic commitments to social integration and liberal-democratic values, and we should interpret any demands or questions they raise about multiculturalism in this light. We should assume that debates over multiculturalism are debates about how best to understand and interpret these shared goals of integration, human rights, and democracy.

If someone demands new media regulations regarding ethnic stereotypes, then, we shouldn't jump to the conclusion that, deep down, they believe in cultural apartheid. And if someone questions whether multiculturalism leads to clitoridectomy, we shouldn't jump to the conclusion that they are racist and intolerant. No doubt there are a few people on both sides who are genuinely intolerant or absolutist. But we shouldn't assume that in advance. We should begin with the assumption that our fellow citizens, on both sides of the debate, have legitimate concerns that deserve a fair hearing.

Second, we should be more specific about the policy options. 'Multiculturalism' is an umbrella term for a wide range of policies, and we need to be clear about which particular policy we are criticizing or defending. Accepting some of these policies does not entail accepting all of them, and each should be assessed on its own merits. We also need to know more about what critics see as the alternatives to multiculturalism. How else might we ensure that the terms of integration are fair? How else might we deal with disturbing trends in race relations? How can we make our democratic system more representative? These questions are dealt with quite differently in Germany, France, and the United States. If critics don't like the Canadian approach, what other models do they propose? Without some sense of the alternatives, it is impossible to evaluate criticisms of multiculturalism.

Finally, we should see what evidence is available on the impact of these different policies. As it happens, there is actually a great deal of information available. One of the results of the federal multiculturalism policy has been, in Freda Hawkins' words, 'a bonanza of remarkable opportunities' for sociologists working in this area in Canada.[4] Since the 1970s, government funding has helped make ethnic relations one of the most intensively studied aspects of Canadian life, and there is now a large literature on multiculturalism and integration in Canada.[5] Moreover, Statistics Canada, which is widely recognized as the best government statistics agency in the world, has excellent census data bearing on many of these questions, data that are easily available in public libraries and now even on the Internet.[6]

We also have considerable evidence about the success of other policy approaches in other jurisdictions; we know a great deal about what works and what doesn't. Of course, looking up the evidence involves more work than armchair speculation does. But at some point speculation must be tested against the facts.

It seems that the usual standards of objectivity and evidence are often not applied in media treatment of multiculturalism. For example, just as I was finishing a draft of this book, *The Globe and Mail* published a two-page feature story on multiculturalism that repeated virtually all the myths and misconceptions outlined in earlier chapters, and described the policy as a failure without citing any evidence.[7] Had this article been written on any other public policy, surely the author would have been expected to provide some evidence for such a claim. Don't the same standards apply to discussions of multiculturalism policy? I am not encouraging media self-censorship on this issue; we have already had too much self-censorship about multiculturalism. Nor do I mean to suggest that we should avoid discussing objections to multiculturalism. On the contrary, we should investigate them—in other words, check the evidence.

If we conducted the debate along these terms, I suspect that multiculturalism would emerge as a well-founded policy for managing ethnocultural relations. On the other hand, perhaps the debate will uncover other approaches that have proven more successful. If so, all the better. My concern is less to defend multiculturalism per se than to get a meaningful debate going in which Canadians can discuss the real issues in an informed way.

Part Two

The Unhappy Marriage of Federalism and Nationalism

Chapter 9

► *Prologue: Taking Nationalism Seriously* ◄

An enormous amount of ink has been spilt on the allegedly disintegrative and divisive impact of Canada's multiculturalism policies. Yet the real threat to Canada's long-term stability is the ongoing failure to reach a satisfactory arrangement with Canada's non-immigrant national minorities: the Québécois and the Aboriginal peoples. To understand the aspirations of these groups we must understand one of the most powerful forces in the modern world, namely, nationalism. Unlike immigrant groups, these national minorities have fought to form themselves (or rather to maintain themselves) as separate and self-governing societies, and have adopted the language of 'nationhood' both to express and to justify this struggle for self-government. Thus it is no coincidence that the Quebec provincial legislature is called the 'National Assembly', or that the main organization of Aboriginal bands is called the 'Assembly of First Nations'. These groups have defined themselves as 'nations' and, as such, they claim the same inherent right of self-determination as other colonized or conquered nations around the world.

Because Canada contains these internal minority nationalisms, it is best seen not as a traditional 'nation state' but as a multination state. We are hardly alone in this respect, even among Western democracies. Other Western states containing powerful minority nationalisms include Belgium (with the Flemish), Switzerland (with the French and Italians), and Spain (with the Catalans and Basques). The crucial question facing Canada, or any other multination state, is how to reconcile these competing nationalisms within a single state.

In such countries the potential risk to social unity from nationalist movements is obvious. One of the defining features of nationalism, historically, has been the quest for an independent state. (Indeed, nationalism is often defined as the view that nations and states should coincide.)[1] Even if they are not explicitly secessionist, nationalists typically insist that the nation is the primary locus of political loyalty and allegiance, so that participation in any supra-national political community is always conditional, depending mainly on how well such participation serves the interests of the primary national community. Once the Québécois, or the Cree, define themselves as a nation, therefore, it seems that their allegiance to Canada can only be derivative and conditional.

Considerations of military or economic security may keep these national groups from pursuing secession. Once an ethnocultural group defines itself as a nation, however, the whole logic of political debate seems to change. Even if independence is not the preferred option, it becomes the benchmark against which other options are measured. The question is not 'Why should we seek more self-governing powers?' but 'Why should we continue to accept limitations on our inherent rights of self-government?' In this way, the threat of secession seems ever-present in multination states.

Yet multination states are not doomed to disintegration. Many have survived and even flourished. Countries like Switzerland, Belgium, and Canada have not only managed their conflicts (so far) in a peaceful and democratic way, but have secured prosperity and individual freedom for their citizens. What has enabled these countries to accommodate minority nationalisms? The most important factor is their nature as federations. In a century when nationalism has torn apart colonial empires and communist dictatorships, and redefined boundaries all over the world, democratic federalism has succeeded in keeping multination states together. No other political structure can make this claim. But federalism is no panacea. On the contrary, the relationship between federalism and nationalism is full of ambiguities and conflicts. Although federalism is a precondition for accommodating minority nationalism, it can easily become yet another source of conflict that fuels separatist sentiments.

While multination federations can survive and flourish, the existence of minority nationalisms dramatically changes, and constrains, their options. Institutions and principles that might work in a single-nation state will not work in a country with powerful minority nationalisms. Even forms of federalism that work in a single-nation state like the United States or Germany will not work in a multination state like Switzerland or Canada.

Many of the participants in the Canadian debate, however, have yet to take full account of the constraints we face. If Canada is to survive, we need to take nationalism much more seriously. We need to understand its nature and dynamics, and the fears and aspirations it generates. We can cope with our contending nationalisms only if we acknowledge them honestly and face up to the challenges that history has bequeathed us as a multination state. Yet many people in Canada—including the leaders of the federal government—have adopted the opposite course of trying to ignore or downplay the reality of minority nationalism in Canada, and obscuring the real challenges in vague talk about diversity, pluralism, and shared values.

The rest of this book is an attempt to sort out the tortured relationship between federalism and minority nationalism. I will try to spell out some of the constraints that minority nationalism imposes on us, and to develop a model of 'multination federalism' that might be responsive to them.

First, in Chapter 10, I will attempt to show why minority nationalism is not a transient phenomenon but an enduring feature of Canada that must be explicitly recognized if we are to secure the willing agreement of national minorities to their continued participation in the country.

Unfortunately, demands for national recognition have revealed a large, and widening, gap between two models of federalism in Canada: the territorial/symmetrical model of federalism dominant in English-speaking Canada, and the multination/asymmetrical model of federalism dominant in Quebec and among Aboriginal peoples. The 'national unity' strategy followed by the federal government for the last ten years can be seen as an attempt to paper over these differences. The government has tried to promote a vague and ambiguous recognition of Quebec while simultaneously emphasizing provincial equality and shared values—a compromise that it hoped would appeal to proponents of both models of federalism. This strategy, reflected in the Meech Lake and Charlottetown Accords, has not worked (to put it mildly), and in Chapter 11 I will discuss why it remains doomed to failure.

If national minorities will not relinquish their nationalist claims, and if the differences cannot be papered over, the only way to keep Canada together is to persuade English-speaking Canadians to accept a multination model of federalism. In Chapter 12 I will explore how and why English-speaking Canadians might come to accept such a conception of Canada and Canadian federalism. Finally, in Chapter 13 I will examine the prospects for such a multination federalism, if it were accepted by English-speaking Canadians. Would it be stable, or merely a stepping-stone on the way to the country's inevitable dissolution?

Chapter 10

> *Two Models of Federalism in Canada* ◄

The fundamental reality of political life in Canada, dating back to the seventeenth century, is the co-existence of distinct national groups on Canadian soil: Aboriginal, French, and English. Many of the pivotal episodes in Canadian political history have centred on attempts to renegotiate the relationships among these national groups. And these relationships remain the most serious threat to the stability of the country.

Why have we had such trouble learning to live with our 'nations within'? Perhaps part of the difficulty is that many Canadians have been reluctant to really accept that these are nations—complete and functioning societies, with their own historic territories, languages, institutions, and cultures. Even people who accept the existence of these nations often fail to see the full implications of this fact for federalism.

In this chapter I will discuss why national recognition is so important (section 1), and how it is linked to territorial self-government (section 2). While the requirement for territorialized national recognition can be met by a federalist system (section 3), it cannot be accommodated within the particular model of 'territorial' federalism accepted by most English-speaking Canadians (section 4). It can be satisfied only within an explicitly 'multination' model of federalism (section 5). I will conclude by focusing on the crux of the difference between these two models of federalism: namely, the issue of 'asymmetry' (section 6).

1. NATIONAL RECOGNITION

Why are the Québécois and Aboriginal peoples in Canada so intent on being recognized as 'nations'? Their insistence on the language of nationhood has been disturbing to some commentators, who view it as inevitably leading to secession. Even those who endorse some notion of self-government for either or both groups often wish to eliminate the language of nations and nationalism from the debate.

Jeremy Webber, for example, argues that we should replace 'nation' with 'political community', because the former term 'carries the assumption that an individual can only have one nation'.[1] Accepting this exclusive conception of nationality implies that Quebecers must decide whether they are 'Quebecers first', in which case they have no real loyalty to Canada and might as well secede, or 'Canadians first', in which case they should relinquish the claim that Quebec has any special status as the forum for national self-government by its people. Webber argues that this is a false choice, and that most Quebecers have a real sense of loyalty to both Quebec and Canada, a multiple allegiance that cannot be captured in the language of either 'Quebec nationalism' or 'Canadian nationalism'. He maintains that the hope for social unity in a country like Canada lies precisely in cultivating these multiple allegiances, which we can do only if we resist the temptation to speak of either Canada or Quebec as a 'nation'.

I agree with Webber that most Québécois, and most Aboriginal people, have a genuine sense of loyalty to Canada as a political community; I also agree that the language of nationalism often obscures this. But we need to understand why national recognition is so important. The fact is that the language of nationalism serves a number of valuable functions for these groups.[2] It provides them with some standing (and, possibly, legal rights) under international law; nations and peoples have claims to self-government under international law that mere political subunits lack. And both Aboriginal peoples and the Québécois have cited international law to support their claims.

The precise scope of these claims is far from clear. The right of national groups to self-determination is affirmed in international law; according to the United Nations' Charter, for example, 'all peoples have the right to self-determination'. However, the UN has not defined 'peoples', and it has generally applied the principle of self-determination only to overseas colonies, not internal national minorities, even when the latter were subject to the same sort of colonization and conquest as the former. This restriction on self-determination to overseas colonies (known as the 'salt-water thesis') is widely seen as arbitrary, especially by national minorities in Canada and elsewhere who insist that they too are 'peoples' or 'nations', and as such have the right of self-determination.

In addition, the language of nationhood adds a historical dimension to such groups' claims, pointing out that current demands are not just political power-grabs by today's élite, but relate to a consistent history of struggles and negotiations that have defined the terms under which the group was incorporated into the country. This sense of history not only provides justification for current demands, but strengthens the sense of collective identity needed to sustain nationalist mobilization.

The language of nationhood also serves to differentiate the claims of national minorities from those of other groups. It is important for Aboriginal peoples and the Québécois to distinguish their claims from those of immigrant groups, on the one hand, and of the nine other provinces, on the other. Unlike immigrants, national groups seek robust forms of self-government, perhaps through some form of federalism. And unlike the other nine provinces, they do not consider the appropriate form of federalism to be a purely 'symmetrical' one that treats all federal sub-units as identical in their rights and powers; as we shall see in section 4, there are powerful reasons to think that a multination state will almost necessarily involve some degree of asymmetry. What distinguishes Aboriginal bands and the province of Quebec from immigrant groups and other provinces is precisely that they are 'nationality-based political units': each of these units provides the forum within which a national group exercises self-government.

Another, larger function of the language of nationhood is to equalize the bargaining power between a majority and national minorities. So long as political issues are discussed in terms of how the majority treats the minority, in a democratic society the presumption will always be that the majority rules. The language of nationhood questions these definitions of majority and minority. By defining the minority as a nation, it converts numerical superiority/inferiority into a co-equal partnership. It is difficult to exaggerate the importance to national minorities of ensuring that they are not defined simply as a minorities, and the language of nationhood is precisely what makes this possible.

Thus there are several strategic reasons for adopting the language of nationhood. But its value is not simply strategic. The fact is that these groups are nations in the sociological sense. They are historical societies, more or less institutionally complete, occupying a given territory or home-land, sharing a distinct language and societal culture.[3]

Finally, it is worth remembering that the power to name itself is one of the most significant powers sought by any group in society, and that respecting this power is seen as a crucial test of respect for the group as a whole.[4] We can see its importance in the efforts made to replace the name 'negro', first with 'Black' and then 'African American'; in the efforts to replace 'crippled' with 'handicapped' and then 'people with disabilities'; and in the efforts of feminists to eliminate sexist language. If Aboriginal peoples have adopted the label 'First Nations', can we seriously ask that they refrain from doing so simply because the term 'nation' makes some non-Aboriginals nervous? Indeed, any attempt to deny national minorities their claims to nationhood will be counter-productive, since it will be seen as an insult, one more denigration of their status as distinct peoples and cultures.

If we wish to avoid the disintegrating effects of minority nationalism in Canada, therefore, our aim should not be to prevent groups from seeing themselves as nations. It should be to break the link between nation and state—to challenge the presumption that an independent state is the only or the best form for national self-government.

2. NATIONS AND TERRITORIES

One ambitious strategy for breaking the link between nation and state is to redefine the national minority's sense of its territory or homeland so that it encompasses the country as a whole, not just one region within it. An example was Pierre Trudeau's strategy of 'sea-to-sea bilingualism', intended to encourage French Canadians to reject the view that they were 'at home' only in Quebec. By redefining the boundaries of the French nation to include all of Canada, official bilingualism would 'shift Quebecers' national identification from Quebec to Ottawa' and undermine the notion that French Canadians' national aspirations could be achieved through the secession of Quebec.[5]

This strategy had no chance of succeeding. Sea-to-sea bilingualism might have been a possibility if the half-million or more French Canadians who moved to the United States had instead settled in the Canadian West. But French Canadians showed little inclination to move West, and whatever inclination they might have had was effectively ended by the execution of Louis Riel, the first in a long series of events (such as the Manitoba schools crisis) and policies that ensured the West would be overwhelmingly English-speaking.[6]

It was right and proper for Trudeau to denounce this history of exclusion and insist that French Canadians should be able to feel at home throughout Canada; the policy of official bilingualism is an appropriate symbolic affirmation of that principle. But there is no chance today that this policy can reverse the reality that it is only in Quebec and parts of New Brunswick and Ontario that francophones can truly live and work within a francophone societal culture.[7] There can be French-language churches and public schools in Alberta, and access to French-language media, but there is no way for francophones to participate meaningfully in the political, economic, or academic life of the province except in English. And the evidence is that despite the best efforts of federal bilingualism policies, francophone communities in the West are both economically marginalized and demographically shrinking.[8]

Thus Quebec will remain the heart of the French-speaking nation in Canada.[9] Indeed, the main effect of sea-to-sea bilingualism has not been to make living outside Quebec a more realistic option for the Québécois, but rather to ensure that living in Quebec remains a viable option for English-speakers. Sea-to-sea bilingualism may have been intended to strengthen the opportunities for francophones outside Quebec, but in Quebec it is widely seen instead as protecting the rights of English-speaking inside the province, whether native-born anglophones or immigrant allophones.

For this reason, unless it is accompanied by recognition of the special status of Quebec, the ideology of sea-to-sea bilingualism is often seen by the Québécois as a threat to their very existence. Most believe that a vibrant francophone culture cannot survive in Canada unless it survives in Quebec, and that the ongoing viability of the French culture in Quebec depends on ensuring that newcomers to the province, whether from other provinces or other countries, integrate into the francophone society. The Quebec provincial government, therefore, must play a pivotal role in maintaining the viability of the French society in Canada, and to fulfil this role it must have the ability to regulate certain language rights. Any conception of sea-to-sea bilingualism that denies this fact is bound to be denounced in Quebec. Attempts to encourage the Québécois to think of themselves as members of a 'nation canadienne-française' stretching from sea to sea may be motivated by a noble ideal—to make francophones feel at home in all of Canada—but are likely to be perceived as weakening the priority of French inside Quebec, without really increasing people's opportunities to live and work in French elsewhere.

In short, there seems to be no chance of reversing the territorialization of the French nation in Canada. It might have been realistic in 1870, but not in 1990. Nor is this problem unique to Canada. The evidence from countries like Belgium and Switzerland suggests a clear trend towards increased territorialization of language communities.[10] The necessity of territorialization is even clearer in the case of Aboriginal peoples (and of course Trudeau never proposed that Aboriginal languages be official languages from sea to sea). If the Nisga'a are to be able to pursue their national aspirations, it will be only in their part of British Columbia, not in New Brunswick.

Thus we need to accept as given both that there will be minority nationalisms in Canada and that these national loyalties will be territorially defined. In other words, we need to accept that Canada is and will remain a *multination* state—a federation of peoples—in which individuals' national identity may differ from, and may conflict with, their identity as Canadian citizens.

The question, then, is what can hold such a multination state together? As I noted earlier, the adoption of the rhetoric of nationhood poses a powerful challenge to political unity, since it changes the background assumptions of political debate and makes the idea of independence the benchmark against which all other options are measured. If we accept that Aboriginal peoples and the Québécois are national minorities, we must also accept that their national community will remain a powerful locus of political allegiance, and that loyalty to Canada will be conditional on respect for their national identity and self-government aspirations.

I don't mean to imply that the loyalty of Quebecers or Aboriginal people to Canada is purely instrumental—that their commitment is solely a function of how well participation in Canada serves to promote their national self-interest. It is clear that the members of these communities do have an independent and non-instrumental commitment to Canada, the bases of which I will explore in the next chapter. But this commitment, though not purely instrumental, may well be conditional—sustainable only on the condition that these communities are able to fulfil their national aspirations within Canada.

3. THE PROMISE OF FEDERALISM

The basic precondition for accommodating the national aspirations of Quebec and the First Nations is some system for dividing and sharing power so as to make meaningful self-government possible. For Quebec, such accommodation has so far been achieved through the federal system. Many commentators argue that federalism can also accommodate Aboriginal communities, either as a 'third order of government' within the existing federal system, exercising a collection of powers carved out of both federal and provincial jurisdictions, or through a form of 'treaty federalism' that predates and exists outside the 1867 Confederation.[11]

In fact, federalism seems the ideal mechanism for accommodating territorially defined national minorities within a multination state.[12] Where such a minority is regionally concentrated, the boundaries of federal subunits can be drawn so that it forms a majority in one of the subunits. Under these circumstances, federalism can provide meaningful self-government for a national minority, guaranteeing its ability to make decisions in certain areas without being outvoted by the larger society.

Quebec is a paradigmatic example. Under the federal division of powers, the province of Quebec has control over issues that are crucial to the survival of the francophone society, including education, language, and culture, as well as significant input into immigration policy. The other nine provinces too have these powers, but the major impetus behind the existing division of powers, and the federal system itself, was the need to accommodate Quebec; when Canada was created in 1867, many English-Canadian leaders wanted a unitary state, like England. Had Quebec not been guaranteed substantial powers—and hence protected against the risk of being outvoted on key issues by the larger anglophone population—the province either would not have joined Canada in 1867, or would surely have seceded sometime thereafter.

Federalism thus provides a constitutionally protected realm of self-government for the national minority while still providing the economic, military, and sociocultural benefits of participation in a larger state. Historically, the most prominent examples of federal systems used to accommodate national minorities are Canada and Switzerland. The apparent stability and prosperity of these countries has led other multination countries (such as India, Malaysia, and Nigeria) to adopt federal systems upon decolonization. Even though many of these federations are facing serious difficulties, there is currently another burst of interest in federalism in multination countries; some are in the process of adopting federal arrangements (Belgium, Spain, Russia) and others are debating whether it would provide a solution to their ethnic conflicts (South Africa).[13]

This widespread interest in federalism reflects a welcome, if belated, acknowledgement that the desire of national minorities to maintain them-selves as culturally distinct and politically autonomous societies must be accommodated. Federalism is one of the few mechanisms available for this purpose. Unfortunately, though, it is no solution to national divisions with-in a multination state. In fact, federalism itself has become a source of divi-sion in Canada. The problem is that French- and English-speaking Canadians have adopted two very different conceptions of federalism, which (following Philip Resnick) I will call 'multination' federalism and 'territorial' federalism.[14] Whereas the former emphasizes the link between federalism and self-government for national minorities, the latter ignores or downplays this link. The public debates over the Meech Lake and Charlottetown Accords revealed clearly that many of our constitutional dilemmas stem from these competing conceptions of federalism.

I will try to uncover the sources of these differing conceptions of feder-alism, starting with the territorial model that is dominant in English-speak-ing Canada (section 4). I will then look at the multination model dominant within Quebec (section 5), before focusing on the crux of the difference between them: asymmetrical rights and national recognition (section 6).

4. TERRITORIAL FEDERALISM

The United States provides a clear example of the 'territorial' conception of federalism. Anglo-Saxon settlers dominated all of the original thirteen colonies that formed the United States. As John Jay put it in the *Federalist Papers*, 'Providence has been pleased to give this one connected country to one united people—a people descended from the same ancestors, speaking the same language, professing the same religion, attached to the same prin-ciples of government, very similar in their manners and customs.' Although Jay exaggerated the ethnic homogeneity of the colonial population,[15] it was true that none of the thirteen colonies was controlled by a national minor-ity; hence there was no need for the original division of powers within the federal system to accommodate ethnocultural divisions.

The status of national minorities became more of an issue as the US began its territorial expansion to the south and west, and eventually into the Pacific. At each step of this expansion, the American government was incorporating the homelands of already settled, ethnoculturally distinct peoples, including American Indians, Chicanos, Alaskan Eskimos, native Hawaiians, Puerto Ricans, and the Chamoros in Guam. And at each step, the question arose whether the American federalist system should be used to accommodate the desire of these groups for self-government.

In the nineteenth century it would have been possible to create states dominated by the Navaho, for example, or by Chicanos, Puerto Ricans, or native Hawaiians. At the time when these groups were incorporated into the United States, they formed majorities in their homelands. However, a deliberate decision was made not to use federalism to accommodate the self-government claims of national minorities. Instead, it was decided that no territory would be accepted as a state unless these national groups were outnumbered within it. In some cases this was achieved by drawing boundaries so that Indian tribes or Hispanic groups were outnumbered (Florida). In others it was achieved by delaying statehood until the numbers of anglophone settlers were great enough (Hawaii, the Southwest). As a result, none of the fifty states can be seen as ensuring self-government for a national minority in the way that Quebec ensures self-government for the Québécois.

Far from helping national minorities, American territorial federalism has hurt them. Throughout most of American history, Chicanos, American Indian tribes, and native Hawaiians have received better treatment from the federal government than from state governments. State governments, controlled by colonizing settlers, have often seen national minorities as obstacles to settlement and resource development, and so have pushed to strip minorities of their traditional political institutions, undermine their treaty rights, and dispossess them of their historic homelands. While the federal government has been complicit in much of the mistreatment, in many cases it has at least attempted to prevent the most severe abuses. We can see the same dynamic at work today in Brazil, where the federal government is trying to protect the rights of Indians in Amazonia against the predations of local state governments.

In short, the people who devised American federalism had no interest in accommodating national minorities. In deciding how to arrange their federal system—from the drawing of boundaries to the sorting out of the division of powers and the role of the judiciary—their aim was to consolidate, then expand, a new country and to protect the equal rights of individuals within a common national community, not to recognize the rights of national minorities to self-government. Insofar as national minorities in the US have achieved self-government, it has been outside—and to some extent despite—the federal system, through the various forms of 'special status' enjoyed by the 'commonwealth' of Puerto Rico, the 'protectorate' of Guam, and the 'domestic dependent nations' of American Indians.

If American federalism was not intended to accommodate ethnocultural groups, why was it adopted? First, like any other mechanism for dividing power, it reduces the danger of tyranny.[16] Second, it provides greater room for policy experimentation and innovation; faced with new issues and problems, each state can adopt differing policies, and those policies that prove most successful can then be adopted more widely. Moreover, as the United States expanded westward and incorporated vast expanses of territory with very different natural resources and patterns of economic development, it became increasingly difficult to conceive how a single, centralized unitary government could be made to work. Some form of territorial devolution was clearly necessary, and the system of federalism adopted by the original thirteen colonies served this purpose very well.

Indeed, any liberal democracy that contains a large and diverse territory will surely be pushed in the direction of some form of federalism, regardless of its ethnocultural composition. The virtues of federalism for large-scale democracies are manifested not only in the United States but also in Australia, Brazil, and Germany. In each of these cases, federalism is firmly entrenched and widely endorsed, even though none of the federal units is intended to enable ethnocultural groups to be self-governing. In some countries, then, federalism is adopted simply because it provides a means by which a single national community can divide and diffuse power. This is the 'territorial' model of federalism, as distinct from 'multination' federalism.

That territorial federalism is the dominant model in English-speaking Canada is reflected both in the insistence that all provinces be equal in their legislative powers and in demands for an American-style 'Triple E' Senate. However, this model is obviously unsatisfactory to the Québécois and Aboriginal peoples, since it says nothing about the accommodation of national minorities. Whether the allocation of powers to territorial subunits promotes the interests of national minorities depends on how the boundaries of those subunits are drawn and which powers are allocated to which level of government. If these decisions about boundaries and powers are not made with the intention of empowering national minorities, then federalism may well worsen the position of national minorities, as has occurred in the United States, Brazil, and other 'territorial federalist' states.

5. Multination Federalism

What would a genuine multination federal system look like? In it, federalism would have to be seen not just as a means by which a single national community can divide and diffuse power, but as a means of accommodating the desire of national minorities for self-government. This is partly a matter of the structure of the federal system: whether the constitutional provisions regarding the boundaries and powers of federal subunits reflect the needs and aspirations of minority groups. But it is also a matter of the underlying ethos of the political culture: whether there is a general commitment to the spirit, as well as the letter, of the federal constitution. A genuine multination federation will tackle new challenges on the basis not of 'majority versus minority', or 'superior versus subordinate', but of consent and shared sovereignty.

The Canadian federation has many of the hallmarks of a genuine multination federation with respect to the Québécois, if not the Aboriginal peoples. Before Confederation, English-speaking Canada West and French-speaking Canada East constituted a single political entity: the united province of Canada.The 1867 Constitution divided that province into two separate political units—English-speaking Ontario and French-speaking Quebec—to accommodate ethnocultural divisions.This decision to create (or, more accurately, to re-establish) a separate province within which francophones formed a clear majority was the crucial first step towards accommodating national self-government within Canadian federalism. Indeed, it was quite possibly the first time in modern history that federalism was used for this purpose.[17]

Many Canadians, however, have not fully accepted a multination model of federalism.This is reflected in the current debates about both Aboriginal self-government and Quebec. (Although I will focus here primarily on Quebec, I will return to Aboriginal self-government at the end of this chapter.) Opposition to the multination model of federalism has emerged explicitly in debates about 'special status' for Quebec, whether that status takes the form of asymmetrical powers or of a 'distinct society' clause. From the point of view of multination federalism, the special status of Quebec is undeniable. It is the only province that is a vehicle for a self-governing national minority; the nine other provinces simply reflect regional divisions within English-speaking Canada. Quebec, in other words, is a 'nationality-based unit', embodying the desire of a national minority to remain a culturally distinct and politically self-governing society, while the other provinces are 'region-based units', reflecting the desire of a single national community to diffuse powers on a regional basis.

In a multination conception of federalism, since nationality-based units and region-based units serve such different functions, there is no reason to assume that they should have the same powers or forms of recognition. In fact, there is every reason to think that they will require some degree of differential treatment. It is almost inevitable that nationality-based units will seek different and more extensive powers than region-based units. As a general rule, we can expect nationality-based units to seek greater and greater powers; region-based units are less likely to do so, and may actually accept a gradual weakening of their powers.

This is reflected in the way the American and Canadian federal systems have developed. It has often been pointed out that the United States began as a strongly decentralized federation, with all residual powers attributed to the states, but has gradually become one of the most centralized, whereas Canada began as a strongly centralized federation, with all residual powers attributed to the federal government, but has gradually become one of the most decentralized.While this is often said to be paradoxical, it is understandable when we remember that the United States is a territorial federation, composed entirely of region-based units. Centralization in the United States, therefore, has not been seen as a threat to anyone's national rights or national identity. By contrast, centralization in Canada threatens Quebec's national aspirations.

This difference has had a profound effect on how the US and Canada have responded to the pressures for centralization in this century. In both countries there have been many occasions—most notably the Depression and the two world wars—when there were strong pressures to strengthen the federal government, at least temporarily. In Canada, these pressures were counterbalanced by the unyielding insistence of French Canadians that the self-governing powers of Quebec be protected, so that any temporary centralization would ultimately be reversed. In the United States, however, there was no such countervailing pressure, and the various forces for greater centralization have gradually and cumulatively won out.

The fact that region-based and nationality-based units typically desire different levels of power is also reflected within both Canada and the United States. For example, while most Québécois want an even more decentralized division of powers, most English-speaking Canadians favour retaining a strong central government.[18] Indeed, it is likely that, were it not for Quebec, Canadian federalism would have succumbed to the same forces of centralization that won out in the United States.

While the region-based American states have gradually lost power, however, we find a very different story if we look at the quasi-federal special-status units used to accommodate national minorities—the Commonwealth of Puerto Rico, for instance, or Indian tribes, or the Protectorate of Guam. In these nationality-based units there is a clear trend towards greater powers of self-government, in order to sustain their culturally distinct societies.[19] The same pattern can be found throughout Europe as well. In Spain, the three nationality-based units (Catalonia, the Basque Country, and Galicia) have demanded greater autonomy than any of the other 14 federal units, or 'Autonomous Communities', such as La Mancha or Extremadura, which simply reflect regional divisions within the majority Spanish national group.[20] Similarly, Corsica seeks greater autonomy than other region-based unit in France. And in the new Russian federation, adopted after the collapse of the Soviet Union, there is considerable asymmetry between the 32 nationality-based units (e.g., Tatarstan, North Ossetia) and the other 56 federal units, which simply reflect regional divisions within the majority Russian national group. The nationality-based units have demanded (and received) not only explicit constitutional recognition as 'nations', but also greater powers than the region-based units.[21]

While many European countries are engaging in forms of regional decentralization, particularly if they were previously highly centralized states, this process is going much farther in countries where the resulting units are nationality-based (e.g., Belgium) rather than region-based (e.g., Italy). And the most extreme assertion of self-government—secession—has been made only by nationality-based units, whether in the former Czechoslovakia, Yugoslavia, or Soviet Union.

In a federal system that contains both region-based and nationality-based units, therefore, it seems likely that demands will arise for some form of *asymmetrical federalism*: a system in which some federal units have greater self-governing powers than others. We see this not only in Quebec's demands, but also in the demands of Aboriginal peoples. Their 'third order of government' will necessarily be markedly asymmetrical.

6. THE 'ASYMMETRY' DEBATE

Here we reach the heart of the issue. At this point, the two models of federalism become not just distinct but incompatible. Guided by a purely territorial model of federalism, the overwhelming majority of English-speaking Canadians reject the idea of 'special status' for Quebec. To grant special rights to one province on the grounds that it is 'distinct', they argue, is somehow to denigrate the other provinces and to create two classes of citizens.[22]

Several commentators have persuasively argued that this view reflects confused moral thinking.[23] Liberal democracies are deeply committed to the principle of the moral equality of persons, and equal concern and respect for their interests. But equality for individual citizens does not require equal powers for federal units. On the contrary, asymmetrical status for nationality-based units can be seen as promoting this underlying moral equality, since it ensures that the national identity of minorities receives the same concern and respect as that of the majority nation. Insofar as English-speaking Canadians view the federal government as their 'national' government, respecting their national identity requires upholding a strong government in Ottawa; insofar as Québécois view the government in Quebec City as their national government, respecting their national identity requires upholding a strong provincial government. Accommodating these differing identities through asymmetrical federalism does not involve any disrespect or invidious discrimination.[24]

Yet this defence of asymmetry presupposes precisely what most English-speaking Canadians deny: namely, that Canada is a multination federation. For most English-speaking Canadians, their 'nation' includes the Québécois and Aboriginal people. English-speaking Canadians do not define their national identity in terms of some subset of Canada, such as a particular province or ethnolinguistic group; they simply see themselves as members of a 'Canadian' nation that includes all citizens, whatever their language or culture, from sea to sea. And so their loyalty to Canada is premised, in part, on the view that all Canadians form a single nation, and that the federal government should act to express and promote this common national identity. On this view, differences among Canadians that are due to language, ethnicity, or region should be respected, of course, but not regarded as dividing Canadians into separate national groups. And while substate groups or provinces should be accorded some autonomy, they should not be seen as having rights of national self-government.

This is why the familiar debate over asymmetry has made no progress.

According to defenders and critics of asymmetry alike, the crux of the debate is the ideal of 'equality'. English-speaking Canadians favour an identical status for all provinces because they think this is what the moral principle of equality requires, and they reject any multination conception of Canada because they think it is inconsistent with this principle. Defenders of asymmetry try to defuse this opposition by showing that asymmetrical rights can be consistent with this deeper principle of equality.

In reality, though, the issue of equality derives from a deeper dispute over nationhood. English-speaking Canadians interpret equality to require identical status for all provinces because any other conception of equality would undermine their sense of Canadian nationhood. As Webber notes, most objections to including a distinct-society clause in the Charlottetown Accord were premised on assumptions about 'what it takes to have a country, about nationalism. To have a real country, the argument ran, the same rules have to apply to everyone; everyone must be treated identically.' He goes on:

> These arguments represented the triumph of a unitary conception of Canadian citizenship. . . . Canadians were Canadians. They should not be treated as French-Canadians or English-Canadians, or even aboriginal or non-aboriginal Canadians. . . . They must be Canadians first, each treated, under the constitution, simply as Canadian. The touchstone for this was the Charter of Rights. At the popular level in English-speaking Canada, Trudeau's attempt to make the Charter the acid test of Canadian nationality had succeeded. Any attempt to vary the application of those rights, taking into account Quebec's uniqueness, was to fiddle with the very basis of Canadian citizenship.[25]

To be sure, English-speaking Canadians argued that asymmetry for Quebec violated the principle of equal rights. But the belief that equality requires symmetrical treatment of all provinces is derived from a prior commitment to the ideal of common nationhood, not vice versa. Asymmetry was rejected not because it violated the general ideal of equality, but rather because it violated the specific sort of equality that is required by, and implicit in, a common nationality.

The derivative role of equality in the Charlottetown debate is shown by the fact that while all critics agreed that asymmetry violates equality, some claimed that asymmetry gives Quebecers more rights than other Canadians, others argued that asymmetry would give Quebecers fewer rights than other Canadians, and yet others alternated between the two views.[26] If the primary concern had been equality, one would expect critics to have been concerned to identify the nature of the inequality—to determine who gained an unfair advantage, or suffered from some unfair burden, as a result of asymmetry. In fact, however, for most critics it was enough to know that asymmetry created a *differential* status for Quebec, and thereby undermined their commitment to a unitary Canadian nationality. Whether these differential rights gave Quebecers more rights or fewer was, for most English-speaking Canadians, a secondary consideration.

So long as English-speaking Canadians cling to this ideal of a unitary Canadian nationality, they will never accept the asymmetry implicit in a multination conception of Canadian federalism. The problem is not simply that English-speaking provinces happen to desire different powers from Quebec. These differences reflect an even deeper difference in the very conception of the nature and aims of political federation. For national minorities like the Québécois, federalism implies, first and foremost, a federation of *peoples*, and decisions regarding the powers of federal subunits should recognize and affirm the equal status of the founding peoples. On this view, to grant equal powers to region-based units and nationality-based units is in effect to deny equality to the minority nation, by reducing its status to that of a regional division within the majority nation. By contrast, for English-speaking Canadians federalism implies above all a federation of *territorial units*, and decisions regarding the division of powers should affirm and reflect the equality of the constituent units. On this view, to grant unequal powers to nationality-based units is to treat some of the federated units as less important than others.

This difference in views of federalism can lead to conflict even when there is little difference between the actual powers demanded by region-based and nationality-based units. For example, some people have proposed a radical across-the-board decentralization, so that all provinces would have the same powers currently demanded by Quebec, thereby avoiding the need to grant 'special status' to Quebec. For many Quebec nationalists, however, this proposal misses the point. The demand for special status is a demand not just for this or that additional power, but also for *national recognition*. As Resnick puts it, 'They want to see Quebec recognized as a nation, not a mere province; this very symbolic demand cannot be finessed through some decentralizing formula applied to all provinces.'[27] Quebec nationalists want asymmetry for its own sake, as a symbolic recognition that Quebec alone is a nationality-based unit within Canada.[28] Although this may seem a petty concern with symbols rather than the substance of political power, we find the same demand in other multination federations.[29]

It is partly for this reason that asymmetry has been so difficult to negotiate within Canada (and other multination federations). I see no prospect for overcoming the impasse unless English-speaking Canadians come to accept a truly multination conception of Canada. Since asymmetrical federalism follows almost necessarily from the idea that Canada is a multination state, whether English-speaking Canadians will accept the former depends on whether they will accept the latter.

7. ABORIGINAL SELF-GOVERNMENT

The demands of Aboriginal peoples for recognition of their inherent right of self-government raise some of the same issues as Quebec's demand for special status. In both cases there is an insistence on national recognition, collective autonomy, distinctive rights and powers, and the equality of peoples. But the situation of Aboriginal peoples is much more complicated.

For one thing, Aboriginal peoples were not included in the original negotiation of the Canadian federation. Thus the boundaries drawn and the division of powers within Canadian federalism took no account of Aboriginal needs and aspirations. Whereas Quebecers can hope to build upon the existing powers of the province of Quebec, Aboriginals have no foothold in the existing federal system from which they can struggle for a genuine multination federation.

Moreover, traditional forms of federalism can serve as mechanisms for self-government only if the national minority forms a majority in one of the federal subunits, as the Québécois do in Quebec. This is not true of most Aboriginal peoples in Canada, who are fewer in number and whose communities are often dispersed across provincial lines. Moreover, except in the north (see below), no redrawing of the boundaries of these federal subunits would create a province or territory with an Aboriginal majority. It would have been possible to create a province dominated by an Indian nation in the nineteenth century, but the massive influx of settlers since then has made that project virtually inconceivable.

For these reasons, among others, many Aboriginal people have suggested that their self-government should be seen as a form of 'treaty federalism' predating the 1867 federation, rather than as a 'third order of government' within the 1867 federation. Their aim is not so much to create a new level of Aboriginal governments within the existing federal system as to redefine (on the basis of existing treaties, combined with the signing of new treaties) a distinctive political status that would stand entirely outside the existing federal system. Like Indian tribes in the United States, Aboriginal communities would be 'federated' to Canada through treaties, but not really part of the federal system per se.

There is one exception, in the north. In 1999 the Northwest Territories will be divided in two, so that the Inuit will form the majority in the eastern half (to be called Nunavut). This redrawing of federal boundaries will make it possible for the Inuit to exercise their right of self-government within the existing federal system, although the Nunavut government will almost certainly have 'asymmetrical' powers compared with other territories and provinces.

For the other Aboriginal peoples in Canada, however, self-government has been primarily tied to the system of reserved lands. Substantial powers have been devolved from the federal government to the band councils that govern each reserve. Indian bands have been acquiring increasing control over health, education, family law, policing, criminal justice, and resource development. Indians want these rights to be affirmed in constitutionally protected treaties, and to be recognized as inherent rights of self-government, not just powers delegated to them by the federal government. Indeed, the Aboriginal demands for self-government are surely more urgent and compelling than the Québécois demands for special status. As the Canadian Human Rights Commission says each year in its annual report, the status of Aboriginal people is the one real human-rights issue that we face in Canada.

The complications of the self-government question are such that it would take a separate book to do justice to it. Indian bands differ enormously in the sorts of powers they desire. Some are too small in land and population, and too poor, to exercise the full range of self-governing powers that they claim as their inherent right. For others, the capacity for self-government will depend on how outstanding land claims are resolved. The recent Royal Commission on Aboriginal Peoples has provided a detailed account of the various models of self-government that Aboriginal peoples could adopt, and of the steps required to achieve it. Part of the difficulty, as the Commission notes, is that it is unclear what the appropriate units of Aboriginal self-government would be. The Commission itself argues that existing Aboriginal bands are simply too small, in general, to exercise meaningful self-government. It suggests that the 600 or so Aboriginal bands should amalgamate into 60 or so 'nations', based on pre-existing cultural and linguistic affinities, and that these larger nations should be seen as having inherent rights of self-government.

This is a serious attempt to grapple with an urgent problem. The current division of the Aboriginal population into 600 'bands' is almost entirely the arbitrary result of the federal Indian Act, which encouraged and sometimes compelled Indians to settle on small plots of land, often far away from other members of their original community. Amalgamating the bands into larger nations would, in one sense, be a return to earlier patterns of Aboriginal community and social organization, adapted to new circumstances.

Whether this is the right strategy for Indians is, of course, for them to decide; this is a matter of ongoing debate within the Aboriginal community. And until we know the relevant units of self-government, it is difficult to provide a more detailed blueprint for achieving it. In the meantime, it is important that Canadians show our willingness to recognize the principle of the inherent right of self-government, and to negotiate in good faith about its appropriate implementation. This is indeed our most urgent obligation of justice in Canada.

For the rest of this book, however, I will focus primarily on the accommodation of Québécois nationalism. Although the issues are for the most part quite different, a better understanding of Québécois nationalism may lead indirectly to a better understanding of our other 'nations within'.

Canadians have shown a somewhat greater willingness to consider 'special status' for Aboriginal peoples than for Quebec. This is not surprising, since attempts to incorporate Indian and Inuit governments under the rubric of the territorial/symmetrical model of federalism are clearly unworkable. Moreover, many Canadians feel a strong sense of guilt for the historical mistreatment of Aboriginal peoples. Yet even here, the presumption that no political units should have differential rights or powers has served to limit support for Aboriginal self-government, and it is possible that the hardening of attitudes towards special status for Quebec has played a part in reducing support for Aboriginal demands. Clarifying the need for multi-nation federalism in the Quebec context may, therefore, indirectly increase support for the rightful claims of Aboriginal peoples.

8. CONCLUSION

We have reached a seemingly insuperable impasse in Canada. The Québécois and Aboriginal peoples insist that Canada must be seen as a multination federation, which in turn requires recognition of the difference between the purely territory-based provinces of English-speaking Canada and the nationality-based units of Quebec and Aboriginal nations. Their demands for national recognition have, if anything, become more adamant over the last two decades.

Yet we know that this 'multination' conception of Canada is implacably opposed by the non-Aboriginal, non-francophone majority. Most English-speaking Canadians view Canada as a single national community—encompassing all citizens, whatever their language, ethnicity, or region—united by bonds of equal citizenship. Polls indicate widespread opposition within English-speaking Canada to any form of 'special status' for Quebec, and this opposition seems to have hardened over the last two decades. Recent polls also indicate a drop in support for the claims of Aboriginal peoples in Canada.

Can anything be done to bridge this widening gulf? I've already argued that it is hopeless to try to persuade our 'nations within' to relinquish their national claims. So that leaves only two options. We can try to paper over our differences and concoct a constitutional formula so vague or ambiguous as to allow the two sides to interpret it in diametrically opposite ways, in accordance with their opposing conceptions of Canadian federalism. This is one way of interpreting the recent federal government's strategy towards Quebec, a strategy that, as I will argue in the next chapter, has no hope of succeeding. The alternative is to try to persuade English-speaking Canadians to accept a multination conception of federalism. I will assess this option in Chapter 12.

Chapter 11

> ▶ *Papering Over the Differences* ◀

Can we find a constitutional formula that is sufficiently vague for both sides to view it as consistent with their opposing conceptions of Canadian federalism? In other words, can we paper over the differences so well that no one will notice the widening gap between English Canada and Quebec? Sometimes it seems that this has been the gist of the federal government's 'national unity' strategy in recent years. As I see it, this strategy has had two main elements: (a) affirming a distinct society clause and (b) emphasizing shared values as the basis for Canadian unity. Neither has succeeded.

1. 'DISTINCT SOCIETY'

A 'distinct society' clause was originally demanded by Quebec as a way of affirming its status as a distinct nation within Canada. However, the clause that was offered to Quebec by the federal government was vague enough that English-speaking Canadians could view it as merely a symbolic gesture, one that would leave untouched the essential equality of provinces. The federal government has, I think, encouraged the Québécois and English-speaking Canadians to adopt these differing interpretations of the distinct society clause—or at least it has done nothing to discourage them. The government has neither affirmed nor denied that Canada is a multination state: it has tried to avoid directly addressing the issue at all. It has tried to fashion constitutional proposals that English-speaking Canadians can interpret as upholding their 'territorial' conception of Canadian federalism (e.g., the Triple-E Senate; symmetrical decentralization of powers), and that the Québécois and Aboriginal people can interpret as upholding their 'multination' conception of federalism (e.g., the distinct society clause; double-majority requirement in the Senate; Aboriginal self-government).

The failure of the Meech Lake and Charlottetown Accords proved that this strategy will not work. The stakes are too high, and the sensitivities too great, for Canadians to be satisfied with such vague and ambiguous proposals. I have already discussed the importance of explicit national recognition for the Québécois and Aboriginal peoples. But the stakes are equally high for English-speaking Canadians. If one starts with a conception of

Canada as a single nation divided into ten equal region-based provinces, then any demand for special status will seem to create first- and second-class citizens.

Moreover, for Quebecers to make their allegiance to Canada conditional upon such a recognition seems to reflect a lack of loyalty to Canada. If Quebecers would secede over the failure of Meech Lake or Charlottetown, they can't have been very committed to Canada in the first place (or so it seems to many English-speaking Canadians). It is one thing to accept an unfair constitutional settlement in the name of Canadian unity; it is another to accept it because one is being 'blackmailed' by people who have no real desire to be Canadians anyway. As Jeremy Webber has pointed out, English-speaking Canadians not only strongly rejected Québécois' demands for asymmetrical powers, they also deeply resented their asymmetrical loyalty—their seeming unwillingness to 'put Canada first'.[1]

I see no way to paper over these differences between the multination conception of Canada endorsed by most Québécois and Aboriginal people and the single-nation conception endorsed by most English-speaking Canadians. Prior to 1982, it might have been possible to formulate a constitutional settlement that avoided the issue of national identities and loyalties. After all, the 1867 BNA Act did not discuss the values or identities of Canadians; nor was it expected to. It was almost entirely a description of the relationship among various levels and institutions of government, with virtually no discussion of the identities and values—or even the rights—of Canadian citizens.

But many Canadians now endorse a more ambitious view of the Constitution, according to which the latter is the proper place to define and affirm one's identities and values. Indeed, this view was explicitly endorsed by the federal government during the Charlottetown debate. As one federal document put it, 'the Constitution must be a framework that reflects our values, our aspirations, and the best of what Canadians really are.'[2] Or, as another federal document put it:

> A constitution has two key purposes: one legal, one symbolic. It sets the rules by which a people govern themselves. But it should also convey a sense of why the rules are drafted as they are, what values shape them, what purposes and characteristics identify the people to whom they relate. All Canadians should be able to relate to the description of the qualities that define the country to which they are bound by birth or choice. As our Constitution stands, that second symbolic component is particularly weak.[3]

We can call this the 'aspirational' view of the Constitution. The promotion of this view began with the patriation of the Constitution in 1982. Trudeau hoped that having a single document expressing the aspirations of Canadians would focus people's allegiance on Canada as a whole, rather than any province or region. It was, in part, an exercise in (pan-Canadian) 'nation-building'. And to a large extent it has worked, particularly in English-speaking Canada. Most English-speaking Canadians now accept that the Constitution should reflect and promote a pan-Canadian identity based on equal citizenship rights.[4]

But the inevitable result was that defenders of minority nationalisms have had to insist that *their* aspirations now be reflected in the Constitution as well. They might once have been willing to accept a document that was silent or ambiguous on these matters, but after Trudeau had given a constitutional stamp of approval to his pan-Canadian nationalism, they had to gain equivalent recognition for their minority nationalisms.

Janet Ajzenstat describes this process as the gradual erosion of the ideal of a 'procedural constitution'—the ideal that a constitution should simply set the ground rules for political debate, but should not entrench any particular political program or ideology.[5] The demand of Quebec nationalists for recognition as a 'distinct society' is an example of such erosion, since it represents an attempt to inscribe a certain substantive (and controversial) nationalist ideology in the constitution. But it was the predictable response to Trudeau's attempt to inscribe his pan-Canadian, anti-nationalist ideology in the 1982 Constitution Act.

As Ajzenstat notes, the dispute between Quebec nationalists who favoured territorial bilingualism and Quebec anti-nationalists who favoured sea-to-sea bilingualism used to be seen as one that should properly be left to ongoing democratic debate. In 1982, however, Trudeau's anti-nationalist vision was given 'constitutional imprimatur'. In fact, many supporters of the 1982 act defended it precisely because it would have the symbolic value of placing a pan-Canadian ideology above the fray of everyday politics. Once the door was opened to using the Constitution as a vehicle for advancing ideological views, however, many other groups—including Quebec nationalists—insisted that their vision also be given constitutional validation. What followed was the 'distinct society' clause, together with the 'Canada clause'[6] and endless debates about how the two clauses relate to each other and to the original Charter of Rights.

According to Ajzenstat, the net result has been to undermine any confidence among Canadians in the idea of a neutral constitution that allows various political ideologies and interests to compete fairly and openly for public allegiance. Instead of standing above these political disputes, the Constitution is now seen as the most important forum for pursuing them. And since we have not yet found a way to recognize these competing ideologies within the same constitution, many Quebec nationalists now see secession as the only way to ensure that the constitutional rules of the game are not biased against them.

In retrospect, Canadians might well come to regret having adopted the ideal of an 'aspirational' constitution. Although we have not yet fully grasped the momentous consequences of this shift, it is already clear that the pre-1982 tactics of 'avoiding the issue' and 'muddling through' will no longer work. Canadians now insist that their identities be recognized in the Constitution. Moreover, members of every identity group are aware of the extent to which other groups have succeeded in gaining 'constitutional imprimatur' for their vision of Canada, and are keenly sensitive to any perceived inequality in the level or form of constitutional recognition. So it is no longer enough that groups can find some part of the Constitution that seems hospitable to their vision of Canada (e.g., the 'distinct society' clause for the Québécois, or the 'Canada clause' for English-speaking Canadians, or the self-government clause for Aboriginals). People also want to know that, within the Constitution, their vision is not subordinated to someone else's. The resulting debates over the wording or placement of different clauses often seem like petty squabbling, but this is the inevitable result of promoting an aspirational conception of the Constitution. Having told people that their values and identities should be recognized in the Constitution, we can hardly expect them to be indifferent to how these various values and identities are related to each other. Put in this context, the attempt to finesse the differences between the multination and territorial conceptions of federalism through a vague and ambiguous 'distinct society' clause was doomed to failure.

2. The Mirage of Shared Values

If the 'distinct society' proposal was intended to fudge the differences between these two models of federalism, the second half of the federal government strategy was intended to turn our focus away from our differences towards our commonalities. Canadians, the government tells us, share more than we realize. In particular, there are many 'shared values' that all Canadians, including Aboriginal people and Québécois, cherish, and because these values are shared across national and linguistic lines, they provide a basis for a common solidarity and allegiance. If only Canadians were more aware of these common values, the government argues, we would have a firmer sense of Canadian unity, and the danger of division along national lines would be diminished.

The rhetoric of shared values is so pervasive in federal government documents that Wayne Norman describes it as 'the official line' concerning the basis of national unity.[7] For example, the 1991 Spicer Commission argued that Canadians are united by their shared commitment to seven values: (1) a belief in equality and fairness; (2) a belief in consultation and dialogue; (3) the importance of accommodation and tolerance; (4) support for diversity; (5) compassion and generosity; (6) attachment to the natural environment; and (7) a commitment to freedom, peace, and non-violent change.[8] A similar list was included in the federal government's background paper *Shared Values: The Canadian Identity*, published to accompany its 1991 constitutional proposals.[9] In both cases (and in several other government documents and reports) it is emphasized that these political values are shared by all national groups in Canada.

The idea that shared values hold democratic states together is a familiar one in democratic theory. According to the American philosopher John Rawls, for example, the source of unity in modern societies is a shared conception of justice. As he puts it, 'although a well-ordered society is divided and pluralistic . . . public agreement on questions of political and social justice supports ties of civic friendship and secures the bonds of association.'[10] Despite its impressive intellectual pedigree, I think this is a profoundly mistaken view of the basis of political stability, at least in multination states like Canada. To be sure, as I emphasized in Part 1, there are shared political principles within Canada; in fact, there is a remarkable degree of consensus on basic liberal-democratic norms, shared not only by French and English, but also by immigrant groups, who internalize these values in a surprisingly short period of time. (The extent to which these values are shared among Aboriginal peoples varies from group to group and is a separate issue.)[11]

However, it is not clear that these principles, in themselves, provide a reason for two or more national groups to stay together in one country. For example, there is a remarkable convergence of political principles between the citizens of Norway and Sweden; but is this any reason for them to regret their break-up in 1905? The fact that they share the same principles doesn't, in itself, mean that they should want to live together in a single state.

Similarly, there has been a pronounced convergence in political principles between English- and French-speaking Canadians over the last thirty years, so that it would now be 'difficult to identify consistent differences in attitudes on issues such as moral values, prestige ranking of professions, role of the government, workers' rights, aboriginal rights, equality between the sexes and races, and conceptions of authority'.[12] If the 'shared values' approach were correct, we should have seen a decline in support for Quebec secession over this period; yet nationalist sentiment has grown steadily. Here again, the fact that anglophones and francophones share the same political principles is not a strong reason to remain together. Deciding to secede would not require the Québécois to abandon their political principles, since they could implement the same principles in their own national state.

This suggests that shared political principles are not sufficient for social unity. If two national groups want to live together under a single state, then sharing political principles will obviously make it easier to do so. But this is not a reason for two national groups to want to live together. The fact that Western Europeans share the same political values does not tell us anything about whether there should be one, or five, or fifteen countries on that part of the European continent.

The insistence by the Québécois that their national autonomy and identity be protected, even though they share the same values as English-speaking Canadians, puzzles many Canadians. It is often seen as a paradox that can only be explained in terms of an irrational 'narcissism of minor differences'.[13] Why else would Quebecers object so strongly to federal government interference in areas of provincial jurisdiction, even when Ottawa's decisions are essentially identical to those that would have been reached by Quebecers themselves?

For example, there is no reason to think that Quebecers object to the substantive principles of the Canada Health Act. If Quebec were exempt from the national standards laid out in that act, they would almost surely adopt the same sorts of standards in their own provincial legislation. Yet many Québécois object to the very idea that the federal government has the authority to dictate standards in areas of provincial jurisdiction. Surely, English Canadians think, this is an irrational attitude that would diminish if only Quebecers understood that we really do share the same values.

This assumption rests on a deep misunderstanding of the nature of nationalism. Having the ability to collectively debate and determine policies on issues that matter to them is not just a *symbol* of nationhood: it is the *substance* or *practice* of nationhood. Having developed a strong sense of national identity, Quebecers want to act together as a political community—to undertake common deliberations, make collective decisions, and co-operate in political goals. They want to make these decisions with each other not because their goals are different from those of other Canadians, or Americans, or Belgians, but because they have come to see themselves as members of the same society, and hence as having responsibilities to one another for the ongoing well-being of that society. That's just what it means to think of one's people as forming a nation.

The failure of English-speaking Canadians to appreciate this point is one of the crucial barriers to resolving our current dilemmas. English-speaking Canadians think that insofar as the Québécois have adopted the same liberal-democratic values as other Canadians, they no longer have any interest in preserving provincial autonomy. If decisions made at the federal level would be essentially identical to those made at the provincial level, why would Quebecers object to national regulation of health care, or education, or pensions? To ask this question is to misunderstand the nature of the desire for self-government, which is based on historical identities and communal solidarities, not distinctive political principles (I will return to this point in Chapter 13).

Indeed, there is no evidence from any multination state that a convergence on political values among national groups reduces the salience or intensity of nationalist demands. Despite the marked convergence in political values between Flemish and Walloons in Belgium, Flemish nationalist sentiment has increased.[14] Similarly, the convergence of political values between the Catalan minority and Castilian majority in Spain has been accompanied by a strengthening, not a diminishing, of nationalist sentiments in Catalonia.[15]

I cannot emphasize this point too strongly. There is no reason either in theory or in the experience of other countries to expect that the existence of 'shared values' among national groups will reduce nationalist conflict. The federal government strategy of compiling endless lists of our shared values, therefore, is simply beside the point. It is certainly important, as I argued in Chapter 4, to emphasize to immigrants that we uphold liberal-democratic values, and that these put a limit on our tolerance of cultural differences. But to emphasize that Aboriginals and Québécois share the same political values as English-speaking Canadians is unhelpful.

One may think that the stubborn assertion of national rights by national minorities reflects a 'narcissistic' preoccupation with their national identity,[16] but this is a reality of multination states. Moreover, one could equally well argue that members of the majority group often have a narcissistic commitment to their conception of national identity. The majority cling to the myth of living in a 'nation-state' whose citizens all share the same national identity, refusing to accept the reality that they live in a multination state. As I will discuss in the next chapter, this is indeed part of our predicament in Canada. We share many political values, but we have deeply conflicting national identities, and Québécois and English-speaking Canadians alike have strong emotional commitments to their conceptions of nationhood.

This is the conflict that must be acknowledged, and tackled head-on, if Canada is to survive. Unfortunately, the recent federal government strategy has been to sidestep rather than to confront it. Both the distinct society clause and the rhetoric of shared values have been attempts to fudge or submerge the reality of these conflicting conceptions of nationhood. As a result, federal initiatives have done nothing either to clarify the nature of the conflict or to reduce its intensity.

3. Conclusion

In the last chapter I argued that there is no realistic chance of getting Québécois or Aboriginal peoples to relinquish their claims for national recognition. In this chapter I have argued that there is no way to provide this recognition without explicitly challenging the dominant English-speaking Canadian conceptions of territorial federalism and common Canadian nationality. The only remaining hope for resolving our constitutional crisis, therefore, is to persuade English-speaking Canadians to adopt an explicitly 'multination' conception of Canadian federalism. The next chapter will consider whether and how that might be achieved.

Chapter 12

► *Rethinking English Canada* ◄

Is English-speaking Canadians' opposition to the multination conception of federalism as implacable as it seems? That is the question I wish to address in this chapter.

The most obvious reason to accept the multination view is that it provides the only alternative to secession. But this is no longer a good enough reason for English-speaking Canadians to accept it. The Meech Lake and Charlottetown debates have shown that English-speaking Canadians cannot be coerced by the threat of secession into accepting something that they find deeply unjust. English-speaking Canadians love Canada and would sacrifice a great deal in its name, but they are not prepared to keep it together by adopting measures that would undermine the very things they love about it. Nor should we regret this fact. Both Québécois and English-speaking Canadians want to live in a country in which they can take pride, and one can hardly take pride in a country that violates one's sense of basic justice, or that is held together only by emotional or economic blackmail.

English-speaking Canadians need, therefore, to be persuaded that the sort of Canada that would result from adopting a multination conception would be just and prosperous, and worthy of their loyalty. This might actually be possible, if we can show two things: (a) that English-speaking Canadians have certain common interests as a linguistic community—interests that are similar in important ways to the interests of Québécois and Aboriginals in the maintenance of their languages and cultures; and (b) that multination federalism provides the fullest and fairest expression of these interests for all groups.

This is not an easy task. To see whether there is any room to manoeuvre here, we need to revisit the reasons why English-speaking Canadians view special status as unfair. As we saw in Chapter 10, while English-speaking Canadians often express their opposition to special status in the language of equality, this concern grows out of an even deeper concern with nationhood. That is, English-speaking Canadians interpret 'equality' as requiring identical rights and powers for all provinces because any other conception of equality would undermine their sense of a common Canadian nationhood.

To persuade English-speaking Canadians to endorse the multination conception of Canada, therefore, we need to directly confront and challenge the ideal of a unitary Canadian nationality. It is not enough to show that this ideal is unacceptable to the Québécois and Aboriginal peoples; and it is not enough to show that there are other legitimate ways of construing equality. We need to go deeper and show not only that the dream of a common national identity is impossible to realize, but also that it is not worth aspiring to.

1. THE INTERESTS OF ENGLISH-SPEAKING CANADA

The crux of the issue is to get English-speaking Canadians to reflect on the interests they share as a language community. This will not be easy, because English-speaking Canadians have little or no sense of group identity—little or no sense that they form a distinct community within Canada. This is reflected in the fact that the idea that English-speaking Canadians constitute a 'nation' has virtually no popular resonance. Nor are there any institutions that have as their explicit mandate the promotion of English-Canadian nationhood. Even those English-speaking Canadians who accept that Aboriginal peoples and the Québécois constitute nations—and that Canada is therefore a multination state—tend to feel that English-speaking Canadians do not form a nation.[1]

From one perspective, this is an admirable characteristic. Lacking any strong sense of ethnocultural nationalism, English-speaking Canadians avoid most of the vices that typically accompany such nationalism. They rarely exhibit xenophobia, exclusionary tendencies, or fear that external influences or internal minorities pose a threat to the 'purity' or 'integrity' of their language and culture. Recent events around the world testify to the benefits of living in a society so lacking in ethnocultural nationalism.

But from another perspective, this tendency to reject ethnocultural nationalism blinds English-speaking Canadians to the fact that they do share certain common interests, and that their conception of pan-Canadian nationalism is strongly influenced by those interests. For example, their conception of Canada as a single national community includes the idea of unrestricted mobility rights, common national standards in social services, and portability in social entitlements, as well as the right to use the English language in courts, schools, and government functions from sea to sea. In short, the idea that Canada forms a single national community means, for English-speakers, that they should be able to live and work in English throughout the country, taking their rights and entitlements with them.

These features of the English-speaking Canadian conception of pan-Canadian nationalism increase not only the mobility of English-speaking Canadians but also their political power. If language rights and standards in social programs are to be national in scope, decisions must be made at the federal rather than the provincial level. And this, in turn, means that decisions will be made in a forum where English-speaking Canadians form an overwhelming majority. By endorsing a pan-Canadian conception of nationhood, English-speaking Canadians ensure that their language rights and social entitlements throughout the country are never vulnerable to the decisions of a political body in which they are a minority. They surely would have been more reluctant to embrace the idea that Canadians form a single nation from sea to sea, and that the federal government should define and promote this common nationhood, if this had reduced, rather than enhanced, their language rights or political power.

By contrast, pan-Canadian nationalism is a threat to the interests of Aboriginal peoples and the Québécois. We can identify three ways in which pan-Canadian nationalism has served English-speaking Canadians at the expense of national minorities:

• First, it operates at the symbolic level to affirm the English-speaking Canadian conception of a single Canadian nationhood, thereby denying the Québécois and Aboriginal conceptions of Canada as a multination state. We saw in Chapter 10 why the demand for national recognition is so important for national minorities, and why the refusal to extend it is seen as an insult.

• Second, at the level of political power, it has operated to increase the range of issues (for instance, in the area of social policy) that are decided in pan-Canadian forums where English-speaking Canadians are a majority, such as the federal Parliament and the federal Supreme Court. It is important to note that this is widely seen as objectionable within Quebec and Aboriginal communities even if the decisions reached in these federal forums are essentially identical to those that would have been reached by Quebecers or Aboriginal people themselves (e.g., the Canada Health Act). The reasons for objection are partly related to the first issue: federal intervention through the spending power is seen as a symbol of English-speaking Canada's indifference to Quebec's national aspirations and its historical rights. In addition, however, as we saw in Chapter 11, having the ability to collectively determine policies on issues that matter to them is not just a symbol of nationhood: it is the substance of Québécois nationhood. Having developed a strong sense of national identity, Quebecers want to act together as a political community: to undertake common deliberations, make collective decisions, and co-operate in the pursuit of political goals. They have come to see themselves as members of the same society, and hence as having responsibilities to each other for the ongoing well-being of that society.

So the Québécois would fight to defend their provincial autonomy against federal encroachment even if they could be guaranteed that the federal government's decisions would be compatible with their own interests and conceptions of justice. But of course there can be no such guarantee. Indeed, as we shall see below, on issues such as language and culture there will almost certainly be conflicts of interest between the English-speaking majority and the Québécois.

Even in areas of social policy, where the interests and the conceptions of justice involved are now very similar among Québécois and English-speaking Canadians, there is no guarantee that the similarities will survive in the future. Guarantees of provincial autonomy are a way of protecting Quebecers against unforseen changes in the political culture of English-speaking Canada. In this respect, it is worth recalling that the Yes camp picked up significant support in the 1995 referendum campaign when it adopted the rhetoric of defending Quebec's social programs against the seeming rightward trend in English-speaking Canada.

• Third, at the level of public policy, there are certain issues on which the interests and identities of English-speaking Canadians directly conflict with those of the Québécois. The most obvious of these is language rights. Anglophones in Quebec have an interest not only in seeing their own language rights protected, but also in being able to ensure that newcomers to Quebec from other provinces or other countries can integrate into their societal culture. (Without such newcomer integration, the English-speaking community in Quebec is in danger of disappearing because of its low birth rate.) And anglophones from other provinces value the opportunity to move to Quebec and live and work within an English-speaking societal culture. The pan-Canadian conception of sea-to-sea bilingualism helps to protect the interests of these English-speaking Canadians. But many Québécois believe that the very survival of the francophone societal culture in Quebec (and hence in Canada) depends on compelling newcomers to integrate into their societal culture. The pan-Canadian conception of bilingualism is therefore perceived as a direct threat to their survival.

Cultural policy is another example. During the Charlottetown negotiations, Quebec sought exclusive jurisdiction over culture. This proposal was vehemently rejected by English-speaking Canadians. That Quebec would seek greater jurisdiction over culture is understandable; possessing a societal culture is the essence of sociological nationhood, and the reproduction of that societal culture is one of the essential goals of nationalism. But it is equally true that cultural life in English-speaking Canada is national in scope. English-speaking Canadians throughout this century have viewed themselves as building a *national* literary or artistic tradition, and have invested their political energies in building national cultural institutions (the Canada Council, National Film Board, the CBC).[2] To give jurisdiction over culture to the provinces would subvert the whole ideal of a national English-speaking culture. Yet to give jurisdiction over culture to the federal government, and to national cultural institutions dedicated to the ideal of a pan-Canadian culture, is perceived as a threat to the French-speaking culture in Quebec.

In short, pan-Canadian nationalism has increased the political power of

English-speaking Canadians, and expanded their opportunities to live and work in English and to express their cultural identity throughout the country. At the same time it has decreased the political power of national minorities and jeopardized their existence as distinct societies. This is not to imply that English-speaking Canadians have consciously adopted pan-Canadian nationalism as a vehicle for advancing the interests of their particular linguistic group. Most English-speaking Canadians have little sense of even forming a distinct group or having common interests. Yet the truth of the matter is that pan-Canadian nationalism is *de facto* a vehicle for promoting the interests of English-speaking Canadians.

We can make the same point in another way. I noted earlier that English-speaking Canadians aren't linguistic nationalists. But let's imagine that they were, and that they were committed to promoting the interests of an English-speaking nation within Canada. What sorts of policies would they endorse? I think they would endorse virtually the same policies in the name of linguistic nationalism that they now endorse in the name of pan-Canadian nationalism. That is, they would insist that all important decisions regarding their rights and entitlement be made in a political body where they form a majority; and they would insist that their mobility and language rights be upheld throughout the country.[3]

Protestations that English-speaking Canadians do not mobilize around a narrow group interest, therefore, ring a bit hollow. As Webber puts it, they

> do not think of Ottawa as the vehicle for a distinctively *English*-Canadian culture. Their allegiance is (they would say) to Canada as a whole, not to a specific linguistic community. . . . [But this is] misleading, hiding the true importance of language to their allegiance. After all, English Canadian political debate expanded beyond provincial boundaries precisely because citizens in many provinces spoke the same language. . . . In any case, English-speaking Canadians have not had the same need to distinguish between allegiance to a linguistic community and allegiance to the truly pan-Canadian community. They could afford to run the two together because, as they were the majority, the distinctive character of their linguistic community was never threatened. . . . Because of their numerical superiority, English-speaking Canadians can afford to focus on a pan-Canadian community, forsaking any direct institutional expression of their linguistic community.[4]

So pan-Canadian nationalism has served as a *de facto* vehicle for the interests of English-speaking Canadians. The earliest expressions of pan-Canadian nationalism, such as the 'Canada First' movement, were explicitly premised on a conservative and imperialist conception of Canada as British in culture and political loyalties. But even the more progressive left-wing expressions of pan-Canadian nationalism that emerged in the 1930s, such as the League for Social Reconstruction, were overwhelmingly led by

English-speaking Canadians who endorsed a strong federal state that would intervene extensively in areas of provincial jurisdiction, thereby reducing the autonomy of national minorities. As Sylvia Bashevkin notes, 'the voices of this nationalism have been overwhelmingly English Canadian,' and their conceptions of pan-Canadian nationalism have 'ignored almost completely' the existence and aspirations of French Canada.[5]

In fact, many Québécois nationalists have wished that English-speaking Canadians had a stronger sense of English-Canadian nationalism. For example, Daniel Latouche expresses exasperation that 'English Canada has always refused to behave as one of the country's founding nations', and decries 'the inability of English Canada to contemplate its own existence as a national collectivity'.[6] Given that nationalism is often tied to notions of exclusion and the quest for power, why would a minority want the majority to relinquish an inclusive, pan-Canadian conception of its interests, and adopt instead a more narrow and nationalist conception of its self-interest?

In part, Québécois nationalists support the development of an English-speaking Canadian nationalism because this would help remove the stigma that many English-speaking Canadians associate with the idea of nationalism, and thus increase their willingness to consider the demands of Québécois nationalism more sympathetically. But there is a deeper reason why Québécois nationalists support the development of English-Canadian nationalism: because it would ensure that English-speaking Canadians would no longer automatically (and often unconsciously) define pan-Canadian nationalism in terms of their own group interests. If English-speaking Canadians had a clearer conception of the interests they possess as members of a linguistic community, they would also understand that these interests are not shared by other Canadians, and so cannot legitimately form the basis for a pan-Canadian nationalism. It would force them to recognize that traditional definitions of pan-Canadian nationalism have involved subordinating the interests and powers of national minorities to those of the English-speaking majority.

Many English-speaking Canadians today would agree that these earlier conceptions of pan-Canadian nationalism were unacceptably biased against the interests of the Québécois and Aboriginal peoples. They accept that any legitimate form of pan-Canadian nationalism must provide some accommodation for the Québécois or Aboriginals, and cannot be merely a vehicle for increasing their own opportunities and political power. Some hoped that the implementation of official bilingualism would be the key to making pan-Canadian nationalism fair to both English- and French-speaking Canadians. But many English-speaking Canadians now accept that official bilingualism was not the panacea Trudeau and others had hoped. As we saw in Chapter 10, it failed to create many meaningful opportunities for francophones to live and work in French outside Quebec, and did nothing to prevent or reverse either the centralizing tendencies of pan-Canadian nationalism or the reduction in the political power and self-governing autonomy of national minorities that centralization entailed.

Thus increasing numbers of English-speaking Canadians recognize the need for a dramatic reformulation of traditional conceptions of pan-Canadian nationalism. They accept that pan-Canadian nationalism not only must be officially bilingual but also must renounce the traditional commitment to a strong federal government. And in recent years some have called for a radically decentralized conception of pan-Canadian nationalism. By endorsing a radical decentralization of power to the provinces, they hope to accommodate the traditional concern of the Québécois for provincial autonomy while still preserving a unitary conception of Canadian nationhood, since this decentralization would apply to all provinces, preserving the ideals of common citizenship and symmetrical federalism.

2. THE MYTH OF DECENTRALIZATION

This move towards decentralization is a last, desperate attempt to preserve the myth of a single Canadian nation. It is the only conception of pan-Canadian nationalism that is remotely plausible, since it at least gestures in the direction of accommodating the interests of the Québécois. But it won't work. In fact, it is unacceptable to both the Québécois and the English-speaking majority.

I've already suggested, in Chapter 10, why any form of symmetrical federalism, even a radically decentralized one, is unlikely to be acceptable to Quebec. For Quebec nationalists, proposals for radical decentralization miss the point. Their demand for special status is a demand not just for more powers, but also for *national recognition*.[7]

But the proposal is equally unacceptable to most English-speaking Canadians. For it is the one form of pan-Canadian nationalism that would actually subvert the interests of English-speaking Canadians and inhibit the expression of their identities and values. It would prevent them from expressing their deep sense of identification with Canada as a whole and from fulfilling their strong desire to act as a political community—to deliberate with other Canadian citizens and to pursue common political projects.

Most English-speaking Canadians believe that the federal government should use its spending power to identify and enforce national standards for important public services and social programs. Indeed, most English-speaking Canadians view support for these sorts of national standards as the very basis of Canadian citizenship. As an 1991 Ontario government document put it, 'where once Canada was linked from sea to sea chiefly by its railways,' we are now linked 'most clearly in our institutions of social policy'.[8] And despite the rise of neo-conservative governments in Alberta and

Ontario, English-speaking Canadians continue to define common citizenship in terms of these national social programs.[9]

For example, there has been no diminution in the overwhelming support in English-speaking Canada for the idea that the federal government should uphold the basic principles of the Canada Health Act, even though health care is one of the clearest areas of provincial jurisdiction. To take another example, in the early 1990s the Royal Commission on New Reproductive Technologies found that English-speaking Canadians were overwhelmingly in favour of federal regulation of new reproductive technologies, even though the basic issues are clearly provincial in jurisdiction (health care and family law). Not only did English-speaking Canadians endorse national regulation, but they simply took it for granted that the federal government could enact such regulations. It was only in Quebec that people raised the question of jurisdiction.[10]

More generally, surveys have repeatedly shown that most English-speaking Canadians have no principled commitment to respecting provincial jurisdiction. On the contrary, their expectations and attributions of responsibility are naturally directed to the federal government even in areas of provincial jurisdiction (the most commonly cited area for federal action is education), and they would support federal intervention in almost any policy area so long as it provided good governance. This is true even in western Canada. While there is slightly higher support for decentralization in the west, this is not connected to any sense that provinces have a *right* to exercise this or that power; there are no policy areas that western Canadians say are *inherently* matters of provincial jurisdiction, in which the federal government has no legitimate right or authority to intervene. What Canadians want is better and more flexible federal-provincial co-ordination, not the rejection of national standards or the protection of inherent provincial rights of self-government.[11]

The fact is that English-speaking Canadians have over time developed their own strong sense of forming a (pan-Canadian) political community. And so they want to act collectively as a political community, not simply as separate provinces. They want to deliberate together, and to make collective decisions, and to create and uphold collective institutions. That is, they too—like the Québécois—want to act as a nation.

Of course, the national identity that English-speaking Canadians have developed is pan-Canadian, including Quebec. This is why English-speaking Canadians view federal legislation as crucial to expressing their national identity. Federal regulation of new reproductive technologies, for example, would allow English-speaking Canadians to express their collective political identity, and to fulfil their deeply felt sense of collective responsibility for each other and for their shared society.

To preserve the ideal of a unitary Canadian nationhood through radical decentralization would therefore be self-defeating. It would preserve the semblance of a common national identity, but only by undermining the whole *raison d'être* of this ideal: to ensure Canadians' ability to express their sense of shared responsibility through collective actions. English-speaking Canadians are undoubtedly willing to accept some limited forms of decentralization, particularly to avoid unnecessary duplication of programs.[12] But this will inevitably fall short of the kind of decentralization demanded by Quebec. After all, English-speaking Canadians can act on their national identity only through the federal government, and so they will not willingly relinquish the sort of federal powers needed to express and sustain this national identity. In particular, English-speaking Canadians would be very reluctant to relinquish the use of the federal spending power to define national standards in health care or education or pensions. They would also be reluctant to relinquish the potential future use of the spending power to create new national social programs (e.g., day care). The current fiscal situation may make any new national social programs unrealistic for the foreseeable future. But I have no doubt that most English-speaking Canadians would like to retain at least the possibility of creating such programs, as a way of further affirming and strengthening their sense of common Canadian citizenship.

Indeed, I think that many English-speaking Canadians, given the choice, would support the transfer of powers upwards from the provincial to the federal government. Consider post-secondary education. I noted earlier that one reason why English-speaking Canadians endorsed pan-Canadian nationalism was that it increased their mobility and economic opportunities throughout the country. But the fact that post-secondary education falls under provincial jurisdiction is a barrier to this mobility. Differences in provincial standards make it difficult for doctors or teachers or mechanics to move from one province to another. I would guess that many English-speaking Canadians would happily transfer jurisdiction over post-secondary education to the federal government, if it meant that their qualifications would be immediately accepted throughout the country. Similarly, I think that many English-speaking Canadians would accept giving the federal government greater powers in the area of environmental regulation.

In the present situation, however, even to mention such ideas is political suicide. How can anyone seriously propose greater centralization of powers in Canada when so many Quebecers find the existing level of centralization unacceptable? Because of the need to accommodate Quebec, English-speaking Canadians refrain from even discussing the idea of allowing the federal government to take over post-secondary education, or using the spending power to create new national social programs in the future. We focus instead on various forms of decentralization, in the hope of finding one that would be substantial enough to accommodate Quebec, but not so great as to undermine English Canada's desire for meaningful national standards and a cohesive national identity.

It should be clear by now that this hope is futile. English-speaking

Canadians and the Québécois will not agree on a division of powers: their national identities are simply too much in conflict. Because English-speaking Canadians can act on their national identity only through the federal government, they will reject any form of decentralization that they see as reducing the federal government's ability to express a common national identity and develop national programs.[13] The Québécois, by contrast, can act on their national identity only through the provincial government, and so will reject any constitutional proposal that does not block, and indeed reverse, federal intervention in areas of social policy.

To many commentators, this is the tragic, unsolvable dilemma at the heart of Canadian political life. Yet it is unsolvable only if we insist on a purely symmetrical form of federalism. If we are willing to relax that insistence, then the deep division between English- and French-speaking Canadians can be seen as an opportunity, for it gives both groups their own strong reasons for preferring asymmetry. I noted earlier that defenders of asymmetry typically claim that asymmetry is needed to give national minorities a fair chance to pursue their interests and identities. That claim is true, I believe, but it has had virtually no success in persuading English-speaking Canadians to support asymmetry.

However, I believe it is equally true that asymmetry is necessary to enable *English-speaking Canadians* to pursue their interests and identities. Asymmetry would allow English-speaking Canadians to continue to use the spending power in areas of provincial jurisdiction, and even to discuss whether they wish to expand the jurisdiction of the federal government in areas such as the environment or post-secondary education. It would, in effect, enable English-speaking Canadians to act more forcefully in defence of their common interests and national identity.

The fact that it is has been impossible even to discuss such proposals for an enhanced federal role, because of Quebec's demands for decentralization, is a source of deep resentment among many English-speaking Canadians.[14] The fact that Quebec is an obstacle to this sort of nation-building is likely one of the reasons why an increasing number of Canadians have hardened their attitudes towards Quebec and now say 'Let them go.' Many English-speaking Canadians would rather see Quebec leave than give up on their desire to act as a nation through the federal government. The paradox is that it is not Quebec's demand for asymmetry that stands in the way of such federal nation-building policies. On the contrary, it is the insistence by English-speaking Canadians on provincial equality that makes such federal initiatives impossible. If English-speaking Canadians accepted asymmetry, then Quebec's demand for special status would not be an obstacle to enhancing the role of the federal government, and English-speaking Canadians could express their national aspirations without fear or guilt that in so doing they are being insensitive to Quebec. As Philip Resnick puts it, we need to free ourselves from the bane that Quebec, ever since the Quiet Revolution, has introduced into our political life, namely, the incessant demand for increased provincial power. If Quebec is a nation, as I have argued, there is a strong case for giving it greatly enhanced powers within a looser Canadian arrangement. But there is no such case for giving enhanced powers to the provinces of English Canada or for watering down those national features that we, as English Canadians, share. Quite the opposite course is called for.[15]

Asymmetry would free us from this 'bane', and from the resentment of Quebec that it has created in English-speaking Canada.

Of course there would be a price to pay: we would have to abandon the dream of a single Canadian nation. It would be legitimate for English-speaking Canadians to pursue the centralizing form of national politics only if they allowed Aboriginal peoples and the Québécois to opt out and preserve their collective autonomy—that is, if they accepted once and for all that Canada is a multination state.

Faced with this choice, I believe that most English-speaking Canadians would endorse asymmetry rather than relinquish the ability to act as a nation. It would be painful to give up the dream of a single pan-Canadian nation. But it was never more than a dream. It arose historically only because English-speaking Canadians ignored and/or denigrated the French and Aboriginal cultures in Canada. Once English-speaking Canadians renounced this paternalistic attitude, the idea of Canada as a single nation became untenable. Besides, a large part of what made the dream inspiring was the way it enabled English-speaking Canadians to develop a sense of nationhood that transcended provincial boundaries. To attempt to salvage the dream by radically decentralizing power to the provinces would preserve only the empty shell of pan-Canadian nationhood, without any of the entitlements, norms of solidarity, or traditions of collective self-government that gave substance to the sense of nationhood.

3. IS ENGLISH-SPEAKING CANADA A NATION?

So far I have argued that English-speaking Canadians should reflect more carefully on the interests they share as a linguistic community, and that they should endorse asymmetry as a way of enabling them to better pursue those interests. This appears to be the only strategy that offers a resolution to our constitutional struggles.

One way to pursue this strategy would be to encourage English-speaking Canadians to view themselves as a 'nation'. This is precisely what many Québécois nationalists have endorsed, and increasing numbers of English-speaking academics are expressing interest in the idea.[16] However, I do not think that the language of 'nationhood' is necessary in this case. It is important for national *minorities* to adopt the language of nationhood, since it helps to limit the vulnerability they would otherwise face as a numerical minority within a democracy. But there is no comparable urgency for the majority to define itself as a nation. What really matters is for English-speaking Canadians to recognize that they have certain common interests as a linguistic group, interests that have historically been taken as definitive of pan-Canadian nationalism but that in fact are not shared by the members of national minorities. Whether or not English-speaking Canadians should define their linguistic group as a 'nation' is a separate question.

Of course, consciously adopting the language of nationhood might provide some benefits. It would help to symbolize English-speaking Canadians' acceptance of the fact that Canada is a multination state, and would affirm the basic equality of the constituent 'nations'.[17] However, to suppose that people can simply change their national identity at will would be a mistake. National identity is something that people feel, and if some people do not feel that they belong to an English-speaking nation within Canada, then there's no point in telling them that they should. Indeed, English-speaking Canadians have historically taken pride in their lack of linguistic nationalism. It would take many years to change this attitude.

Moreover, there would be difficulties even naming this 'nation'. 'English Canada' runs the danger of being interpreted in an ethnically exclusive way, as if descendants of British colonists were truer 'English Canadians' than the descendants of Italian or Ethiopian immigrants. 'English-speaking Canada' avoids this ethnic connotation (which is why I have used it in this book), but it is both over- and under-inclusive.[18] Neither of these terms really captures the essence of a sociological nation: a societal culture constituted by a set of societal institutions employing a common language.

I suspect that if we do manage to find an acceptable form of asymmetry, English-speaking Canadians will over time develop a stronger sense of forming a 'nation'. As Alan Cairns suggests, this will likely at first take the form of a 'residual' nationalism—a form of national identity that is only reluctantly adopted when the preferred forms of pan-Canadian nationalism have proven unworkable.[19] But over time it may evolve and take on a more positive form.

Still, that is a long way off. And it would be a mistake to wait for it. We need to find a way to persuade English-speaking Canadians to adopt the multination conception of Canada even if they themselves continue to define their national identity in pan-Canadian terms. The crucial question is how to persuade English-speaking Canadians that while their nation may encompass the country as a whole, they also have interests as a linguistic group, interests that can best be promoted through some form of asymmetrical multination federalism.

4. CONCLUSION

The 'national unity' crisis in Canada is often explained in terms of the rise of Quebec nationalism in the 1960s and 1970s, and (usually to a lesser extent) the more recent resurgence of Aboriginal nationalism. These forms of minority nationalism are powerful sources of conflict in Canada, and they need to be accommodated through some form of federalism.

But the crisis is equally a result of the rise of a particular form of nationalism among English-speaking Canadians. The latter have adopted a form of pan-Canadian nationalism that emphasizes the role of the federal government as the embodiment and defender of their national identity. English-speaking Canadians have a deep desire to act as a nation, which they can do only through the federal government; they also have come to define their national identity in terms of certain values, standards, and entitlements that can be upheld from sea to sea only through federal intervention in areas of provincial jurisdiction. In short, the only way for English-speaking Canadians to express their national identity is to undermine the provincial autonomy that has made it possible for Quebecers to express their national identity.

The problem in Quebec-Canada relations, therefore, is not simply that Quebecers have developed a strong sense of political identity that is straining the bounds of federalism. It is also that Canadians outside Quebec have developed a strong sense of pan-Canadian political identity that strains the bounds of federalism. Both of these political identities are complex and deeply rooted psychological phenomena, grounded in history, territory, and common institutions. There is a myth, popular among many liberals, that whereas Quebec's political identity is grounded in irrational factors such as language and history, English-speaking Canada's political identity is grounded in a rational commitment to principles of freedom and democracy. In reality, both identities are complex mixtures of political principles and historical bonds. The fact that English-speaking Canadians share a commitment to freedom and democracy does not explain their deeply felt desire to act as a single pan-Canadian collectivity rather than as separate provinces. This too is a contingent and affective desire rooted in history and a shared sense of belonging that has transcended provincial boundaries.

This suggests that if we are ever to accommodate the demands of Quebec nationalism, we need to look more honestly at the development of English-speaking Canada's political identity. It also suggests that if we are to find a lasting settlement to our constitutional predicament, we need to find a political arrangement that can accommodate both of these political identities. We need to find a form of federalism that will allow Quebec to act on its deeply felt sense of national political identity without preventing English-speaking Canadians from acting on their equally deeply felt desire to act as a collectivity, and not simply as discrete provinces. We need, in short, to find some form of asymmetrical multination federalism.

Chapter 13

> ## *The Bonds of Social Unity* ◄

In the last few chapters I have tried to describe a form of 'multination' federalism that would be responsive to Canada's diversity and that might allow all of Canada's national groups to protect and promote their interests and identities. However, I confess I am not overly optimistic that English-speaking Canadians will accept such a multination conception of federalism. For one thing, there have already been several clear and careful attempts to defend such a conception to English-speaking Canadians, most recently in books by Philip Resnick, Jeremy Webber, Charles Taylor, and Kenneth McRoberts. If English-speaking Canadians are unenthusiastic about multination federalism, it isn't because there has been a shortage of qualified advocates promoting and defending it.

Moreover, many English-speaking Canadians are suffering from constitutional fatigue and have no interest in rehashing these issues. And whatever generosity towards Quebec may have once existed has been replaced with indifference. This is reflected in the view one often hears in English-speaking Canada that we must reject Quebec's constitutional demands because 'We keep giving Quebecers more and more, but they're never satisfied.' In reality, during the many rounds of constitutional negotiation over the last thirty years, not a single one of Quebec's constitutional demands has ever been accepted. The only constitutional reform that has taken place—the 1982 patriation—was informed by Trudeau's ideological hatred of Quebec nationalism, and was supported by every province except Quebec. In short, in thirty years of constitutional debate and reform, Quebec has consistently been the loser, not the winner.

As Jeremy Webber notes, Quebecers

were accused of dominating Canada, yet the constitution had been patriated without their consent. Amendments had addressed western concern over resource taxation, had protected the education rights of official-language minorities, had guaranteed (in general terms) aboriginal rights, and had recognized Canada's multicultural heritage, but in all the years of discussion not one amendment had been adopted at the request of the Quebec government, not one amendment had addressed the traditional concerns of Quebec with the spending power, the division of powers, disallowance, or the recognition of Quebec's distinctiveness.[1]

Despite this record, English-speaking Canadians have managed to persuade themselves that they have already given too much to Quebec. This suggests that any defence of multination federalism may fall on deaf ears.

Yet it would be wrong to present too stark a picture of English-speaking Canadian attitudes towards Quebec. The fact that English-speaking Canadians have come to feel this way is understandable, given the way recent debates have unfolded. If one listens only to separatist leaders like Lucien Bouchard or Jacques Parizeau, then it does seem that no matter what English-speaking Canada offers to Quebec, it will be rejected as insufficient. During the Meech Lake and Charlottetown debates, English-speaking Canadians engaged in long and anguished discussions about their constitutional proposals, only to have them dismissed out of hand by separatists and told that these proposals were an 'insult' to Quebec. English-speaking Canadians rightly resent this.

But of course separatist leaders have staked their careers on the claim that meaningful federal reform is impossible, and so they have a vested interest in undermining and trivializing any offer from English-speaking Canada. If Bouchard and Parizeau spoke for all Quebecers, there would indeed be little reason for maintaining a generous and open-minded attitude towards reform of the federal system. But they do not speak for all Quebecers. On the contrary, most Quebecers sincerely seek a renewed federation. Despite the continued rejection of their constitutional demands, they have twice voted against secession and in favour of yet another attempt at reforming the federation. These Quebecers—the 'soft nationalists'—are not dismissive of English-speaking Canada's offers, and seek good-faith negotiations. If English-speaking Canadians were able to see this strand of Quebec public opinion, which often gets submerged beneath the rhetoric of separatist leaders, they might be more willing to consider Quebec's demands. And then, perhaps, the mutual benefits of multination federalism might become visible.

So it is not inconceivable that a consensus on a new form of federalism could emerge. But this raises one last question. How long would the victory last? Is multination federalism a stable form of political organization? Or is it too fragmented and divided to be capable of producing the sort of allegiance, trust, and solidarity among its citizens that a stable democracy requires? I do not think there is any way to rule out the possibility that multination federalism will eventually dissolve into a more confederal arrangement, or perhaps outright secession; this threat will always be present (section 1). However, I will offer some tentative reasons for thinking that such a system might endure and prosper (sections 2–4).

1. THE SOURCES OF INSTABILITY

The potential for instability is endemic to multination federations, and we must learn to live with it. Canadians have a tendency to personalize our political conflicts, and to blame our problems on the personality of particular politicians. Some people talk as if French-English relations were going smoothly until Pierre Trudeau began his ideological attack on Quebec nationalism; Trudeau's defenders respond that the current crisis would not have arisen had Brian Mulroney (the 'sorcerer's apprentice') not tried to appease Quebec nationalists by reopening the Constitution. Others blame our problems on the intransigence of Réne Lévesque, or Clyde Wells, or Jacques Parizeau.

But if we look at multination federations around the world, it becomes clear that Canada's problems are not reducible to individual personalities. Everything we know about multination federations suggests that they are, and will remain, deeply divided societies. Belgium, Switzerland, Spain, India, Nigeria, Russia—all face enduring tensions, and they will never exhibit the level of social and political unity characteristic of single-nation countries.

Why is this? Part of the explanation is that multination states face certain difficult and divisive issues that single-nation states simply do not face—conflicts over language, national culture, and the division of powers. We saw in Chapter 12 why these issues pose some of the most intractable problems of ethnocultural accommodation in modern states. Another part of the explanation, however, is that multination states can generate only a relatively weak and conditional sense of loyalty among their national minorities. National minorities see themselves as distinct 'peoples' whose existence predates that of the country they currently belong to. And as separate peoples, they see themselves as possessing inherent rights of self-government. Although they are currently part of a larger country, they do not consider this fact to mean that they have renounced their original rights of self-government; they have simply transferred some aspects of their self-governing powers to the larger polity, on the condition that other powers remain in their own hands. In countries formed by the federation of two or more national groups, the authority of the central government is therefore seen as derivative, limited to the powers that each constituent nation agreed to transfer to it. And these national groups often see themselves as having the (moral) right to take back these powers and withdraw from the federation if they feel that the original terms of federation have been broken.

To put it another way, the basic claim made by national minorities is not simply that the political community is culturally diverse (as immigrants typically claim). Instead, the claim is that there is more than one political community, and that the authority of the larger state cannot be assumed to take precedence over the authority of the constituent national communities. If democracy is the rule of 'the people', national minorities claim that there is more than one people, each with the right to rule themselves. Multination federalism divides the people into separate 'peoples', each with its own historic rights, territories, and powers of self-government; and each, therefore, with its own political community. They typically view their own political community as primary, and the value and authority of the larger federation as derivative.

Hence the sort of loyalty that multination states can claim is much more conditional and mediated than in single-nation states. When immigrants demand multiculturalism or group representation, they take the larger political community for granted, and seek greater inclusion in it. By contrast, the pursuit of self-government by national minorities reflects a desire to weaken the bonds with the larger political community, and in fact to question its very nature, authority, and permanence.

Of course I am speaking here of political perceptions, not historical facts or legal formalities. That national minorities existed on Canadian soil long before 1867 cannot be doubted, but whether Confederation is accurately viewed as a pact between 'two founding nations' is a subject of endless debate. Similarly, the real intentions underlying Aboriginal treaties—including the extent to which these treaties involved retaining or relinquishing sovereignty—can be debated. What matters is not so much historical reality as present-day perceptions. If a group today has a strong sense of national identity, and a strong belief in its right of self-government, then it will tend to view the larger federation as having only derivative authority, whatever the historical facts.

So multination states face difficult issues that single-nation states do not; yet the sense of loyalty they can draw on to resolve these issues is relatively weak. Further, the more a federal system is genuinely multination—the more it recognizes and affirms the demand for self-government—the more it will strengthen the belief that national minorities are separate peoples with inherent rights of self-government, whose participation in the larger country is conditional and revocable. And if the attachment of national minorities to the larger state is conditional, then sooner or later one can expect conditions to change so that the benefits of staying within the federation become subject to question and debate. In addition, federalism provides national minorities with the experience of self-government, so that they will tend to feel increasingly confident of their ability to go it alone. Finally, federal systems create territorially demarcated subunits, the boundaries of which provide the obvious boundaries for a potential independent state. Federalism thereby helps to settle what would otherwise be an explosive question—namely, the question of what territory a seceding group can take with it. And insofar as the boundaries of this province were drawn to include the traditional heartland of the national minority, the seceding group is assumed to have some *prima facie* historical claim to that territory (i.e., it is historically 'their' land).[2]

Moreover, the economic and military costs of secession have fallen in recent years. In the past, national minorities needed to join larger countries to gain access to economic markets, or to ensure military security. But these benefits of federalism can now be achieved through confederal arrangements (like the European Community), international agreements (like the North American Free Trade Agreement), and the gradual strengthening of international law. If Quebec or Catalonia seceded, they would still be able to participate in continental or international free trade and security arrangements.

For all these reasons, our goal cannot be to eliminate once and for all the threat of secession. Although the American political philosopher John Rawls argues that citizens of a liberal democracy should view themselves as members of 'one cooperative scheme in perpetuity',[3] this sort of unconditional allegiance cannot be expected in multination federations.

2. SOURCES OF SOCIAL UNITY

And yet, despite all these tendencies towards secession, the fact is that Quebecers have consistently voted to stay in Canada. Indeed, it is a remarkable fact that no multination federation in the West has yet fallen apart. Paradoxically, multination federations appear to combine a very weak sort of unity with surprising levels of resilience and stability.

In thinking about social unity, therefore, we must be modest in our aims. The sort of unity that we can achieve is very different from the kind that single-nation states often possess. We cannot expect national minorities to express unconditional allegiance to Canada, or to 'put Canada first'. The only sort of unity we can hope to achieve is one that will allow national minorities to give primacy to their national identity and conditional allegiance to Canada, that will co-exist both with the firm belief among national minorities that they have the right to secede and with ongoing debate about the conditions under which it would be appropriate to exercise that right.

If we lower our sights in this way, there are grounds for cautious optimism. There is no reason to take the ever-present possibility of secession as proof that a multination federation will fail and secession must occur. On the contrary, the experience gained to date in Canada and abroad suggests that democratic multination federations are remarkably resilient: weak bonds of social unity may nonetheless be enduring, and conditional allegiances may nonetheless be powerful.

This puts survey data on Quebecers' identification with Canada in a new light. For example, recent polls show that over half of Quebecers attach priority in their self-identify to their status as Quebec citizens, compared with 15 to 30 per cent who attach priority to Canadian citizenship.[4] Pessimists see such findings as evidence that Canada is on the verge of breaking up. But this sort of privileging of Quebecers' national identity should be expected, not attacked or resented. To expect Quebecers to sub-ordinate their national identity to a pan-Canadian identity is to invoke a standard of unity that is appropriate only for single-nation states. The appropriate test of unity in a multination state like Canada is one that takes it for granted that Quebecers will privilege their national identity, but asks whether this identity co-exists with a significant sense of identification and solidarity with other Canadians.

And on that question the evidence is clear. Some 70 per cent of Quebecers say they would be willing to make personal sacrifices that would benefit only Canadians outside Quebec. This reflects a striking degree of attachment to Canada and other Canadians, which is matched by the attachment of other Canadians to Quebec. Concrete manifestations of this mutual attachment can be seen in the generous way English-speaking Canadians responded to the 1996 floods in Quebec, and the way Quebecers reciprocated during the 1997 Red River flood.

What is the source of this bond? Liberal political theorists have typically argued that the 'shared' liberal-democratic values of individual freedom, social justice, democracy, and peace provide the bond of solidarity in modern democratic states. But as we saw in Chapter 11, these shared values cannot explain Quebecers' attachment to Canada, since they could implement the same principles in their own independent state. And in fact the convergence in political values between English and French over the last thirty years has been accompanied by an increase, not a decrease, in nationalist sentiment.

Communitarians offer a different account of social unity, although it too involves a version of what Wayne Norman calls the 'ideology of shared values'.[5] Communitarians rightly insist that any plausible account of social unity must be particularized: that is, it must show why people have an attachment to a particular historical political community like Canada. Principles of justice, they point out, are an inadequate basis for social unity, since they are shared by many countries and thus cannot explain attachment to a particular historical community.

What can support social unity, communitarians claim, is a common allegiance to certain substantive ends or conceptions of the good life—in other words, a shared 'way of life'. This shared way of life encompasses not just principles of individual freedom and equal opportunity, but also beliefs about what sorts of goals are worth pursuing with that freedom and opportunity. Promoting solidarity in a political community involves identifying the shared ways of life that are particular to that community and developing a 'politics of the common good' around them, as distinct from the liberal 'politics of rights', which emphasizes principles of procedural justice and people's ability to form and pursue their own individual conceptions of the good.[6]

The problem with this account is that there are no such shared ends in modern societies. The members of a political community, at least in a modern liberal state, do not share conceptions of the good or traditional ways of life. This is true both for Canada as a whole and for each of the component national groups within it. The members of a national group share a language and history, but often disagree fundamentally about the ultimate ends in life. Indeed, disagreement about the value of different ways of life is arguably the defining feature of liberal societies.

Quebec provides a nice illustration. Before the Quiet Revolution the Québécois generally shared a rural, Catholic, conservative, and patriarchal conception of the good. Today, after a rapid period of liberalization, most people have abandoned this traditional way of life, and Québécois society now exhibits all the diversity of any modern society: atheists and Catholics, gays and heterosexuals, urban yuppies and rural farmers, socialists and conservatives, and so on. To be a 'Québécois' today, therefore, simply means to be a participant in the francophone society of Quebec. And francophones in Quebec no more agree about conceptions of the good than do anglophones in Canada or the United States.

If the communitarian 'shared way of life' approach were correct, we should have witnessed a weakening in Québécois identity and a decline in support for secession over this period. Yet nationalist sentiment has grown consistently. Whatever unites the Québécois today, it is not a shared conception of the good life. And if there are no shared conceptions of the good within each national group, then the communitarian approach cannot explain what unifies two or more national groups in a multination state.

There is a common problem in the liberal and communitarian approaches. Both give an overly cerebral account of social unity in terms of shared normative beliefs regarding justice or the good life. Social unity cannot be based on shared beliefs because conceptions of the good are not widely shared within national groups, and principles of justice are too widely shared across them.

3. SHARED IDENTITIES IN A MULTINATION STATE

The real basis for social unity, I believe, is not shared *values* but a shared *identity*. A shared conception of justice throughout a multination political community does not necessarily generate a shared identity, let alone a shared citizenship identity that will supersede rival national identities. Conversely, the lack of a shared conception of the good does not preclude a shared identity. People decide whom they want to share a country with by asking whom they identify with, whom they feel solidarity with. What holds Americans together, despite their disagreements over the good life, is the fact that they share an identity as Americans. Conversely, what keeps Swedes and Norwegians apart, despite their shared principles of justice, is the lack of a shared identity.

Where does this shared identity come from? In single-nation states, shared identity typically derives from commonality of language, culture, and maybe even religion. But these are precisely the things that are typically not shared in a multination state. What then is the basis of a common identity in a multination state? In some countries, such as the United States, the basis for a shared identity seems to be pride in certain historical achievements (e.g., the founding of the American republic). This shared pride is one of the bases of the strong sense of American political identity, and is constantly reinforced in school curricula and in the citizenship education literature given to immigrants.

In many multination countries, however, history is a source of division between national groups. The people and events that spark pride among members of the majority nation often generate a sense of betrayal among the national minority. English-speaking Canadians honour Sir John A. Macdonald for his role in building the country; French Canadians revile him for ordering the execution of Riel. English-speaking Canadians take pride in their contributions to the two world wars; French Canadians resent their treatment during the two conscription crises. And so on.

Some commentators suggest that we should therefore focus solely on those features of a country's history that are sources of shared pride, and ignore features that are divisive. For example, Andrew Oldenquist argues that information about American history 'should be taught so as to provide grounds for developing pride and affection', and that children will 'not acquire affection for our country by being told that we exterminated Indians, lynched Blacks, and slaughtered Vietnamese'.[7] But this approach would require a very selective, even manipulative, retelling of history.[8] Furthermore, it is quite unnecessary. History has a role in creating a shared identity regardless of whether we share a *pride* in it. The fact that English, French, and Aboriginal people share a history in Canada has helped to shape a shared Canadian identity—an identification with Canadian political institutions and symbols—even though each of these groups has very different interpretations and assessments of that history. (Indeed, to emphasize pride in history simply takes us back to the 'shared values' approach since it presupposes a shared normative assessment of that history.)

History is important, I would argue, because it defines the shared context and framework within which we debate our *differing* values and priorities. We grow up with this framework and learn to situate issues within it. It becomes the implicit background for our thinking, providing the symbols, precedents, and reference points by which we make sense of issues. Over time, it becomes an important part of our identity.

For example, consider the role of race in the United States. Race is one of the most divisive issues in that country. According to the 'shared values' or 'shared pride' approach, race can therefore play no role in defining a common American identity: race, on this view, is an obstacle to a common American identity, not one of the building-blocks of that identity. This is surely false. In fact, one of the most distinctive features of the American identity is an intense preoccupation with race. To be an American is, in part, to have a deep and personal sense of the importance of race. To be an American is, in part, to know that slavery, the civil war, segregated schools, Martin Luther King, and Black ghettos are defining features of the American experience. Race is the explicit topic of many American public debates; even more important, it also is the implicit subtext underlying many more. Any discussion of topics like welfare, unemployment, crime, drugs, political apathy, free speech, or foreign policy is 'race-coded'. Race is the quintessential American conversation.

Of course Americans disagree—sometimes violently—on what to do about race issues, from welfare reform to affirmative action. (It is precisely *because* these disagreements are so vehement that race is so important.) So there is no sense in which race forms a 'shared value' for Americans, or in which Americans have a 'shared pride' in the civil war or Malcolm X. Rather, the history of race relations is a formative and distinctive fact of the American experience, one that underlies Americans' sense of who they are and of what issues they need to confront.[9]

Once we recognize that history matters for many reasons, not just as a source of shared pride, we can reinterpret the role of the US Constitution in American identity. Americans cherish the Bill of Rights and the Declaration of Independence, and loyalty to the Constitution is a defining feature of the American identity. Most commentators maintain that the privileged status of the Constitution rests on its role as the embodiment of certain political principles. For example, Edward Luttwak argues that 'Americans have no shared national culture to unite them as the French or Italians have. . . . What [they] have in common are their shared beliefs in the principles of the Constitution.'[10] This, I think, is quite misleading. The feminist National Organization of Women and the Michigan Militia both appeal to the Constitution, but they hardly share the same political principles. Similarly, the Aryan Nation and the National Association for the Advancement of Coloured People (NAACP) both argue that they are fighting to defend the Constitution, but their principles are diametrically opposed.

Americans define their identity in terms of the Constitution not because it embodies shared values, but because it is the starting-point of their national conversation. Like race, it is one of the reference points by which Americans orient their debate. Immigrants to the US quickly pick up on the symbolic importance of the Constitution. As John Harles shows, when immigrants seek to express their willingness to become 'American' they do so by affirming their support for the Constitution. Yet they often do this before they understand the actual 'principles' that it propounds.[11]

Jeremy Webber argues that Canadians are similarly united by their participation in what he calls 'the Canadian conversation'.[12] He argues that English, French, and Aboriginal people grow up listening to this conversation, and that it becomes a part of all of our identities. Thus John A.

Macdonald and Louis Riel are both part of the Canadian identity, not because we all share pride in their actions, but because they helped to define the institutions within which we continue our conversation, and because they helped to shape the issues that we still need to confront. As he puts it, 'we may find that what we most value is the health, vitality, and flexibility of our national conversation.' What would define Canadian patriotism, then, is 'its commitment to the distinctively Canadian conversation and that conversation's distinctive vernaculars.' Webber goes on to say:

> Lying behind this conception of patriotism is an understanding of why [countries] are important to their citizens. They are important not because they pursue a long list of constitutionalized goals with which all citizens agree, but because they serve as forums for discussion and decision making. They serve as the framework, in other words, for democratic self-government. They provide the structures through which we come together, deliberate about the objectives we should pursue, and take steps as a society to achieve them. We value our country because we value the particular character of its public debate. That specific debate is ours, one we know and care about. . . . And over time, the unique character of its debate marked us. We may well wish to change parts of that debate. In extreme cases, we may seek to escape it altogether. But generally we will be drawn to work for change from within the debate for the simple reason that it is ours. It concerns our community, and speaks in terms we understand.[13]

I think there is a great deal of truth in Webber's account. Yet it raises as many questions as it answers. The fact that people grow up identifying with this historical conversation does not really explain why they can't come to tire of participating in it. Charles Taylor expresses the hope that citizens will 'find it exciting and an object of pride' to continue this sort of conversation, in which we collectively build a society founded on our differing conceptions of history and of the future.[14] But he also admits that some people might weary of the endless negotiations and complications that such a conversation entails.

There are real, if intangible, benefits to this sort of conversation. As Petr Pithart, the former prime minister of Czechoslovakia, put it, reflecting on the country's dissolution:

> In the last 55 years, the Czechs have lost—as co-tenants in their common house—Germans, Jews, Ruthenians, Hungarians and Slovaks. They are now, in effect, an ethnically cleansed country, even if it was not by their own will. It is a great intellectual, cultural, and spiritual loss. This is particularly true if we consider central Europe, which is a kind of mosaic. We are still living touristically from the glory of Prague, which was a Czech-German-Jewish city and a light that reached to the stars. But you cannot win elections with that kind of argument.[15]

Similarly, it would be a 'great intellectual, cultural and spiritual loss' if Canada dissolved. What Pithart says of Prague applies equally well to Montreal. What makes Montreal a distinctive city is precisely that it has been the meeting point of English and French, as well as Aboriginals and immigrant groups. If Montreal's 'visage linguistique' had always been that of a purely French (or purely English) city, it would not be the great city that it is—a source of pride to Quebecers and Canadians generally. And if Quebec were to secede, the inevitable diminishment of the historical non-French communities in Montreal—WASPs, Jews, Italians, Greeks, and so on—would be a dramatic impoverishment.

Unfortunately, it is not easy to articulate these losses, and (as Pithart notes) it is not clear how powerful such arguments really are in people's minds. Still, whatever the explanation, the fact is that Canadians have exhibited a desire to continue the national conversation. Canadians identify enough with each other, and with our shared history, to find the prospect of stopping the conversation unacceptable.

4. ERODING THE BONDS OF SOLIDARITY

Would moving in the direction of a more explicitly multination federation strengthen or weaken the existing bonds among Canadians? Since the real source of these bonds remain murky (to me, at least), it is difficult to predict with certainty what would promote or diminish them. But we can hazard a few guesses.

I think there are two conditions under which these bonds might be eroded: (a) if national minorities lost a direct sense of participation in the decision-making processes of the Canadian state; and (b) if national minorities lost their trust in the fairness of these decision-making processes. How would multination federalism affect each of these requirements?

First, to maintain their sense of allegiance to Canada, it is important that individual Quebecers and Aboriginal people participate *directly* in the larger Canadian conversation, not simply via their subunits (e.g., the Quebec provincial government). It is perhaps inevitable in a multination state that the members of national minorities will be most strongly influenced by the more local conversation within their own subunits. But they must feel that the larger Canadian conversation is theirs as well. For example, when a conflict arises between the Quebec provincial government and the federal government, this must not be seen by Quebecers as a conflict between 'us' and 'them', but rather a conflict between two levels of conversation, both of which Quebecers view as 'ours', and both of which have shaped Québécois identity.[16]

It is a great virtue of multination federalism, I think, that it preserves such a direct connection. In this respect it is quite unlike confederal arrangements such as the 'sovereignty-association' proposed by the Parti Québécois or the 'partnership' model proposed by Roger Gibbins.[17] Under such confederal proposals, Quebecers would have very few, if any, tangible connections to the rest of Canada. They would have no direct personal participation or representation in the government of Canada. Their link with the rest of Canada would consist solely in the fact that some of their provincial politicians and bureaucrats would meet on a regular basis with politicians and bureaucrats from the rest of the country. Under some such proposals, Quebecers might not even have the right to work outside Quebec. I do not see how such an arrangement could be stable over the long term.

Confederal proposals are often defended on the grounds that Quebecers' attachment to Canada is 'symbolic', and that this symbolic attachment would be satisfied by such things as a shared passport and currency, even if they had no other connection to the rest of the country. But this, I think, misconstrues the nature and source of Quebecers' commitment to Canada. They feel attached to Canada because they helped to build the country, from sea to sea to sea, and because they have continued to play an active role in the governing of Canada as a whole. They are proud to be Canadians because they have played a visible, often decisive, role in making Canada the country it is today. They have provided some of the most important politicians and bureaucrats at the federal level— including a disproportionate share of prime ministers—and some of the most important policy decisions of the federal government can be traced to the influence of Quebecers in Ottawa. This is why Quebecers view themselves as participants in the Canadian conversation, and not just in a Quebec conversation.

If this historical connection between Quebecers and the Canadian state were broken, would they continue to feel a symbolic attachment to it? If Quebecers no longer exercised any visible influence and power in the day-to-day operations of the Canadian state, and perhaps faced restricted mobility rights in the rest of Canada, would they continue to think of it as their country? Would they continue to take pride in being Canadians if they had no influence on Canada's accomplishments? And once this symbolic attachment to Canada started to fade, as it surely would, confederal options would offer no obvious economic or political advantages over outright secession.[18]

The great virtue of a multination federalism, by contrast, is that it would preserve a direct sense of connection to, and participation in, pan-Canadian institutions.[19] The fact is that federalism has provided an important avenue for Quebecers to make a difference in Canada as a whole, and any confederal model that closes off this avenue is unlikely to survive for long. Multination federalism, by contrast, would protect this essential source of attachment to Canada, and thereby help secure its own long-term stability.[20] It would provide tangible benefits and sources of attachment that would reduce the appeal of secession.

The second way in which the bonds of social unity might erode is if the level of distrust between majority and national minorities increases. Federalism requires give and take, the willingness to make sacrifices for others now, in the firm assurance that others will reciprocate down the road. Even the best-designed federal system will not work if this sense of trust is missing. Canadians today exhibit a significant level of trust. But it is threatened from two directions. On the one hand, English-speaking Canadians may doubt the commitment of the Québécois to stay in the federation. After all, the ultimate goal of nationalism has typically been an independent state. How can we be sure that the Québécois aren't just biding their time, waiting for a more opportune moment to secede? And if federalism is just a temporary stepping-stone to secession, why should we bother to make any concessions? Why make sacrifices for people who have no commitment to our country?

On the other hand, Quebecers may have doubts about the majority's commitment to the principles of federalism. As I noted in Chapter 10, federalism involves renouncing the model of 'majority versus minority', or 'superior versus subordinate', and replacing it with a model of co-equal sovereigns. Many Quebecers doubt that English-speaking Canadians have really renounced their ultimate power of majority rule and accepted the principle that Quebec's sovereignty cannot be infringed in areas of provincial jurisdiction. They fear that many English-speaking Canadians view federalism as a technicality that they can override when they feel strongly enough about an issue. Why should Quebecers make sacrifices to maintain a federal system without any assurance that their autonomy will be respected?

These are the sources of the distrust that we see on both sides in Canada today. And the distrust is not entirely baseless. Some Québécois separatists do invoke a teleology of nationhood that treats federalism as an 'abnormal' stunting of healthy national development, even as they negotiate for greater powers within the federation. Conversely, the English-speaking majority has not done all it can or should to renounce its power of majority rule. It has not renounced the disallowance power, or given provinces an equal say in the appointment of justices to the Supreme Court—in both cases contradicting the principle of co-equal sovereigns. More generally, as we saw in Chapter 12, many English Canadians are indifferent to issues of provincial jurisdiction.

Would moving closer to a multination form of federalism increase or reduce the danger of distrust? It would almost certainly reduce the level of distrust among Quebecers, in part because the institutions of multination federalism would more firmly protect their national identity and autonomy from threats by English-speaking Canadians. Equally important, though, the very act of accepting multination federalism would be evidence that English-speaking Canadians do not wish to threaten Quebec's autonomy. It would both reduce the fear of such threats to Quebec and provide greater institutional protection against them.

Whether multination federalism would decrease the level of distrust among English-speaking Canadians is more difficult to predict. English-speaking Canadians might view a call from Quebec for multination federalism as proof that Quebecers are not really committed to Canada, especially if separatist leaders discuss multination federalism as just a stepping-stone to 'normal' national development. On the other hand, the perception among English-speaking Canadians that Quebecers lack any commitment to Canada, and that their demands will escalate until they reach their goal of independence, is based on a dramatic misrepresentation of the past thirty years. The fact is that Quebecers have not yet received any of the constitutional amendments they have requested; yet they have twice rejected secession. It is difficult to think of clearer evidence that they are committed to Canada, and to trying to find a fair accommodation within Canada. If English-speaking Canadians could be disabused of their misperception of Quebec then perhaps they too would find reasons to reduce their mistrust.

So I am inclined to think that moving towards a multination federalism would not erode the existing bonds of social unity in Canada, and could indeed strengthen them. As I emphasized earlier, the sorts of bonds one finds in multination states are inherently weak—at least compared with the social bonds one finds in single-nation states—and they co-exist with the ever-present potential for secession. But they may nonetheless be enduring.

Moreover, despite recent changes in the international environment, the costs of secession remain high, or at any rate unpredictable. This is particularly true in the Canadian case, given the conflict between Québécois and Aboriginal people over territory. Aboriginal people in the north of Quebec have said they have the right to stay in Canada even if the rest of Quebec secedes, so that an independent Quebec would include only the southern part of the province. Some anglophone groups have suggested that English-majority towns in Quebec should also have the right to stay in Canada if they wish. The risk of violence from such 'partitionist' movements cannot be entirely excluded. A majority of Quebecers are unlikely to accept such risks if they have achieved a workable form of multination federalism.[21]

5. CONCLUSION

Canadians are rightly concerned about national unity, and with ensuring that any new institutions would secure the loyalty and allegiance of citizens. Yet too often we have adopted the wrong standard for measuring unity and allegiance. We have defined unity and loyalty as the elimination of the very idea of secession. This is not a reasonable or realistic standard for any multination state, including Canada.

Rather than try to make secession impossible or unthinkable, we should instead focus on identifying the benefits that Canadians gain from living in a multination federation. As I have tried to show in the last two chapters, multination federalism provides benefits to both Québécois and English-speaking Canadians—benefits that cannot be gained through symmetrical federalism, sovereignty association, or outright secession. Thus my own view is that multination federalism could be stable—and a source of pride at home and abroad—if only we knew how to get there from here.

The two parts of this book, focusing on ethnic groups and national minorities respectively, describe two very different sides of ethnocultural relations in Canada. In the case of ethnic groups, increasing numbers of Canadians are rejecting a policy of multiculturalism that has been, by all statistical measures, a success, and that has been adopted as a model by other Western immigrant countries. As we saw in Chapter 1, Canada does a better job of integrating ethnic groups today than it did before the adoption of multiculturalism, and it does a better job than any country that has not adopted multiculturalism.

In the case of national minorities, by contrast, most English-speaking Canadians seem to be clinging stubbornly to a model of federalism that has demonstrably failed, not only in Canada but in other Western multination states as well. As we saw in Chapter 10, the American model of symmetrical/territorial federalism is appropriate for single-nation states, but is unworkable in countries containing minority nationalisms.

Yet the situations of ethnic groups and national minorities in Canada do share something in common. In each case, Canadians seem unable or unwilling to learn either from our own experience or from the experience of other countries. We seem unwilling to learn from our successes in the case of multiculturalism, and unwilling to learn from our failures in the case of minority nationalism.

Why is this? There are probably many factors at play. Part of the explanation, however, is that many Canadians seem to regard ethnocultural politics as so irrational and unpredictable that the past provides no reliable guide to the future. This view is reflected in the way many Canadians swing between two extremes when discussing these issues. On the one hand, there is a widespread pessimistic belief that ethnocultural politics are 'out of control', with an ever-expanding cycle of more groups making more demands, leading to the eventual disintegration of Canadian society. On the other hand, many of the same people also express the remarkably optimistic belief that if we just stand firm and refuse to cave in to the demands of multiculturalists and nationalists, then all those demands will fade away and we can go back to the good old days before the rise of 'identity politics'. The demands of ethnocultural groups are treated like a contagious virus that could multiply infinitely, or could disappear overnight.

I hope this book has made clear why both extremes are mistaken. Ethnocultural politics are here to stay: they reflect enduring realities of a society with an extraordinary level of ethnocultural diversity. But the demands of ethnocultural groups in Canada are not endless or unpredictable. On the contrary, they work within fairly narrow constraints.

In Part 1 I tried to show that there are clear and predictable limits on the sorts of demands made by ethnic groups formed through immigration. Their demands for multiculturalism have not created any dramatic change in the basic trends of integration, nor were they intended to do so. Multiculturalism policies are situated within a much larger structure of social and political institutions that are taken as given. Demands for multiculturalism are simply demands for modest changes to the terms of integration.

In Part 2 I tried to show that the demands of national minorities, though very different from those of ethnic groups, are equally predictable. Aboriginal peoples and Québécois, like national minorities around the world, have adopted a nationalist project. That is, they seek to maintain themselves as separate and self-governing societies—with their own legal, educational, social, and political institutions—alongside the larger majority society. This nationalist project generates a number of predictable demands regarding national recognition and collective autonomy.

So ethnocultural politics in Canada are not particularly mysterious. The dynamics we see here are of the same kind that we see in other Western democracies, and they are the sorts of dynamics one would expect to find in an ethnoculturally diverse country. Immigrant groups, indigenous peoples, and national minorities all face distinctive circumstances, and their demands are predictable responses to those circumstances. Not only can we predict these dynamics, but we have also learned a great deal about how to manage them. We know quite a bit about which policies work well and which are doomed to failure.

The fact that ethnocultural politics are predictable in these ways does not mean that there are easy solutions to all our conflicts. Predictable conflicts are not necessarily are easy to resolve, particularly when they involve competing nationalisms. But understanding these constraints should help us put our conflicts back into perspective, and enable us to deal with them in a more pragmatic way. Once we recognize that there is a stable and coherent core to these demands, and that they will neither disappear nor expand infinitely, then perhaps we can adopt a more flexible and open-minded approach to resolving them.

In the end, ethnocultural politics are not that different from other areas of public policy. They are predictable and constrained, not mysterious and unstable. And so they can be managed. We have the experience to address ethnocultural issues in Canada in a fair and mutually beneficial way. If we allow ethnocultural relations to deteriorate, as I fear we are doing, it is not because we do not know how to manage diversity, or because ethnocultural politics are inherently divisive and uncontrollable. It is because we have lost the will, and the confidence, to learn from our own experience.

▶ *The Multiculturalism Policy of Canada* ◀

WHEREAS the Constitution of Canada provides that every individual is equal before and under the law and has the right to the equal protection and benefit of the law without discrimination and that everyone has the freedom of conscience, religion, thought, belief, opinion, expression, peaceful assembly and association and guarantees those rights and freedoms equally to male and female persons;

AND WHEREAS the Constitution of Canada recognizes the importance of preserving and enhancing the multicultural heritage of Canadians;

AND WHEREAS the Constitution of Canada recognizes rights of the aboriginal peoples of Canada;

AND WHEREAS the Constitution of Canada and the *Official Languages Act* provide that English and French are the official languages of Canada and neither abrogates or derogates from any rights or privileges acquired or enjoyed with respect to any other language;

AND WHEREAS the Citizenship Act provides that all Canadians, whether by birth or by choice, enjoy equal status, are entitled to the same rights, powers and privileges and are subject to the same obligations, duties and liabilities;

AND WHEREAS the Canadian Human Rights Act provides that every individual should have an equal opportunity with other individuals to make the life that the individual is able and wishes to have, consistent with the duties and obligations of that individual as a member of society, and, in order to secure that opportunity, establishes the Canadian Human Rights Commission to redress any proscribed discrimination, including discrimination on the basis of race, national or ethnic origin or colour;

AND WHEREAS Canada is a party to the *International Convention on the Elimination of All Forms of Racial Discrimination*, which Convention recognizes that all human beings are equal before the law and are entitled to equal protection of the law against any discrimination and against any incitement to discrimination, and to the *International Covenant on Civil and Political Rights*, which Covenant provides that persons belonging to ethnic, religious or linguistic minorities shall not be denied the right to enjoy their own culture, to profess and practise their own religion or to use their own language;

AND WHEREAS the Government of Canada recognizes the diversity of Canadians as regards race, national or ethnic origin, colour and religion as a fundamental characteristic of Canadian society and is committed to a policy of multiculturalism designed to preserve and enhance the multicultural heritage of Canadians while working to achieve the equality of all Canadians in the economic, social, cultural and political life of Canada;

(1) It is hereby declared to be the policy of the Government of Canada to:

(a) recognize and promote the understanding that multiculturalism reflects the cultural and racial diversity of Canadian society and acknowledges the freedom of all members of Canadian society to preserve, enhance and share their cultural heritage;
(b) recognize and promote the understanding that multiculturalism is a fundamental characteristic of the Canadian heritage and identity and that it provides an invaluable resource in the shaping of Canada's future;
(c) promote the full and equitable participation of individuals and communities of all origins in the continuing evolution and shaping of all aspects of Canadian society and assist them in the elimination of any barrier to such participation;
(d) recognize the existence of communities whose members share a common origin and their historic contribution to Canadian society, and enhance their development;
(e) ensure that all individuals receive equal treatment and equal protection under the law, while respecting and valuing their diversity;
(f) encourage and assist the social, cultural, economic and political institutions of Canada to be both respectful and inclusive of Canada's multicultural character;
(g) promote the understanding and creativity that arise from the interaction between individuals and communities of different origins;
(h) foster the recognition and appreciation of the diverse cultures of Canadian society and promote the reflection and the evolving expressions of those cultures;
(i) preserve and enhance the use of languages other than English and

French, while strengthening the status and use of the official languages of Canada; and

(j) advance multiculturalism throughout Canada in harmony with the national commitment to the official languages of Canada.

(2) It is further declared to be the policy of the Government of Canada that all federal institutions shall:

(a) ensure that Canadians of all origins have an equal opportunity to obtain employment and advancement in those institutions;
(b) promote policies, programs and practices that enhance the ability of individuals and communities of all origins to contribute to the continuing evolution of Canada;
(c) promote policies, programs and practices that enhance the understanding of and respect for the diversity of the members of Canadian society;
(d) collect statistical data in order to enable the development of policies, programs and practices that are sensitive and responsive to the multicultural reality of Canada;
(e) make use, as appropriate, of the language skills and cultural understanding of individuals of all origins; and
(f) generally, carry on their activities in a manner that is sensitive and responsive to the multicultural reality of Canada.

Excerpts from the Canadian Multiculturalism Act, July 1988

Notes

INTRODUCTION

1 Leslie Laczko, 'Canada's Pluralism in Comparative Perspective', *Ethnic and Racial Studies* 17, 1 (1994): 20–41.

2 Wayne A. Cornelius, Philip L. Martin, and James F. Hollifield, eds, *Controlling Immigration: A Global Perspective* (Stanford: Stanford University Press, 1995): 14.

3 See Ted Gurr, *Minorities at Risk: A Global View of Ethnopolitical Conflict* (Washington: Institute of Peace Press, 1993); Jeff Spinner, *The Boundaries of Citizenship: Race, Ethnicity and Nationality in the Liberal State* (Baltimore: Johns Hopkins University Press, 1994); Michael Walzer, *On Toleration* (New Haven: Yale University Press, 1997).

1: SETTING THE RECORD STRAIGHT

1 Trudeau in *House of Commons Debates*, 8 Oct. 1971: 8545–6.

2 Freda Hawkins, *Critical Years in Immigration: Canada and Australia Compared* (Montreal: McGill-Queen's University Press, 1989): 221.

3 Neil Bissoondath, *Selling Illusions: The Cult of Multiculturalism in Canada* (Toronto: Penguin, 1994); Richard Gwyn, *Nationalism Without Walls: The Unbearable Lightness of Being Canadian* (Toronto: McClelland and Stewart, 1995).

4 The passages quoted in this paragraph can be found on pages 111, 110, 98, and 133 of *Selling Illusions*.

5 Schlesinger, *The Disuniting of America* (New York: Norton, 1992): 138. According to his analysis, the United States is witnessing the 'fragmentation of the national community into a quarrelsome spatter of enclaves, ghettoes, tribes . . . encouraging and exalting cultural and linguistic apartheid' (137–8). Bissoondath argues that the same process is occurring in Canada.

6 The passages quoted in this paragraph are from pages 274, 8, and 234 of *Nationalism Without Walls*.

7 Robert Fulford, 'Do Canadians want ethnic heritage freeze-dried?', *Globe and Mail*, 17 Feb. 1997.

8 Citizenship and Immigration Canada, *Citizenship and Immigration Statistics* (Ottawa: Public Works, 1997), Table G2 and Table 1.

9 The remaining differences between citizens and permanent residents relate to (a) minority language rights; (b) protection against deportation; and (c) access to a few sensitive bureaucratic positions, none of which are relevant to most immigrants.

10 The average length of residence before naturalization is 7.61 years, with

immigrants from the UK taking the longest (13.95 years); immigrants from China, Vietnam, and the Philippines all take under five years on average (Citizenship Registrar, Multiculturalism and Citizenship Canada, 1992). In 1971, only five per cent of the Americans eligible to take out citizenship in Canada chose to do so. See Karol Krotki and Colin Reid, 'Demography of Canadian Population by Ethnic Group' in J.W. Berry and Jean Laponce, eds, *Ethnicity and Culture in Canada: The Research Landscape* (Toronto: University of Toronto Press, 1994): 26.

11 For surveys of the political participation of ethnocultural groups in Canadian politics, see the three research studies in Kathy Megyery, ed., *Ethnocultural Groups and Visible Minorities in Canadian Politics: The Question of Access*, vol. 7 of the Research Studies of the Royal Commission on Electoral Reform and Party Financing (Ottawa: Dundurn Press, 1991); Jean Laponce, 'Ethnicity and Voting Studies in Canada: Primary and Secondary Sources 1970–1991' in Berry and Laponce, eds, *Ethnicity and Culture*: 179–202; and Jerome Black and Aleem Lakhani, 'Ethnoracial Diversity in the House of Commons: An Analysis of Numerical Representation in the 35th Parliament', *Canadian Ethnic Studies* 29, 1 (November 1997): 13–33.

12 Daiva Stasiulus and Yasmeen Abu-Laban, 'The House the Parties Built: (Re)constructing Ethnic Representation in Canadian Politics' in Megyery, ed., *Ethnocultural Groups*: 14; cf. Alain Pelletier, 'Politics and Ethnicity: Representation of Ethnic and Visible-Minority Groups in the House of Commons', in ibid.: 129–30.

13 Geoffrey Martin, 'The COR Party of New Brunswick as an "Ethnic Party"', *Canadian Review of Studies in Nationalism*, 23, 1 (1996): 1–8.

14 For evidence of the quick absorption of liberal-democratic values by immigrants, see James Frideres, 'Edging into the Mainstream: Immigrant Adults and their Children' in S. Isajiw, ed., *Multiculturalism in North America and Europe: Comparative Perspectives on Interethnic Relations and Social Incorporation in Europe and North America* (Toronto: Canadian Scholars' Press, 1997); Jerome Black, 'The Practice of Politics in Two Settings: Political Transferability Among Recent Immigrants to Canada', *Canadian Journal of Political Science* 20, 4 (1987): 731–53. Studies show that students born outside Canada, as well as students for whom English was not a first or home language, knew and valued their rights as much as their Canadian-born, English-speaking counterparts. See, for example, Charles Ungerleider, 'Schooling, Identity and Democracy: Issues in the Social-Psychology of Canadian Classrooms' in R. Short et al., *Educational Psychology: Canadian Perspectives* (Toronto: Copp Clark, 1991): 204–5.

15 Hawkins, *Critical Years*: 279.

16 Some 63 per cent of immigrants have neither English nor French as their mother tongue, yet only 309,000 residents in the 1991 Census couldn't speak an official language. Most of these were elderly (166,000 were over 55). See Brian Harrison, 'Non Parlo né inglese, né francese' (Statistics Canada: Census of Canada Short Article Series, #5, September 1993).

17 Derrick Thomas, 'The Social Integration of Immigrants', in Steven Globerman, ed., *The Immigration Dilemma* (Vancouver: Fraser Institute, 1992): 224.

18 Susan Donaldson, 'Un–LINC-ing Language and Integration: Future Directions for Federal Settlement Policy' (M.A. thesis, Department of Linguistics and Applied Language Studies, Carleton University, 1995).

19 Morton Weinfeld, 'Ethnic Assimilation and the Retention of Ethnic Cultures', in Berry and Laponce, eds, *Ethnicity and Culture*: 244–5.

20 Jeffrey Reitz and Raymond Breton, *The Illusion of Difference: Realities of Ethnicity in Canada and the United States* (Toronto: C.D. Howe Institute, 1994): 80; Leo Driedger, *Multi-Ethnic Canada: Identities and Inequalities* (Toronto: Oxford University Press, 1996): 277.

21 Driedger, *Multi-Ethnic Canada*: 263.

22 John Mercer, 'Asian Migrants and Residential Location in Canada', *New Community* 15, 2 (1989): 198.

23 Thomas, 'Social Integration': 240, 247.

24 Orest Kruhlak, 'Multiculturalism: Myth versus Reality', unpublished paper prepared for the Institute for Research on Public Policy project 'Making Canada Work: Towards a New Concept of Citizenship' (1991): 10.

25 For example, the naturalization rate of immigrants who arrived in the US in 1977 is around 37 per cent. The comparable rate in Canada is between 70 per cent and 80 per cent, and is much higher in some multicultural groups (e.g., 95 per cent of the Vietnamese refugees have become citizens). For a comparative study of naturalization policies and trends, see Dilek Cinar, 'From Aliens to Citizens: A Comparative Analysis of Rules of Transition' in Rainer Baubock, ed., *From Aliens to Citizens: Redefining the Legal Status of Immigrants* (Aldershot: Avebury, 1994): 65. For the case of Vietnamese 'boat people' in Canada, see Frideres, 'Edging into the Mainstream'.

26 Krotki and Reid, 'Demography': 40.

27 Reitz and Breton, *The Illusion of Difference*: 80–1.

28 Ibid., 60.

29 See Cinar, 'From Aliens to Citizens': 65; Stephen Castles and Mark Miller, *The Age of Migration: International Population Movements in the Modern World* (London: Macmillan, 1993): 220–1; Sarah Wayland, 'Religious Expression in Public Schools: Kirpans in Canada, Hijab in France', *Ethnic and Racial Studies* 20, 3 (1997): 545–61.

30 Angus Reid, *Canada and the World: An International Perspective on Canada and Canadians*. The polling data is available on the Angus Reid web-site at www.angusreid.com. Australia came second on this question, with 71 per cent of respondents agreeing that ethnic groups get along well in Australia.

31 As Freda Hawkins notes, multiculturalism was adopted in both countries in the 1970s 'for the same reasons and with the same objectives' (*Critical Years*: 214). And they have evolved in similar directions since the 1970s, from an emphasis on cultural maintenance to issues of public participation and institutional accommodation. For a detailed comparison of their origins, see Hawkins, 'Multiculturalism in Two Countries: The Canadian and Australian Experience', *Review of Canadian Studies* 17, 1 (1982): 64–80. For a more up-to-date account, see James Jupp, *Explaining Australian Multiculturalism* (Canberra: Centre for Immigration and Multicultural Studies, Australian

National University, 1996), and Stephen Castles, 'Multicultural Citizenship in Australia' in Veit Bader, ed., *Citizenship and Exclusion* (London: St Martin's Press, 1997).

32 Similarly, Fulford argues that the multiculturalism policy disapproves of inter-marriage and inter-ethnic friendships ('Do Canadians want ethnic heritage freeze-dried?').

2: Putting Multiculturalism into Perspective

1 For a typical statement of this contrast, see Michael Ignatieff, *Blood and Belonging: Journeys into the New Nationalism* (New York: Farrar, Straus and Giroux, 1993).

2 Michael Walzer, 'Comment' in Amy Gutmann, ed., *Multiculturalism and the 'Politics of Recognition'* (Princeton: Princeton University Press, 1992): 100–1. See also Walzer, *What It Means to Be an American* (New York: Marsilio, 1992): 9.

3 Preston Manning, *The New Canada* (Toronto: Macmillan, 1991): 317.

4 Gwyn, *Nationalism Without Walls* (Toronto: McClelland and Stewart, 1995): 273.

5 Gerald Johnson, *Our English Heritage* (Westport, Conn.: Greenwood Press, 1973): 119.

6 On the ubiquity of this process around the world, see Ernest Gellner, *Nations and Nationalism* (Oxford: Blackwell, 1983); Benedict Anderson, *Imagined Communities: Reflections on the Origin and Spread of Nationalism* (London: New Left Books, 1983).

7 Charles Taylor, 'Nationalism and Modernity' in J. McMahan and R. McKim, eds, *The Morality of Nationalism* (New York: Oxford University Press, 1997): 34.

8 For a sympathetic account of Lord Durham's motives for recommending assimilation of the French, emphasizing his hope that this would lead to greater freedom and equality for French Canadians, see Janet Ajzenstat, *The Political Thought of Lord Durham* (Kingston: McGill-Queen's University Press, 1988).

9 Walker Connor, 'The Politics of Ethnonationalism', *Journal of International Affairs* 27, 1 (1973): 20; cf. Ted Gurr, *Minorities at Risk: A Global View of Ethnocultural Conflict* (Washington: Institute of Peace Press, 1993).

10 E. Weber, *Peasants into Frenchmen: The Modernization of Rural France 1870–1914* (London: Chatto and Windus, 1976).

11 The old sign law, known as Bill 101, forbade the use of languages other than French on signs on most commercial establishments in Quebec. This excessive law was struck down by both provincial and federal courts as a violation of Quebec's own Charter of Rights, and has been replaced with a more moderate sign law. This new law still requires the use of French on most commercial signs, but allows for languages other than French alongside it.

12 Obviously this doesn't apply to refugees. People who flee their homeland to avoid persecution cannot be said to have chosen to immigrate. While their subjective motivations differ from those of immigrants, however, their objective circumstances within Canada are similar in terms of the feasibility of nation-building. Like immigrants, they arrive as individuals or families, and so

lack the territorial concentration or corporate institutions needed for nation-alist mobilization.

13 For example, if the German government persists in making it difficult for long-term Turkish residents (and their children and grandchildren) to gain citizenship, one would expect Turks to press for greater powers of self-gov-ernment, so that they can create and perpetuate a separate and self-governing society alongside the German society to which they are denied entry. But this is not the preference of the Turks, who, like immigrants in other liberal democracies, want to become full and equal participants in German society. The historical record suggests that forms of self-government will be sought by immigrant groups within liberal democracies only if they face unjust bar-riers to their full integration and participation in the mainstream society.

14 Gwyn, *Nationalism*, 156.

3: RENEGOTIATING THE TERMS OF INTEGRATION

1 Kenneth McRoberts, *Misconceiving Canada: The Struggle for National Unity* (Toronto: Oxford University Press, 1997): Chapter 5.

2 For an overview of multiculturalism 'at work', see Augie Fleras and Jean Elliot, *Unequal Relations: An Introduction to Race, Ethnic and Aboriginal Dynamics in Canada*, 2nd edn (Scarborough: Prentice Hall, 1996): Chapter 11. They dis-cuss concrete examples of multiculturalism at work vis-à-vis religious holi-days, policing, the media, and schooling.

3 Under Muslim family law, a husband can unilaterally divorce his wife, with-out cause or formal procedure, simply by orally declaring 'I divorce you' three times. This is called a *talaq* divorce, meaning an oral and unilateral divorce. Where such divorces are legally sanctioned, as in India, the consequences can be very grave for women, especially when combined with other features of Muslim family law (e.g., the unequal division of property after divorce). See the discussion of the famous 'Shahbano' case in Zakia Pathak and Rajeswari Rajan, 'Shahbano', *Signs: Journal of Women in Culture and Society* 14, 3 (1989): 558–82.

4 The failure to recognize the role of common institutions is noted by Ian Angus, *A Border Within: National Identity, Cultural Plurality and Wilderness* (Montreal: McGill-Queen's University Press, 1997): 164–5.

5 For an overview of these developments in multiculturalism policy, see Fleras and Elliot, *Unequal Relations*: 330–5. Even in the early 1970s, the main aim of the policy was to encourage not folk culture but, for example, academic analyses of ethnicity in Canada, and studies of inter-ethnic attitudes in Canada.

6 Bissoondath, *Selling Illusions* (Toronto: Penguin, 1994): 82–3, 87–8.

7 Many Muslims in America were understandably pleased when President Clinton, for the first time in American history, invited an Islamic cleric to cel-ebrate Ramadan at the White House, and declared that Islam was an American religion.

8 Shelagh Day and Gwen Brodsky, 'The Duty to Accommodate', *Canadian Bar Review* 75 (1996): 433–73.

9 See Susan Donaldson, 'Un–LINC-ing Language and Integration: Future Directions for Federal Settlement Policy' (M.A. thesis, Dept. of Linguistics and Applied Language Studies, Carleton University, 1995). See also Barbara Burnaby, 'Official Language Training for Adult Immigrants in Canada: Features and Issues' in B. Burnaby and A. Cumming, eds, *Socio-Political Aspects of ESL* (Toronto: Ontario Institute for Studies in Education, 1992). See also the articles in the same volume by Giltrow and Colhoun (on Mayan immigrants), Klassen (on Latino immigrants), and Cumming and Gill (on immigrants from India), all of which discuss the obstacles to learning ESL faced by many groups of newcomers. For related discussions, see J.S. Frideres, 'Visible Minority Groups and Second-Language Programs: Language Adaptation', *International Journal of the Sociology of Language* 80 (1989): 83–98.

10 Jim Cummins, 'Heritage Language Learning and Teaching' in J.W. Berry and Jean Laponce, eds, *Ethnicity and Culture in Canada: The Research Landscape* (Toronto: University of Toronto Press, 1994): 452. See also David Corson, 'Towards a Comprehensive Language Policy: The Language of School as a Second Language', *Education Canada* (Summer 1995): 48–60.

11 See Chapter 1, note 14.

12 See Angus, *Border Within*: 166.

13 Gwyn, *Nationalism*: 202. As a result, he says, 'Increasingly, English-Canadian culture will be a culture of the hinterland, of the farms, of small towns, and of the cities' (p. 117).

14 For evidence of this appreciation, see Canadian Ethnocultural Council, *Canada for All Canadians*, brief submitted to the House of Commons and Senate Special Joint Committee on Renewed Canada (Ottawa: Canadian Ethnocultural Council, 1992).

15. C. McAll, *Class, Ethnicity and Social Inequality* (Montreal: McGill-Queen's University Press, 1990): 169.

16. Jean Burnet, 'Multiculturalism, Immigration, and Racism', *Canadian Ethnic Studies* 7, 1 (1975): 36.

4: THE LIMITS OF TOLERANCE

1 Bissoondath, *Selling Illusions*: 138–9. The term 'female circumcision' covers many different practices, some of which (e.g., ritual scarring) are not very different from male circumcision. I assume that Bissoondath has in mind the more extreme forms, which are clearly incompatible with Canadian legal norms. To avoid confusion, I will refer to this practise as 'clitoridectomy', not 'circumcision'.

2 Gwyn, *Nationalism Without Walls*: 189.

3 John Rawls, *A Theory of Justice* (London: Oxford University Press, 1971): 13.

4 See my 'Minority Group Rights: The Good, The Bad and the Intolerable', *Dissent* 43, 3 (Summer 1996): 22–30.

5 It's important to note, for example, that immigrant groups from countries where clitoridectomy is practised have not sought the right to continue this practice in Canada. Indeed, when the federal government consulted these groups in 1995, there was 'unanimous consent' that, with the appropriate edu-

cation and support, the practice can and should be stopped in Canada. See Lula Hussein et al., *Female Genital Mutilation: Report on Consultations Held in Ottawa and Montreal* (Ottawa: Department of Justice, Research and Statistics Section, WD1995–8e, 1995): 31. The closest example we have of an immigrant group seeking an internal restriction is the request, in the wake of the Rushdie affair, by a small Muslim group to have the right to opt out of the Canadian judicial system in favour of Islamic law. This example is frequently cited (e.g., by Bissoondath: 139), but it was in fact a blip in the debate, unsupported by any major ethnocultural group, and quickly disappeared.

6 Yasmeen Abu-Laban and Daiva Stasiulus, 'Ethnic Pluralism under Siege: Popular and Partisan Opposition to Multiculturalism', *Canadian Public Policy* 18, 4 (1992): 379.

7 Gwyn, *Nationalism*: 197.

8 Bissoondath, *Selling Illusions*: 139.

9 Ibid.: 138–9.

10 *What Is Multiculturalism?* (Canberra, Department of the Prime Minister, Office of Multicultural Affairs, April 1995).

11 For a clear statement of these three principles, and the moral contract more generally, see *Let's Build Quebec Together: Vision: A Policy Statement on Immigration and Integration* (Quebec City: Ministère des Communautés culturelles et de l'Immigration du Québec, 1990).

12 Bissoondath: 197.

13 Gwyn: 183–4.

14 For a comparison of Quebec and Canada's policies towards the integration of immigrants, see Linda Pietrantonio, Danielle Juteau, and Marie McAndrew, 'Canadian-Style Multiculturalism and Quebec-Style Integration: Similarities and Differences', *Profile* 5, 1 (1997). As they note, the usual tendency to view these opposed approaches is 'part of a false debate' (12). At one point, Bissoondath seems to recognize this. He admits that 'Quebec had simply made *de jure* what was *de facto* elsewhere in the country: if a Spanish-speaker arrived in Toronto, he would necessarily have to live much of his life—to engage with the society—in English' (197). But in fact learning an official language is not just a *de facto* necessity under the federal policy: it is a *de jure* requirement, reflected in laws on citizenship, schooling, access to government training programs, and so on. Both the Quebec and federal policies have a *de jure* requirement of linguistic and institutional integration. Only in Quebec, however, is this requirement highlighted by policy-makers, and in the public debate.

15 Gwyn: 189.

16 This was particularly evident, for example, in Sheila Finestone's response to Bissoondath's book, which implied that a good Canadian would not question the multiculturalism policy.

17 Tariq Modood, 'Establishment, Multiculturalism, and British Citizenship', *Political Quarterly* 65, 1 (1994), 64; cf. Freda Hawkins, *Critical Years in Immigration: Canada and Australia Compared* (Montreal: McGill-Queen's University Press, 1989): 217.

5: A CROSSROADS IN RACE RELATIONS

1 I will use the terms 'racial minorities' and 'visible minorities' interchangeably to refer to non-white, non-Aboriginal groups, including Blacks, Chinese, Koreans, Filipinos, Indo-Pakistanis, West Asians and Arabs, Southeast Asians, Latin Americans, and Pacific Islanders.

2 Kenneth Karst, 'Paths to Belonging: The Constitution and Cultural Identity', *North Carolina Law Review* 64 (1986): 325.

3 William Julius Wilson, *The Declining Significance of Race* (Chicago: University of Chicago Press, 1978).

4 Edward Sagarin and Robert Kelly, 'Polylingualism in the United States of America: A Multitude of Tongues Amid a Monolingual Majority' in William Beer and James Jacob, eds, *Language Policy and National Unity* (Totowa: Rowman and Allenheld, 1985): 26–7.

5 Adeno Addis, '"Hell Man, They Did Invent Us": The Mass Media, Law and African Americans', *Buffalo Law Review* 41 (1993).

6 John Ogbu, 'Diversity and Equity in Public Education: Community Forces and Minority School Adjustment and Performance' in R. Haskins and D. MacRae, eds, *Policies for America's Public Schools: Teachers, Equity and Indicators* (Norwood, NJ: Ablex Publishers, 1988): 164–5.

7 Nathan Glazer, *Ethnic Dilemmas: 1964–1982* (Cambridge: Harvard University Press, 1983): 184, 284. In his most recent book, Glazer acknowledges that his earlier belief that Blacks could follow the immigrant model of integration was mistaken, and accepts that distinctive Black-focused policies are needed to improve their situation. See Glazer, *We Are All Multiculturalists Now* (Cambridge: Harvard University Press, 1997).

8 Michael Walzer, 'Pluralism in Political Perspective' in Will Kymlicka, ed., *The Rights of Minority Cultures* (Oxford: Oxford University Press, 1995): 153–4.

9 Cecil Foster, *A Place Called Heaven: The Meaning of Being Black in Canada* (Toronto: HarperCollins, 1996): 318–19; Frances Henry, *The Caribbean Diaspora in Toronto: Learning to Live with Racism* (Toronto: University of Toronto Press, 1994): 18.

10 Dorothy Williams, *Blacks in Montreal 1628–1986: An Urban Demography* (Cowansville: Éditions Yvon Blais, 1989): 7–14, 17–18.

11 Ibid.: 30, 45.

12 Ibid.: 80–81. On the extent to which recent Caribbean immigrants have 'hijacked' the race agenda in Canada, see Foster, *A Place*: 25–6.

13 Williams, *Blacks in Montreal*: 44.

14 See, for example, Adrienne Shadd, 'Where Are You Really From? Notes of an "Immigrant" from North Buxton, Ontario' in Carl James and Adrienne Shadd, eds, *Talking about Difference: Encounters in Culture, Language and Identity* (Toronto: Between the Lines Press, 1994): 14.

15 Augie Fleras and Jean Elliot, *Unequal Relations: An Introduction to Race, Ethnic and Aboriginal Dynamics in Canada*, 2nd edn (Scarborough: Prentice Hall, 1996): 105.

16 Peter Rose, 'Asian Americans: From Pariahs to Paragons' in James S. Frideres,

ed., *Multiculturalism and Intergroup Relations* (New York: Greenwood Press, 1989): 107–22.

17 Stephen Lewis, *Report on Race Relations in Ontario* (Toronto: Office of the Premier, 1992): 2.

18 See, for example, Henry, *The Caribbean Diaspora*: Chapter 5.

19 See ibid.: 219–22; Foster, *A Place*: 189; Augie Fleras, 'Media and Minorities in a Post-Multicultural Society' in J.W. Berry and Jean Laponce, eds, *Ethnicity and Culture in Canada: The Research Landscape* (Toronto: University of Toronto Press, 1994): 267–92.

20 For a discussion of double standards regarding punishment in jails, see the Interim Report of the Commission on Systemic Racism in the Ontario Criminal Justice System, *Racism Behind Bars: The Treatment of Black and Other Racial Minority Prisoners in Ontario Prisons* (Toronto, 1995): 48–9. On the schools, see Toronto Board of Education's 1988 report *Education of Black Students in Toronto: Final Report of the Consultative Committee*: 33, and appendix E: 4.

21 R. Breton et al., *Ethnic Identity and Equality: Varieties of Experience in a Canadian City* (Toronto: University of Toronto Press, 1990): 199–201.

22 For interesting examples, see Henry Codjoe, 'Black Nationalists Beware! You Could be Called a Racist for Being "Too Black and African"' in James and Shadd, eds, *Talking about Difference*: 235.

23 See Shadd, 'Where Are You Really From?': 11; Williams, *Blacks in Montreal*: 4.

24 On 'subliminal racism' in Canada, and how it differs from red-necked and polite racism, see Fleras and Elliot, *Unequal Relations*: 71–8. They describe subliminal racism as reflecting a contradiction between the values of social equality and individual freedom. This seems to me quite unhelpful. So far as I can tell, it is rather a contradiction between people's general beliefs about freedom/equality and their more specific habits, dispositions, and emotions.

25 For a discussion of how the changing status of Coloureds in South Africa is related to a racialized discourse of 'respectability', see Jeremy Seekings and Courtney Jung, '"That Time Was Apartheid: Now It's the New South Africa"' in Will Kymlicka and Ian Shapiro, eds, *Ethnicity and Group Rights* (New York: New York University Press, 1997): 504–39.

26 J.W. Berry and R. Kalin, 'Multicultural and Ethnic Attitudes in Canada', *Canadian Journal of Behavioural Studies* 27 (1995): 301–20; cf. Leo Dreidger, *Multi-Ethnic Canada: Identities and Inequalities* (Toronto: Oxford University Press, 1996): 264.

27 For evidence regarding African Americans, see Ogbu, 'Diversity and Equity': 164–5.

28 Patrick Solomon, 'Academic Disengagement: Black Youth and the Sports Subculture from a Cross-National Perspective' in Lorna Erwin and David MacLennan, eds, *Sociology of Education in Canada* (Toronto: Copp Clark Longman, 1994): 191. Indeed, as Solomon notes, the drop-out rate actually underestimates the problem, since many Blacks stay in school only for the sports, without any real interest in academic achievement (189); he argues that students within this 'sports subculture' have *de facto* 'dropped out'.

29 Andrew Hacker, *Two Nations: Black and White, Separate, Hostile and Unequal* (New York: Ballantine, 1992); Foster, *A Place*: 115.

30 See Henry, *The Caribbean Diaspora*: 144. Elsewhere, unfortunately, Henry discusses 'Black youth' in a way that makes it unclear whether the trends apply to both Caribbean-born and native-born Blacks.

31 See, for example, Toronto Board of Education, *Education of Black Students*, passim.

32 On the differences between Canadian and American models of Black-focused schools, see Foster, *A Place*: 130–4.

33 See Toronto Board of Education, *Education of Black Students*; Henry, *The Caribbean Diaspora*: chapter 6; Lewis, *Report on Race Relations*: 20–1; Solomon, 'Academic Disengagement'; Keren Braithwaite, 'The Black Student and the School: A Canadian Dilemma' in Simeon Chilungu and Sada Niang, eds, *African Continuities/L'Héritage africain* (Toronto: Terebi, 1989): 195–214; George Dei, 'Reflections of an Anti-Racist Pedagogue', in *Sociology of Education in Canada*: 290–310, and Dei, '(Re)Conceptualizing Black Studies in Canadian Schools', *Canadian and International Education* 24, 1 (1995): 1–19.

34 I don't mean to imply that racism in Canada is the only, or even the primary, explanation for the difficulties facing young Caribbean Black adults today. For one thing, some of those who are in the greatest difficulty (those caught up in crime, drugs, gangs) are recent arrivals in Canada, and received most of their education in Jamaica, with Black teachers and a curriculum designed by Black educators. It would be implausible to argue that the one or two years of schooling they've had in Canada are solely responsible for such outcomes. In at least some of these cases, the problem must have started much earlier, and the worst that can be said is that Canadian schools have failed to rescue people who were already in danger of falling through society's cracks.

35 For a discussion of this issue, see Toronto Board of Education, *Education of Black Students*: 33–4; appendix E: 4–5.

36 Lewis, *Report on Race Relations*: 17.

37 For a discussion of this issue see Henry, *The Caribbean Diaspora*: Chapter 4.

38 On this point I agree with Gwyn, *Nationalism*: 174–6.

39 For the impact of affirmative action on women in Canada, see Pat and Hugh Armstrong, 'Lessons from Pay Equity', *Studies in Political Economy* 22 (1990).

40 See House of Commons Special Committee on Participation of Visible Minorities in Canadian Society, *Equality Now!* (Ottawa, 1984).

6: CAN MULTICULTURALISM BE EXTENDED TO NON-ETHNIC GROUPS?

1 For a classic statement of this shift, see Jean Cohen, 'Strategy or Identity: New Theoretical Paradigms and Contemporary Social Movements', *Social Research* 54, 4 (1985): 663–716; see also Enrique Larana, Hank Johnston, and Joseph Gusfield, eds, *New Social Movements: From Ideology to Identity* (Philadelphia: Temple University Press, 1994).

2 William Carroll, 'Introduction: Social Movements and Counter-Hegemony in a Canadian Context' in *Organizing Dissent: Contemporary Social Movements*

in Theory and Practice (Toronto: Garamond Press, 1992): 7.

3 In the rest of this chapter I will focus primarily on the gay male community, since more has been written about it than about the lesbian community. Many of the historical trends and current issues affecting gays also apply to lesbians, although lesbian communities tend to be smaller in size.

4 Foucault, *History of Sexuality*, quoted in Steven Epstein, 'Gay Politics, Ethnic Identity: The Limits of Social Constructionism' in Edward Stein, ed., *Forms of Desire: Sexual Orientation and the Social Constructionist Controversy* (New York: Garland Publishing, 1990): 250. Similarly, Cathy Cohen notes that 'Sodomous acts, once thought to be wayward individual behaviour, were redefined, largely by medical professionals, as signalling some inherent or fundamental flaw in the character of an individual. Further, all those participating in such behaviour were understood as a distinct or distinguishable group in society' ('Straight Gay Politics: The Limits of an Ethnic Model of Inclusion' in Will Kymlicka and Ian Shapiro, eds, *Ethnicity and Group Rights* [New York: New York University Press, 1997]: 584–5).

5 As Brian Walker notes, speaking specifically of the gay community, 'One creates culture by creating institutions, and these new institutions in turn make possible new forms of identity' ('Social Movements as Nationalisms', unpublished paper, Department of Government, Harvard University, 1995: 14).

6 Epstein, 'Gay Politics, Ethnic Identity', 243, 255. As he notes, this acceptance of groups as legitimate actors in the political process had the paradoxical effect that gays were given legitimacy as a group, even when homosexual acts were still criminalized (255).

7 Ibid.: 256.

8 Stephen Murray notes that, as measured by standard sociological criteria, gays in Toronto are as much a 'community' as ethnic groups are. For example, 'more than half of these active participants in the gay community live in less than 2 percent of the total land mass of Metropolitan Toronto' ('The Institutional Elaboration of a Quasi-Ethnic Community', *International Review of Modern Sociology* 9 [1979]: 168). Indeed, 'to the extent that the gay community has succeeded in creating new institutional supports that link individuals into the community and provide their lives with a sense of meaning, gays may now be more "ethnic" than the original ethnic groups' (Epstein, 'Gay Politics, Ethnic Identity': 281).

9 See Stephen Murray, 'Components of Gay Community in San Francisco' in Gilbert Herdt, ed., *Gay Culture in America: Essays from the Field* (Boston: Beacon Press, 1992): 125.

10 Hank Johnston argues that 'a source of continuity with the past' is what differentiates traditional ethnonationalist movements from most new social movements ('New Social Movements and Old Regional Nationalisms' in Larana et al., eds, *New Social Movements*: 282). But he is primarily comparing ethnic groups with peace groups, environmentalists, and anti-poverty groups. Gay groups, by contrast, are building precisely this sense of historical continuity. On the construction of a gay history, see Walker, 'Social Movements': 10.

11 Murray, 'Components': 116–23.

12 'Introduction: Culture, History, and Life Course of Gay Men' in Herdt, ed., *Gay Culture in America*: 5.

13 Oliver Sacks, *Seeing Voices: A Journey into the World of the Deaf* (Berkeley: University of California Press, 1989): xi.

14 Most Deaf people in Canada use ASL, although there is a separate sign language in Quebec (Langue des Signes Québécois), and some in Nova Scotia use a sign language related to British Sign Language rather than ASL. See Carol Padden and Tom Humphries, *Deaf in America: Voices from a Culture* (Cambridge: Harvard University Press, 1988): 3.

15 Ibid.: 2; cf. Sacks: xi.

16 Sacks, *Seeing Voices*: 26.

17 Compare John Stuart Mill's comment, typical of the nineteenth-century prejudice against national minorities: 'Nobody can suppose that it is not more beneficial to a Breton, or a Basque of French Navarre, to be brought into the current of the ideas and feelings of a highly civilised and cultivated people—to be a member of the French nationality, admitted on equal terms to all the privileges of French citizenship . . . than to sulk on his own rocks, the half-savage relic of past times, revolving in his own little mental orbit, without participation or interest in the general movement of the world. The same remark applies to the Welshman or the Scottish Highlander as members of the British nation' (*Considerations on Representative Government* [1861] in *Utilitarianism, On Liberty, Considerations on Representative Government*, ed. H.B. Acton [London: J.M. Dent and Sons, 1972]: 395). Mill also opposed the attempts of the Québécois to maintain a distinct francophone society in Canada, and encouraged their assimilation into the more 'civilized' English culture. See Bhikhu Parekh, 'Decolonizing Liberalism' in Aleksandras Shtromas, ed., *The End of 'Isms'?* (Oxford: Blackwell, 1994): 91.

18 Sacks, *Seeing Voices*: 25.

19 Padden and Humphries, *Deaf in America*: 2.

20 For this evidence, see Sacks, *Seeing Voices*, and Padden and Humphries, *Deaf in America*.

21 Sacks: 127.

22 Ibid.: 136–7.

23 Padden and Humphries: 44.

24 This is reflected in the different orientations of the national organization for the Deaf, as compared with organizations serving adults who have lost their hearing in later life. The former focus on developments in sign language, the portrayal of the Deaf in the media, and developing Deaf-run social services. The latter focuses on medical treatments and devices. See Padden and Humphries: 43.

25 For this definition of lifestyle enclaves, see Robert Bellah et al., *Habits of the Heart: Individualism and Commitment in American Life* (Berkeley: University of California Press, 1985): 72–5. Bellah implies that gays are just a lifestyle enclave, not a genuine 'community'.

26 Murray, 'Components': 114–16; cf. Mark Blasius, 'An Ethos of Lesbian and Gay Existence', *Political Theory* 20, 4 (1992): 655.

27 Walker, 'Social Movements': 1.

28 For this shift, see Jean Crête and Jacques Zylberberg, 'Une problématique floue: l'autoreprésentation du citoyen au Québec' in Dominique Colas, Claude Emeri, and Jacques Zylberberg, eds, *Citoyenneté et nationalité: perspectives en France et au Québec* (Paris: Presses Universitaires de France, 1991): 425–30; and Joseph Carens, 'Immigration, Political Community, and the Transformation of Identity: Quebec's Immigration Policies in Critical Perspective' in Carens, ed., *Is Quebec Nationalism Just?* (Montreal: McGill-Queen's University Press, 1995): 20–81.

29 See *Final Report*, vol. 2: 239. For a partial defence of the practice, however, see Gerald Alfred, *Heeding the Voices of Our Ancestors* (Toronto: Oxford University Press, 1995): 163–75.

30 Walker, 'Social Movements': 4, 9.

31 Dennis Altman, 'What Price Gay Nationalism?' in Mark Thompson, ed., *Gay Spirit: Myth and Meaning* (New York: St Martin's, 1987): 18–19, quoted in Blasius, 'An Ethos of Lesbian and Gay Existence': 668n.12.

32 Epstein, 'Gay Politics': 256n.37. As Murray notes, only 4 per cent of gays in the San Francisco gay community were born there ('Components of Gay Community': 125).

33 Larry Kramer, *Reports from the Holocaust: The Making of an AIDS Activist* (New York: St Martin's, 1989): 257, quoted in Blasius, 'An Ethos', 648. Kramer quotes Hannah Arendt: 'The simple truth is that Jews will have to fight anti-Semitism everywhere or else be exterminated everywhere.' The same is true, he argues, for gays.

34 Blasius, 'An Ethos': 647.

35 Epstein, 'Gay Politics': 274–5.

36 Epstein: 277–9, 282. It's true that members of immigrant groups typically acquire a sense of their ethnic identity as children, whereas gay identity arises later on. But immigrant ethnicity—particularly for subsequent generations—can remain a fairly latent and symbolic identity for long periods of time, until circumstances lead to its activation and mobilization. In this respect, immigrant ethnicity is similar to gay ethnicity. As Epstein puts it, 'if "ethnicity" is to serve even as an analogy for comprehending gay and lesbian group identity, then ethnicity must be understood as something that is neither an absolutely inescapable ascription nor something chosen and discarded at will; as something neither there from birth, nor something one joins like a club; as something that makes one neither fundamentally different from others, nor fundamentally the same. It is in the dialectics between choice and constraint, and between the individual, the group and the larger society, that "identities", "ethnic identities", and "gay and lesbian identities" emerge' (281, 285–6). Moreover, the increasing importance of sexuality to modern identities means that gay identity, even if it is 'secondary', is nonetheless particularly important to self-respect and personal autonomy (269).

37 Cohen, 'Straight Gay Politics': 603, drawing on two recent (1994) American surveys (588).

38 Ibid.: 602–3.

39 Cohen and others also criticize this ethnic model for the way it encourages

group leaders to impose a false internal homogeneity on the group, ignoring or marginalizing those group members who may not seem sufficiently 'respectable' to the larger society (Cohen: 10–11; cf. Didi Herman, *Rights of Passage: Struggles for Lesbian and Gay Legal Equality* [Toronto: University of Toronto Press, 1994]: 6; Epstein, 'Gay Politics': 292).

40 As Murray notes, there is a common myth that many gays 'abandoned careers to move to San Francisco, taking any job available just to live there', accepting marginal jobs simply to be close to the 'sexual playground'. However, there is no evidence to support this myth (Murray, 'Components': 128–34).

41 Blasius, 'An Ethos': 647.

42 For a discussion of recent efforts to introduce sexual orientation into the school curriculum in Toronto, see Helen Lenskyj, 'Going Too Far? Sexual Orientation(s) in the Sex Education Curriculum' in Lorna Erwin and David MacLennan, eds, *Sociology of Education in Canada* (Toronto: Copp Clark Longman, 1994): 278–89. Gays believe that it is very important to present gay lives in a positive manner in the schools, since there is strong evidence that gay teenagers who lack positive role models are at much greater risk of suicide. Yet according to Lenskyj, the original curriculum regarding gay sexual orientation 'clung to a disease model and a clinical perspective. There was a strong emphasis on suicide; family conflict; high-risk sexual practices; promiscuity; loneliness; alienation from parents, siblings, and friends—all presumably aimed at alleviating right-wing fears about unduly "attractive" portrayals of gay and lesbian "lifestyles"' (284). As Brian Walker notes, gays believe strongly that they have a 'duty of rescue' to protect young gays from suicide, and this 'explains why gay people cannot leave gay culture as a matter for the private sphere, and why there is such a deep disagreement of principle between them and the right-wing groups which advocate the complete banning of positive representations of gay life from state institutions' ('Social Movements as Nationalisms', 15).

43 See Herman, *Rights of Passage*: 44, 146, on the need for gays in Canada to challenge majority notions of gender roles and 'coupledom'. See also Epstein, 'Gay Politics': 252–3.

44 Sacks, *Seeing Voices*: 128n.

45 Padden and Humphries, *Deaf in America*: 113; cf. Sacks: 32n. In this sense, the Deaf pose the clearest challenge to the idea that only ethnocultural groups can form 'nations' or 'societal cultures'. But they are the exception proving the rule that societal cultures are tied to a common language, for what has made the idea of a Deaf societal culture meaningful is precisely that they have their own language, which sets them apart from the larger society.

46 Padden and Humphries estimate that the number of Deaf people throughout all of North America is only 'a few hundred thousand' (5).

47 Sacks: 137.

48 Padden and Humphries: 116.

49 Sharon Stone and Joanne Doucette, 'Organizing the Marginalized: The DisAbled Women's Network' in Sue Findlay et al., eds, *Social Movements/ Social Change: The Politics and Practice of Organizing* (Toronto: Between the Lines Press, 1988): 84.

50 I have tried to discuss some of these confusions in the American debate in *Multicultural Citizenship: A Liberal Theory of Minority Rights* (Oxford: Oxford University Press, 1995): Chapter 4.

7: TOWARDS A MORE REPRESENTATIVE DEMOCRACY

1 Although there were Aboriginal representatives at many of the crucial nego-tiations leading up to the Charlottetown Accord, they were left out of other important sessions. Similarly, representatives of various women's groups were included in some provincial delegations, but only for some sessions.

2 Indeed, 'middle-class status is a virtual prerequisite for candidacy for major office' (Raymond Wolfinger, quoted in Royal Commission on Electoral Reform and Party Financing, *Reforming Electoral Democracy: Final Report*, vol. 1 (Ottawa: Supply and Services, 1991): 102. The statistics are from ibid.: 93–6 and 192, based on the 1986 Census.

3 For these more recent studies, see Jerome Black and Aleem Lakhani, 'Minority Women in the 35th Parliament', *Canadian Parliamentary Review* 20, 11 (1997); Daiva Stasiulus, 'Participation by Immigrants, Ethnocultural/Visible Minorities in the Canadian Political Process', paper presented to the Metropolis Research Domain Seminar, Montreal, November 1997.

4 These options are discussed in *Reforming Electoral Democracy*: 93–121.

5 See Lisa Young, 'Electoral Systems and Representative Legislatures: Consideration of Alternative Electoral Systems' (Ottawa: Canadian Advisory Council on the Status of Women, 1994).

6 See ibid.

7 For a fuller discussion of these proposals, see my 'Group Representation in Canadian Politics' in Leslie Seidle, ed., *Equity and Community: The Charter, Interest Advocacy, and Representation* (Montreal: Institute for Research on Public Policy, 1993): 61–89. The material in the rest of this chapter draws extensive-ly on this earlier work.

8 See Lisa Young, 'Gender Equal Legislatures: Evaluating the Proposed Nunavut System', *Canadian Public Policy* 23, 3 (1997): 306–16.

9 *Reforming Electoral Democracy*: 149.

10 Beverley Baines argues that the principle of ensuring representation for com-munities of interest should extend to women. See her '"Consider Sir ... On What Does Your Constitution Rest?" Representational and Institutional Reform', *Conversations Among Friends: Proceedings of an Interdisciplinary Conference on Women and Constitutional Reform* (Edmonton: Centre for Constitutional Studies, University of Alberta, 1992): 56.

11 *Reforming Electoral Democracy*: 152–3.

12 See ibid.: 149–50, and Lani Guinier, 'No Two Seats: The Elusive Quest for Political Equality', *Virginia Law Review* 77, 8 (1991): 1413–1514.

13 Judy Rebick and Shelagh Day, 'A place at the table: the new Senate needs gender equality, minority representation', *Ottawa Citizen*, 11 Sept. 1992: A11.

14 For a summary of the conference, and the shift in focus generated by the demands of NAC, see *Renewal of Canada Conferences: Compendium of Reports*

(Ottawa: Privy Council Office, 1992).

15 Canada West Foundation, *Regional Representation: The Canadian Partnership* (Calgary: Canada West Foundation, 1981): 9.

16 For a detailed account of the history of this notion of representation, see Hanna Pitkin, *The Concept of Representation* (Berkeley: University of California Press, 1967): Chapter 4.

17 Anne Phillips, 'Dealing with Difference: A Politics of Ideas or a Politics of Presence', *Constellations* 1, 1 (1994): 76. Phillips herself does not endorse this view.

18 Anne Phillips, *The Politics of Presence* (Oxford: Oxford University Press, 1995), especially Chapter 1.

19 See Christine Boyle, 'Home-Rule for Women: Power-Sharing Between Men and Women', *Dalhousie Law Journal* 7 (1983): 797–8.

20 Melissa Williams, *Voice, Trust, Memory: Marginalized Groups and the Failings of Liberal Representation* (Princeton: Princeton University Press, forthcoming).

21 Pitkin, *Concept of Representation*: 73, quoting Alfred DeGrazia.

22 Roger Gibbins, 'Electoral Reform and Canada's Aboriginal Population: an assessment of Aboriginal Electoral Districts' in Robert A. Milen, ed., *Aboriginal Peoples and Electoral Reform in Canada*, vol. 9 of the research studies of the Royal Commission on Electoral Reform and Party Financing (Toronto: Dundurn Press, 1991): 171. For an in-depth discussion of the relevance of the Maori model for Canada, see Fleras, 'Aboriginal Electoral Districts for Canada: Lessons from New Zealand', in ibid.

23 Baines, 'Consider, Sir': 56.

24 Anne Phillips, 'Democracy and Difference: Some Problems for Feminist Theory', *Political Quarterly* 63, 1 (1992): 85.

25 For a detailed discussion of this problem in the British context, see ibid.: 89.

26 Phillips, 'Dealing with Difference': 7.

27 Iris Marion Young, 'Polity and Group Difference: A Critique of the Ideal of Universal Citizenship', *Ethics* 99, 2 (1989): 257.

28 Ibid.: 259; cf. Young's *Justice and the Politics of Difference* (Princeton: Princeton University Press, 1990): 183–91.

29 The Supreme Court has recognized that the principle of 'one person, one vote' may not secure 'effective representation' for minorities (*Reference Re Electoral Boundaries Commission Act* [1991] 81 D.L.R. [4th] 16).

30 See Boyle, 'Home-Rule for Women': 791.

31 This representation may take the form of a permanent seat on the Court, or of a seat only in cases that directly affect the group. This is the model used by the International Court of Justice, which allows each country that is party to a particular dispute to nominate one member to the Court when that case is being heard. Some Aboriginal people have suggested that such a model might be appropriate for Aboriginal representation on the Supreme Court.

32 Part of the oversimplification is that while Aboriginal self-government involves transferring powers from the federal government to Aboriginal communities, which then become exempt from federal legislation, there is

also a distinctive trust relationship between Aboriginal peoples and the federal government that gives the latter more authority over the former than it has over other Canadians. Because of Section 91(4) of the BNA Act, which gives it the exclusive power to legislate in matters relating to Indians and Indian lands, the federal government provides certain services to Aboriginals that other Canadians receive from provincial governments. This distinctive trust relationship provides an argument in favour of increased Aboriginal representation in Parliament, an agreement that helps to counterbalance the presumption that enhanced Aboriginal self-government reduces the necessity of Aboriginal representation in Parliament (see *Reforming Electoral Democracy*: 181–2).

33 Special Joint Committee on a Renewed Canada, *Report* (Ottawa: Supply and Services, 1992): 52.

34 Indeed, the original granting of the vote to Status Indians in 1960 was largely the result of international pressure; Indians themselves saw enfranchisement as a threat to their status as self-governing nations. See Alan Cairns, 'Aboriginal Canadians, Citizenship and the Constitution' in *Reconfigurations: Canadian Citizenship and Constitutional Change* (Toronto: McClelland and Stewart, 1995).

35 Claims based on disadvantage would apply equally to urban, non-status Indians, who may have no meaningful self-government powers, whereas claims based on self-government would apply most clearly to Status Indians on reserves. See the discussion in Gibbins, 'Electoral Reform and Canada's Aboriginal Population': 181–2. Gibbins argues that off-reserve Aboriginal people should be represented in the House of Commons through Aboriginal Electoral Districts, whereas those on self-governing reserves should be represented in Ottawa primarily through delegates of their tribal governments sitting on inter-governmental bodies.

36 Young, *Justice and the Politics of Difference*, 187.

37 Young, 'Polity and Group Difference': 261.

38 Phillips, 'Democracy and Difference': 89.

39 Young, 'Polity and Group Difference': 187–9.

40 For example, civil service employment equity programs identify four categories of disadvantaged people: women, Aboriginals, visible minorities, and people with disabilities.

41 Section 15(2) says that the constitutional prohibition on discrimination does not preclude affirmative action-type programs aimed at ameliorating the conditions of 'disadvantaged individuals or groups'. In interpreting this clause, the Supreme Court has had to develop criteria for determining which groups count as 'disadvantaged', and these criteria would be relevant for determining which groups are entitled to group representation.

42 However, the Canadian Ethnocultural Council (CEC) has 'long advocated that a tradition, written or unwritten, be established to ensure some minority presence' on the Supreme Court (CEC, 'A Dream Deferred: Collective Equality for Canada's Ethnocultural Communities' in Michael Behiels, ed., *The Meech Lake Primer: Conflicting Views of the 1987 Constitutional Accord* [Ottawa: University of Ottawa, 1989]: 342). For in-depth discussions of the

strategies for including ethnocultural and visible minority groups, see the essays collected in Kathy Megyery, ed., *Ethno-Cultural Groups and Visible Minorities in Canadian Politics: The Question of Access*, vol. 7 of the Research Studies of the Royal Commission on Electoral Reform and Party Financing (Ottawa: Dundurn Press, 1991).

43 Phillips, 'Dealing with Difference': 34n.9.

44 Rebick and Day, 'A place at the table'.

45 Guinier, 'No Two Seats': 1434–7.

46 A related question is whether group representatives (however many there are) should have special powers (such as a veto) in areas directly affecting their group. This seems most plausible—indeed, almost essential—for group representation based on claims of self-government. Since the justification of group representation in this case is to protect powers of self-government from federal intrusion, a veto in areas of concurrent or conflicting jurisdiction seems a logical mechanism. Whether group representation based on systemic disadvantage leads to special veto powers (e.g., veto powers for women senators over decisions regarding reproductive rights, as Iris Young suggests) is more complicated, and would depend on the nature of the disadvantage.

47 For a particularly comprehensive discussion of one model, see *Reforming Electoral Democracy*: 170–85.

48 Bernard Grofman, 'Should Representatives Be Typical of their Constituents?', in B. Grofman et al., eds, *Representation and Redistricting Issues* (Lexington, Mass.: D.C. Heath, 1982): 98; emphasis in original.

49 Phillips, 'Democracy and Difference': 86–8.

50 Phillips, *Politics of Presence*: 54.

51 See *Reforming Electoral Democracy*: 149 (on communities of interest), and Special Joint Committee, *Report*: 41 (on regional representation).

52 *Reforming Electoral Democracy*: 93.

53 Robert Dahl, *Democracy and its Critics* (New Haven: Yale University Press, 1989), chapters 10–14.

8: A Truce in the Multiculturalism Wars?

1 Neil Bissoondath, *Selling Illusions* (Toronto: Penguin, 1994): 143.

2 Richard Gwyn, *Nationalism without Walls* (Toronto: McClelland and Stewart, 1995): 6.

3 Ibid.: 147.

4 Freda Hawkins, *Critical Years in Immigration: Canada and Australia Compared* (Montreal: McGill-Queen's University Press, 1989): 227.

5 For a summary of the literature, see the comprehensive overview in J.W. Berry and Jean Laponce, eds, *Ethnicity and Culture in Canada: The Research Landscape* (Toronto: University of Toronto Press, 1994): 260.

6 For interesting information on ethnocultural groups in Canada, see the 'country profiles' at http://cicnet.ingenia.com.

7 Gina Mallet, 'Multiculturalism: Has Diversity Gone Too Far?' *Globe and Mail*, 15 March 1997: D1–D2.

9: TAKING NATIONALISM SERIOUSLY

1 Ernest Gellner, *Nations and Nationalism* (Oxford: Blackwell, 1983): 6.

10: TWO MODELS OF FEDERALISM IN CANADA

1 Jeremy Webber, *Reimagining Canada: Language, Culture, Community and the Canadian Constitution* (Montreal: McGill-Queen's University Press, 1994): 24.

2 On the adoption of the language of nationhood by the Québécois and Aboriginal people, see Jane Jenson, 'Naming Nations: Making Nationalist Claims in Canadian Public Discourse', *Canadian Review of Sociology and Anthropology* 30, 3 (1993): 337–57; Alan Cairns, 'The Fragmentation of Canadian Citizenship' in William Kaplan, ed. *Belonging: The Meaning and Future of Canadian Citizenship* (Montreal: McGill-Queen's Press, 1993): 181–220; Gerald Alfred, *Heeding the Voices of our Ancestors: Kahnawake Mohawk Politics and the Rise of Native Nationalism* (Toronto: Oxford University Press, 1995).

3 On the concepts of 'societal culture' and 'institutional completeness', see Chapter 2. For the relationship between institutionally complete societal cultures and sociological accounts of nationhood, see my *Multicultural Citizenship* (Oxford: Oxford University Press, 1995): Chapter 5.

4 See Paul Chartrand, '"Terms of Division": Problems of Outside-Naming for Aboriginal People in Canada', *Journal of Indigenous Studies* 2, 2 (1991): 2.

5 For discussions of Trudeau's attempts to shift Quebecers' national identification from Quebec to Ottawa, and the role of bilingualism in this strategy, see Webber, *Reimagining Canada*: 50–62; Kenneth McRoberts, *Misconceiving Canada: The Struggle for National Unity* (Toronto: Oxford University Press, 1997): Chapter 4.

6 See John Conway, *Debts to Pay: English Canada and Quebec from the Conquest to the Referendum* (Toronto: Lorimer, 1992): 37–44.

7 Webber, *Reimagining*: 243; McRoberts, *Misconceiving*: 248.

8 McRoberts, *Misconceiving*: 86–8, 103–6.

9 Some people argue that this focus on Quebec is comparatively recent and so potentially reversible. After all, the term 'Québécois' displaced 'French-Canadian' only in the last few decades. But this is misleading. The term 'Québécois' emerged as the Quebec provincial government displaced the Catholic Church as the main defender of French-Canadian nationalism. But even earlier Church-led forms of French-Canadian nationalism viewed Quebec as the homeland of the nation. See Webber, *Reimagining*: 40–50; McRoberts, *Misconceiving*: Chapter 1.

10 On Belgium, see Robert Senelle, 'Constitutional Reform in Belgium: From Unitarism towards Federalism' in Murray Forsyth, ed., *Federalism and Nationalism* (Leicester: Leicester University Press, 1989): 51–95; on Switzerland, see Gerda Mansour, *Multilingualism and Nation Building* (Clevedon: Multilingual Matters, 1993): 109–11. For a more general theoretical account of the 'territorial imperative' in multilingual societies, see Jean Laponce, *Languages and their Territories* (Toronto: University of Toronto Press,

1987).

11 J.A. Long, 'Federalism and Ethnic Self-Determination: Native Indians in Canada', *Journal of Commonwealth and Comparative Politics* 29, 2 (1991): 192–211; David Elkins, *Where Should the Majority Rule? Reflections on Non-Territorial Provinces and Other Constitutional Proposals* (Edmonton: Centre for Constitutional Studies, University of Alberta, 1992); James Youngblood Henderson, 'Empowering Treaty Federalism', *University of Saskatchewan Law Review* 58, 2 (1994).

12 Daniel Elazar is perhaps the most eloquent proponent of the view that federalism is the ideal political arrangement for multination states. See his *Federalism and the Way to Peace* (Kingston: Institute of Intergovernmental Affairs, Queen's University, 1994); and *Exploring Federalism* (Tuscaloosa: University of Alabama, 1987). For other discussions of the idea of diffusing minority nationalisms within federal systems, see Robert Howse and Karen Knop, 'Federalism, Secession and the Limits of Ethnic Accommodation: A Canadian Perspective', *New Europe Law Review* 1, 2 (1993): 269–320; Wayne Norman, 'Towards a Normative Theory of Federalism' in Judith Baker, ed., *Group Rights* (Toronto: University of Toronto Press, 1994).

13 See the discussion of the 'federalist revolution' in Elazar, *Exploring Federalism*: Chap. 1.

14 Philip Resnick, 'Toward a Multination Federalism' in Leslie Seidle, ed.. *Seeking a New Canadian Partnership: Asymmetrical and Confederal Options* (Montreal: Institute for Research on Public Policy, 1994): 71.

15 Alexander Hamilton, James Madison, and John Jay, *The Federalist Papers* (New York: Bantam, 1982). Jay ignores not only the sizeable Black population, but also pockets of non-English immigrants (particularly Germans) and Indian tribes (most of whom had been dispossessed of their lands).

16 This is the main reason given by Madison in *The Federalist Papers*; see number 10: 54, 61 in the Bantam edition. The belief that federalism helps prevent tyranny was one reason why federalism was imposed by the Allies on Germany after the Second World War. It was supposed to help prevent the re-emergence of nationalist or authoritarian movements.

17 Some people argue that Switzerland was 'the first modern federation built upon indigenous ethnic and linguistic differences that were considered permanent and worth accommodating' (Daniel Elazar, 'The Role of Federalism in Political Integration' in *Federalism and Political Integration*, ed. D. Elazar [Ramat Gan, Israel: Turtledove Publishing, 1987]: 20). But as Forsyth notes, the old Swiss confederation, which existed for almost 500 years, was composed entirely of cantons that were Germanic in ethnic origin and language. While French- and Italian-speaking cantons were added in 1815, the decision to adopt a federal structure was not taken primarily to accommodate these ethnolinguistic differences. According to Murray Forsyth, the Canadian federation of 1867 was the first case where a federal structure was explicitly adopted to accommodate national minorities (Forsyth, 'Introduction' in *Federalism and Nationalism*, 3–4).

18 See the discussion and references in Chapter 12.

19 For a survey of the rights of national minorities in the United States, see

Sharon O'Brien, 'Cultural Rights in the United States: A Conflict of Values', *Law and Inequality Journal* 5 (1987): 267–358; Judith Resnik, 'Dependent Sovereigns: Indian Tribes, States, and the Federal Courts', *University of Chicago Law Review* 56 (1989): 671–759; Alexander Aleinikoff, 'Puerto Rico and the Constitution: Conundrums and Prospects', *Constitutional Commentary* 11 (1994): 15–43.

20 Some of the remaining 14 Autonomous Communities are not simply regional divisions, but form culturally distinct societies, even if they are not self-identified as distinct 'nations'. This is true, for example, of the Balearic Islands, Valencia, and Asturias, where distinct languages or dialects are spoken. But many of the communities do not represent distinct ethnocultural or linguistic units. For a discussion of Spain's Autonomous Communities and their varying levels of ethnocultural distinctiveness, see Audrey Brassloff, 'Spain: The State of the Autonomies' in Forsyth, ed., *Federalism and Nationalism*, 24–50.

21 Graham Smith, 'Russia, Ethnoregionalism and the Politics of Federation', *Ethnic and Racial Studies* 19, 2 (1996): 392, 395. It is interesting to note that Russia contemplated adopting an American-style model of symmetrical/territorial federalism, but national minorities were 'outraged at [the plan] to deny special status and to acknowledge their cultural difference' (395), and instead Russia quickly adopted an explicitly multinational/asymmetrical model of federalism. It's also worth noting that one of these 32 nationality-based units—Chechnya—has since declared its independence.

22 On English-speaking Canadian opposition to special status, see Alan Cairns, 'Constitutional Change and the Three Equalities' in Ronald Watts and Douglas Brown, eds, *Options for a New Canada* (Toronto: University of Toronto Press, 1991): 77–110; David Milne, 'Equality or Asymmetry: Why Choose?', ibid.: 285–307; Andrew Stark, 'English-Canadian Opposition to Quebec Nationalism' in R. Kent Weaver, ed., *The Collapse of Canada?* (Washington: Brookings Institute, 1992): 123–158; Stéphane Dion, 'La Fédéralisme fortement asymétrique' in Seidle, ed., *Seeking a New Canadian Partnership*: 133–52, who cites a poll showing 83 per cent opposition to special status. See also the articles by Resnick and Milne in the same book. A certain amount of *de facto* asymmetry in powers has been a long-standing aspect of Canadian federalism, but as these authors note, most English-speaking Canadians have been unwilling to formally recognize or entrench this in the Constitution, let alone to extend it.

23 See, for example, Charles Taylor, 'Shared and Divergent Values' in Watts and Brown, eds, *Options for a New Canada*: 53–76; Webber, *Reimagining*: 232–51.

24 English-speaking Canadians sometimes say to Québécois, 'Why can't we all be Canadians first, and members of provinces second?' But this involves asking the Québécois to subordinate their national identity, whereas for English-speaking Canadians it involves strengthening their national identity. Where is the 'equality' in such a demand?

25 Webber, *Reimagining*: 142–3; cf. Guy Laforest, *De la Prudence* (Montreal: Boréal, 1993): 191–2.

26 See Webber, *Reimagining*: 142.

27 Resnick, 'Towards a Multination Federalism': 77.

28 Changes to the boundaries of the Northwest Territories will soon create a new nationality-based unit, controlled by the Inuit, to be known as 'Nunavut'.

29 For other examples, see Petr Pithard, 'Czechoslovakia: The Loss of the Old Partnership' in Seidle, ed., *Seeking a New Canadian Partnership*: 164; Brassloff, 'Spain': 35; Smith, 'Russia': 392, 395.

11: PAPERING OVER THE DIFFERENCES

1 Jeremy Webber, *Reimagining Canada: Language, Culture, Community and the Canadian Constitution* (Montreal: McGill-Queen's University Press, 1994): 4–5, 156–9.

2 Government of Canada, *Shared Values: The Canadian Identity* (Ottawa: Supply and Services, 1991): 2.

3 Government of Canada, *Shaping Canada's Future Together: Proposals* (Ottawa: Supply and Services, 1991): 9.

4 For discussions of this nation-building aspect of Trudeau's constitutional reforms (and its striking success in English-speaking Canada), see Rainer Knopff and F.L. Morton, 'Nation-Building and the Canadian Charter of Rights and Freedoms' in Alan Cairns and Cynthia Williams, eds, *Constitutionalism, Citizenship and Society in Canada* (Toronto: University of Toronto Press, 1985); Alan Cairns, *Disruptions: Constitutional Struggles from the Charter to Meech Lake* (Toronto: McClelland and Stewart, 1991): 43–5; Kenneth McRoberts, *Misconceiving Canada* (Toronto: Oxford University Press, 1997): Chapters 6–7.

5 Janet Ajzenstat, 'Decline of Procedural Liberalism: The Slippery Slope to Secession' in J. Carens, ed., *Is Quebec Nationalism Just?* (Montreal: McGill-Queen's University Press, 1995): 120–36. For a related discussion of how the patriation of the 1982 Constitution reduced the possibility of papering over our competing conceptions of nationhood, see David M. Thomas, *Whistling Past the Graveyard: Constitutional Abeyances, Quebec and the Future of Canada* (Toronto: Oxford University Press, 1997). Thomas explains that the 1867 constitution contained a deliberate 'abeyance' on the question of Quebec's status. This decision to avoid a clear statement on this issue was remarkably stable for over a century; it was, in Thomas's term, a 'settled unsettlement'. But the pressures for a clearer statement have increased, in part because of the 1982 patriation.

6 The 'Canada clause' was intended to provide a list of the 'defining characteristics' of Canada, including democracy, multiculturalism, gender equality, the rights of Aboriginal peoples, and official bilingualism. If the 'distinct society' clause was intended to provide explicit constitutional recognition for Quebec, the Canada clause was intended to provide explicit recognition to a wide range of other groups (women, ethnic groups, official language minorities, Aboriginal peoples), and thereby make all groups feel equally recognized in the new constitutional settlement. Unfortunately, many people felt that the Canada clause did not really provide 'equal' recognition to other groups, since it did not occupy an equally prominent place within the Constitution.

7 Norman, 'The Ideology of Shared Values' in Carens, ed., *Is Quebec Nationalism*

Just?: 138. My discussion in this section is strongly influenced by Norman's analysis.

8 Citizens' Forum on Canada's Future, *Report to the People and Government of Canada* (Ottawa: Supply and Services, 1991): 33–44.

9 Government of Canada, *Shared Values*. For another example, see the Beaudouin-Dobbie Committee report (Special Joint Committee on a Renewed Canada, *Report* (Ottawa: Supply and Services, 1992): 9.

10 Rawls, 'Kantian Constructivism in Moral Theory', *Journal of Philosophy* 77, 9 (1980): 540.

11 See Brian Schwartz, *First Principles, Second Thoughts: Aboriginal Peoples, Constitutional Reform and Canadian Statecraft* (Montreal: Institute for Research on Public Policy, 1986), for a discussion of the varying degrees of support for liberal-democratic principles among the main Aboriginal groups during constitutional conventions on Aboriginal rights of the mid-1980s.

12 Stéphane Dion, 'Le Nationalisme dans la convergence culturelle' in R. Hudon and R. Pelletier, eds, *L'Engagement intellectuel: mélanges en l'honneur de Léon Dion* (Sainte-Foy: Presses de l'Université Laval, 1991): 301; Dion, 'Explaining Quebec Nationalism' in R. Kent Weaver, ed., *The Collapse of Canada?* (Washington: Brookings Institute, 1992): 99; cf. Charles Taylor, 'Shared and Divergent Values' in R. Watts and D. Brown, eds, *Options for a New Canada* (Toronto: University of Toronto Press, 1991): 54.

13 Michael Ignatieff, *Blood and Belonging* (New York: Farrar, Straus and Giroux, 1993): 21.

14 W. Peterson, 'On the Subnations of Europe' in N. Glazer and D. Moynihan, eds, *Ethnicity: Theory and Experience* (Cambridge, Harvard University Press, 1975): 208.

15 Alistair Hennessy, 'The Renaissance of Federal Ideas in Contemporary Spain' in Murray Forsyth, ed., *Federalism and Nationalism* (Leicester: Leicester University Press, 1989): 11–23.

16 For a more detailed discussion of this 'narcissism' charge, see my 'From Enlightenment Cosmopolitanism to Liberal Nationalism' in Steven Lukes and Martin Hollis, eds, *The Enlightenment: Then and Now* (London: Verso, forthcoming).

12: RETHINKING ENGLISH CANADA

1 Some commentators wish to encourage the development of a sense of English-Canadian nationhood (e.g., Philip Resnick, *Thinking English Canada* [Toronto: Stoddart, 1994]); others oppose such a development (e.g., Jeremy Webber, in *Reimagining Canada* [Montreal: McGill-Queen's University Press, 1994]: 278). But both agree that such a sense of nationhood does not yet exist.

2 As Kenneth McRoberts notes, 'no other province endorsed Quebec's position that jurisdiction for culture belonged exclusively to the provinces. The artistic community across Canada Outside Quebec mobilized in defense of national cultural institutions and the federal government's role in supporting them' ('In Search of Canada "Beyond Quebec"' in McRoberts, ed., *Beyond Quebec: Taking Stock of Canada* (Montreal: McGill-Queen's University Press,

1995): 17.

3 If English Canadians were consciously motivated by a linguistic nationalism, they might be reluctant to accept official bilingualism outside Quebec. This is the one clear concession English-speaking Canadians have made to the ideal that pan-Canadian nationalism is not simply a form of English-speaking nationalism in disguise. But of course many English-speaking Canadians *are* reluctant to accept bilingualism outside Quebec. Moreover, as I noted in Chapter 10, official bilingualism does not threaten the interests of English-speaking Canadians the way it threatens the interests of francophones within Quebec. It is, therefore, a small price to pay for all the ways in which pan-Canadian nationalism promotes their shared interests.

4 Webber, *Reimagining*: 210; cf. Ian Angus, *A Border Within: National Identity, Cultural Plurality and Wilderness* (Montreal: McGill-Queen's University Press, 1997): 24–6. Notice the way English-speaking Canadians and national minorities respond to the labels of 'majority' and 'minority'. As we saw in Chapter 10, national minorities are concerned to ensure that basic issues relating to their status as separate and self-governing societies are not described in the language of 'majority vs minority', since in a democracy the assumption is that the majority should rule. One might think, therefore, that a majority group like English-speaking Canadians would be happy to self-consciously describe themselves as the majority group. But as Webber notes, they can in fact afford to view themselves simply as individual members of the country as a whole, without distinguishing themselves as members of a particular (majority) subset of the country.

5 Sylvia Bashevkin, *True Patriot Love: The Politics of Canadian Nationalism* (Toronto: Oxford University Press, 1991): 26–7. For a discussion of the history of pan-Canadian nationalism, see Bashevkin, Chapters 1–2. She notes that pan-Canadianism has historically rested 'on a vision of federal supremacy and authority that is at odds with the decentralist reality of Confederation', and on the equating of 'national interest' with 'federal action' (26–7). See also Roger Gibbins' claim that what is described as pan-Canadian nationalism in the West is in fact 'a variant best suited to a Canada without Quebec' ('Western Canada: "The West Wants In"' in McRoberts, ed., *Beyond Quebec*: 46).

6 Latouche, *Canada and Quebec, Past and Future: An Essay*, vol. 70 of the Research Studies of the Royal Commission on the Economic Union (Toronto: University of Toronto Press, 1986): 74.

7 Moreover, even the most radical proposals for decentralization still typically insist on the federal definition and protection of language rights, and so are unacceptable to the Québécois for this reason as well.

8 Government of Ontario, *A Social Charter for Canada: Making Our Shared Values Stronger* (Toronto: Ministry of Intergovernmental Affairs, 1991): 1.

9 See Citizens' Forum on Canada's Future, *Report to the People and Government of Canada* (Ottawa: Supply and Services, 1991): Figure 2 (158); Resnick, 'Toward a Multination Federation' in L. Seidle, ed., *Seeking a New Canadian Partnership: Asymmetrical and Confederal Options* (Montreal: Institute for Research on Public Policy, 1994): 73; Suzanne Peters, *Exploring Canadian*

Values: Foundations for Well-Being (Ottawa: Canadian Policy Research Networks, 1995).

10 I discuss the Royal Commission's experience, and how it sheds light on the conflicting national identities in Canada, in 'The Paradox of Liberal Nationalism', *Literary Review of Canada* 4, 10 (1995): 13–15.

11 See David Elton, 'Public Opinion and Federal-Provincial Relations: A Case Study in Alberta' in J. Peter Meekison, ed., *Canadian Federalism: Myth or Reality*, 3rd edn (Toronto: Methuen, 1977): 52–3; and the more recent data in Ekos Research Associates, *Rethinking Government* (Ottawa, April 1995). Needless to say, this indifference to the principles of federalism drives Quebec nationalists up the wall, and makes them despair of ever reforming the federation to truly achieve recognition and protection for their national identity and autonomy.

12 It is important to distinguish decentralization of policy-making *jurisdiction*—i.e., changes to the federal division of powers—from the decentralized *administration* of policies. There are often good reasons to give local or regional offices more control over the administration of policies—e.g., to bring control 'closer to the people'. But this has nothing to do with the division of powers. The federal government is just as capable of decentralizing the administration of its policies as a provincial government is. The issue, therefore, is not whether social programs should be administered in a decentralized way, but rather whether these programs—however they are administered—should have to meet certain national standards set by the federal government.

13 As Bashevkin notes, this is true even of those English-speaking Canadians who are sympathetic to Québécois nationalism. While they endorse Quebec's right to pursue collective national projects, they nonetheless have 'indicated little willingness to surrender *their* structural vehicle for accomplishing such ends—namely, the federal state' (*True Patriot Love*: 164). And why should they?

14 See, for example, the rather angry tone of Reg Whitaker's discussion of this issue in 'With or Without Quebec' in J.L. Granatstein and Kenneth McNaught, eds, *'English Canada' Speaks Out* (Toronto: Doubleday, 1991): 20.

15 Resnick, *Thinking English Canada*: 85.

16 Resnick, *Thinking English Canada*; and various essays in *'English Canada' Speaks Out*, especially those by Reg Whitaker and Richard Gwyn.

17 Developing a sense of nationhood would also enable English-speaking Canadians to adopt a common voice if and when we have to negotiate with a sovereign Quebec. This often seems to be Resnick's main concern.

18 On this debate see McRoberts, 'In Search of Canada': 7–13; Resnick, *Thinking English Canada*: 21–34; Angus, *Border Within*: 24–6. McRoberts rejects the term 'English Canada'; Resnick and Angus support it.

19 Cairns, 'The Fragmentation of Canadian Citizenship' in William Kaplan, ed., *Belonging: The Meaning and Future of Canadian Citizenship* (Montreal: McGill-Queen's University Press, 1993): 194.

13: THE BONDS OF SOCIAL UNITY

1 Jeremy Webber, *Reimagining Canada* (Montreal: McGill-Queen's University

Press, 1994): 159. There are other examples of this sort of biased perception. For example, it is often said that western Canadians resist Quebec's demands for special status because the idea of a French-English duality has little reality in the West, where francophones are often outnumbered by various immigrant groups. But of course it's precisely *because* there is such a small francophone presence in the West that it is so important for the Québécois to ensure that Quebec has a special status as defender of the French language and culture. The relative absence of francophones in the West is not an objection to special status for Quebec: it is precisely one of the reasons why this is necessary.

2 This is only a *prima facie* claim, since the territory encompassed by the federal subunit may include the homeland of other national groups. This is a serious issue in Quebec, where the northern part of the province is the historic homeland of various indigenous peoples. These indigenous groups argue that their right of self-determination is as strong as that of the Québécois, and that if Quebecers vote to secede, they may decide to stay in Canada, so that an independent Quebec would only include the southern part of the province. See, on this, Mary Ellen Turpel, 'Does the Road to Quebec Sovereignty Run Through Aboriginal Territory?' in D. Drache and R. Perin, eds, *Negotiating with a Sovereign Quebec* (Toronto: Lorimer, 1992).

3 John Rawls, quoted in Allen Buchanan, *Secession: The Morality of Political Divorce* (Boulder: Westview Press, 1991): 5.

4 *L'Actualité* 17, 11 (July 1992); Kenneth McRoberts, *Misconceiving Canada* (Toronto: Oxford University Press, 1997): 183, 247. For other polls to this effect, see Richard Johnston and André Blais, 'Meech Lake and Mass Politics: The "Distinct Society" Clause', *Canadian Public Policy* 14 (Supplement; 1988): 33–8.

5 Norman, 'The Ideology of Shared Values' in J. Carens, ed., *Is Quebec Nationalism Just?* (Montreal: McGill-Queen's University Press, 1995).

6 For the contrast between a politics of the common good and a politics of rights, see Michael Sandel, 'The Procedural Republic and the Unencumbered Self', *Political Theory* 12, 1 (1984): 81–96. This is only a crude thumb-nail sketch of communitarianism; for a more systematic exposition and critique of communitarian views see my *Contemporary Political Philosophy* (Oxford: Oxford University Press, 1990): Chapter 6.

7 Andrew Oldenquist, quoted in American Association of School Administrators, *Citizenship: Goal of Education* (Arlington: AASA Publications, 1987): 26.

8 This raises some important questions about the nature of citizenship education, and the legitimacy of selective and manipulative use of history in schools, which I discuss in 'Education for Citizenship' in Terence McLaughlin and Mark Halstead, eds, *Education in Morality* (London: Routledge, forthcoming).

9 As Webber puts it, 'societies that seem to have the clearest "national character" are often defined more by their disagreements than by their agreements. It isn't so much what citizens agree upon as the way in which they disagree that is important. It is the distinctive structure of their fundamental debates—

the issues that preoccupy their public life, the ways in which those issues are posed, the kinds of solutions discussed—that give a society its distinctive cast' (*Reimagining*: 186). Webber himself invokes debates over race in the US as an example of this phenomenon.

10 Luttwak, *The Endangered American Dream* (New York: Harcourt & Brace, 1991): 73. Cf. Arthur Schlesinger, *The Disuniting of America* (New York: Norton, 1992): 83.

11 John Harles, *Politics in the Lifeboat: Immigrants and the American Democratic Order* (Boulder: Westview Press, 1993): 83–4, 122, 129.

12 Webber, *Reimagining*: 29–33, 186–92, 309–19. For a related account of the bases of Canadian unity, see James Tully, *Strange Multiplicity: Constitutionalism in an Age of Diversity* (Cambridge: Cambridge University Press, 1995): 196–8.

13 Webber, *Reimagining*: 192–3.

14 Charles Taylor, 'Shared and Divergent Values' in R. Watts and D. Brown, *Options for a New Canada* (Toronto: University of Toronto Press, 1991): 76.

15 Petr Pithard, 'Czechoslovakia' in Leslie Seidle, ed., *Seeking a New Canadian Partnership* (Montreal: Institute for Research on Public Policy, 1994): 198. It is not quite true to say that it 'was not by their own will' that Czechs now live in a country that is for the most part ethnically homogeneous. Czechs did not wish the secession of Slovakia, but most certainly supported the expulsion of the Germans after the Second World War.

16 See Robert Howse and Karen Knop, 'Federalism, Secession and the Limits of Ethnic Accommodation', *New Europe Law Review* 1, 2 (1993): 285–8.

17 Roger Gibbins, 'The Institutional Parameters of a Quebec-Canada Partnership' in Guy Laforest and Roger Gibbins, eds, *Beyond the Impasse: Toward Reconciliation* (Montreal: Institute for Research on Public Policy, 1998).

18 On the (lack of) benefits of confederalism compared to entering NAFTA as an independent state, see the paper by Kenneth Norrie and Michael Percy in *Beyond the Impasse*.

19 The participation of Quebecers in the governing of Canada will be different from that of other Canadians. Asymmetrical powers for Quebec will likely entail asymmetrical representation and participation in Ottawa (see my 'Group Representation in Canadian Politics' in Leslie Seidle, ed., *Equity and Community: The Charter, Interest Advocacy, and Representation* [Montreal: Institute for Research on Public Policy, 1993]: 61–89). But this participation will nonetheless be real and tangible, and a viable source of ongoing attachment to Canada.

20 The importance of this factor is often neglected, because from a purely statistical point of view it appears insignificant. Relatively few Quebecers in fact exercise their option to work outside Quebec, or to work in federal institutions that affect the rest of Canada. For obvious reasons, francophone Quebecers are less likely than other Canadians to move to another province. But the fact that this is an option, however infrequently exercised, helps explain why Quebecers continue to exhibit a strong attachment to Canada. To put the point most starkly, Quebecers today can imagine their sons or daughters becoming federal cabinet ministers. The chances of this actually occurring are extremely low, of course, but if that possibility for influencing

the future of Canada goes, so too does much of their motivation for caring about being Canadian.

21 Secession also carries some economic costs, and it would be possible for English-speaking Canada to increase these costs by threatening to block Quebec's entry into NAFTA. But if a country can be kept together only by threats, perhaps it is no longer worth the effort. In any event, it is unlikely that English-speaking Canadians would carry through on such a threat, since it would involve imposing considerable costs on themselves.

Index

Aboriginal peoples, 3, 6; attachment to Canada, 131, 134–5; 'blood quantum' membership rules, 96; and federalism, 129; group representation, 104–5, 106, 109, 113, 114, 117, 118–19; land claims, 145; national identity, 10; national recognition, 127, 128, 130–2; political status, 1–2; in Quebec, 180; self-government, 113, 114, 144–6; 'special status', 146

Affirmative action, 42, 43, 45, 63, 86–8

African Americans: alienation of, 83; Black nationalism, 77; distinguished from both immigrant groups and national minorities, 75, 76, 78; relations with immigrant groups, 76; segregation, 75–6; term, 132

Ajzenstat, Janet, 149

Altman, Dennis, 97

Amish, 30

Anti-racism education, 42, 43

Asymmetry, 130, 141–3; see also Federalism, 'multination'

Australia, 56, 57; federalism, 138; immigration, 1, 44; limits to multiculturalism, 66; multiculturalism policy, 21–2

Baines, Beverley, 111

Bashevkin, Sylvia, 159

Beaudoin-Dobbie Commission, 114

Belgium, 2, 128, 134, 135, 140, 152, 169

Bilingualism, 2; 'sea-to-sea', 133–4, 149, 157, 60; territorial, 149

Bissoondath, Neil, 16–17, 18–20, 22, 60, 64–5, 67, 121

Blacks, Canadian, 9; and affirmative action programs, 86–8; Black-focused schools, 42, 52, 84–6; Black Loyalists, 78; Caribbean immigrants, 78–9; political representation, 110–11 (see also Representation, group); segregation, 78, 79; single-parent families, 87; US influences, 83, 86; see also African Americans; Minorities, visible

Blasius, Mark, 99–100

Bloc Québécois, 18

Bouchard, Lucien, 168

Boyle, Christine, 110, 112–13

Brazil, 138

British North America Act (1867), 148

Broadcasting guidelines, 42, 64

Burnet, Jean, 59

Cairns, Alan, 165

Calgary constitutional conference (1992), 108

Canada, colonial history, 1, 5–6, 138–9

Canada First movement, 158

Canada West Foundation, 108

Canadian Race Relations Foundation, 89

Canadian Radio-television and Telecommunications Commission (CRTC), 36

Canadians, English-speaking, 10; attitudes towards Aboriginal self-government, 146; attitudes towards Quebec, 11, 139, 141, 142–3, 146, 167–8; common interests, 154, 155–60; conceptions of Canada, 141–3, 147–8, 154–5; and federalism, 141–3, 147; national identity, 141; nationalism, 155–63, 166; rea-